JAPANESE LINKED POETRY

Japanese Linked Poetry

AN ACCOUNT WITH TRANSLATIONS

OF RENGA AND HAIKAI SEQUENCES

BY EARL MINER

PRINCETON UNIVERSITY PRESS   1979

Preface

LIKE ALL other literature that may be thought truly important, the linked poetry of Japan makes a dual claim: to sameness and difference. Its claim to sameness means that it offers us a valued kind of knowledge of ourselves and our world that is recognizably like that provided by other important literature. Without such a valid claim, any literature is trivial. Its claim to difference means that the knowledge it gives is also determined by, appreciated for, the distinct terms on which it gives. Without such a valid claim, one thing would be too like the next. In all important literary matters we seek the valued sameness, importance, or we would not seek at all. But we discover it only through difference. Otherwise one work of literature, one parochial kind, would suffice for the whole world.

Such characteristics do not apply to non-aesthetic knowledge. Only the aesthetic welcomes the different and defies obsolescence in the appearance of subsequent examples. The novel is not diminished by the Homeric poems nor they by it. But differences can easily be underestimated. The novel is only two and a half centuries old. Only a minority of people have seen plays performed by actors before them on a stage. Very few people can scan more than one kind of poetry, and most read it, if they do, as an eccentric kind of prose. Some of the differences are, then, not so valuable and are not inherent in our subject. Others are crucial. Of all the kinds of poetry known to me, Japanese linked poetry has the fairest claim to be thought as different, as unusual, as poetry can be and yet also be important, the same.

"Linked poetry" designates two kinds, renga and haikai. Both have histories stretching over centuries, with the great age for renga occurring in the fifteenth and sixteenth centuries, and with that for haikai in the seventeenth and eighteenth. Both are typically composed by (let us say) three poets at a single sitting, working in alternation to compose three-line and two-line stanzas up to a given number. The method of composition seems casual, as close to randomness as intelligibility might allow. Yet linked poetry is also governed by elaborate canons, rules, and principles. It has been said that two decades are necessary for a poet to learn the rules well enough to compose naturally and to show a talent. After twenty years, the rules become important enough to be broken when their purpose is better served another way. These and other features will make clear that linked poetry is genuinely different. From such difference comes the same meaningfulness we insist on in all literature. Two poets can illustrate this. The renga master Sōgi assisted in defining not only his own poetic kind but also principles of other literary kinds after him. The haikai master Bashō is quite simply the poet whom Japanese themselves have most taken to their hearts.

An author of a literary study is also a student of literature and therefore a guest in its palace. An author is also host in a book bearing the author's name. For linked poetry, I find that I must play the role of servant or guide. Much of this study is, then, devoted to introduction and commentary. The seven chapters in Part One deal with linked poetry in several sets of terms: in the history of Japanese literature, as renga, as haikai, and as a special kind in world literature. Only in the last, the seventh chapter of Part One, am I fully the guest-host. It excites me to think, as I propose there in some detail, that linked poetry gives us what we cannot know on its terms elsewhere: narrative without plot, narrative made up of lyric units. Part Two offers two renga sequences, and Part Three four haikai sequences—in translation and with commentary. No one is likely to mistake my translations for the original, but study of the original also has allowed me the happiest of roles as a guest. I offer as well many translations of poems and passages of poems or prose. The prose includes pronouncements by various important critics and poets of linked verse.

In Parts Two and Three each sequence has its introduction and appears with a stanza represented on facing pages. To the left there is a transliteration of the Japanese and a translation, stanza numbers, and the name of the composer of each stanza (unless one poet has composed the whole). To the right there is commentary on each stanza. Some of the commentary is explanatory, some analytical, some appreciative. Some—and the most important—is schematic. The scheme is indebted to Yamada Yoshio and Konishi Jin'ichi, especially to Professor Konishi, as the method has been fully used for but one sequence, in a book by Professor Konishi in Japanese. It has never been used in English, as far as I am aware. And it has never been used at all before in full for five of the six sequences given here. That is a matter of some hazard, to which I shall return.

This approach has derived from various experiments in teaching and with physical layout on the page. It seeks to solve the problem of dealing with stanzas that have three related but distinguishable existences: as individual poetic units, as stanzas combining with predecessors to make a single poem, and as stanzas combined with successors to make another single poem. Can there be another poetic tradition elsewhere in which an individual unit has three such existences? If that were not unusual enough, a given stanza (though possessing such close semantic connections as to make an integer with its predecessor and successor) possesses *nothing* continuously integral with any other stanza. That is why we call it linked or chain poetry. As in a chain, where a given link joins with the one before and the one after, but no other, so does each stanza. And as a chain with one hundred links has a beginning and an end, so does a linked poem with one hundred stanzas. Only the first stanza is added to no predecessor; only the last has no other added to it. We find the central art of linked poetry in the adding or joining of stanzas. Often an addition effects profound semantic change in a stanza. For this reason, and because each stanza makes a part of a poem with two others, my translations give each stanza twice. So are they read by the Japanese, and so each transliteration is also given twice.

To speak of what is "continuously integral" excludes some large matters. In fact a sequence of linked poetry has many means of joining into wholeness those links which do not touch. There are parts defined by a "rhythm" derived from music, parts defined by the method of setting down on sheets, and parts defined by topics that may well run well beyond two stanzas or that must not be repeated for seven or a hundred stanzas. The sheets on which sequences are set down must have flower stanzas, and the sides of the sheets must have moon stanzas, usually in particular places. Some topics are in place and some out of place on the front side of the first sheet. I might go on, but it will be clear that the stanzas making up linked semantic integers, each with two others, also possess semantic integrity as part of a whole sequence in which wholeness derives not merely from immediate connection, but from sequence otherwise meaningfully conceived. That is to say, linked poetry is plotless narrative.

The shifting juncture of individual stanzas leads to an extraordinary poetic fluidity. The fact has led me to a procedure new to my translations of Japanese poetry. In Part One and elsewhere will be found some translations from the five-line tanka poems of the court. For them I have employed the methods Robert H. Brower and I used in *Japanese Court Poetry* (1961), later used by each of us on other occasions. For renga and haikai alike, however, I have felt the need for a procedure answering to the flexible, often abstruse, broken, and ambiguous syntax of the original. The reader of these translations will encounter a kind of English almost stripped of its capitals and punctuation. Why this should seem necessary would require an explanation tediously long when one example may serve. The most famous renga stanza is that which opens *One Hundred Stanzas by Three Poets at Minase.*

Yuki nagara	Despite some snow
yamamoto kasumu	the base of hills spreads with haze
yūbe kana	the twilight scene

Here and where possible elsewhere, I have sought to follow the sequences of lines in the original, although that is not always feasible. But let us consider what might be gained or lost by adding punctuation and such.

> Despite some snow,
> The base of hills spreads with haze:
> The twilight scene.

But the clarity gained by such discipline has meant the loss of another meaning.

> Despite some snow,
> The base of hills spreads with haze
> The twilight scene.

The verb, "kasumu," "spreads with haze," describes features of both the hills and the twilight, working backwards and forwards. Other features of linked poetry have led me to the same conclusions about presentation, although I realize the kind of burden that this exacts from the reader. Yet the originals are much more difficult than my translations.

The preceding paragraphs will also have shown another convention I have used. Japanese words are quoted or italicized only when English words would be—for particular kinds of stress. Consultation with experienced editors has led me to the conclusion that italics and quotation marks are used to assist where convenience is important. When a stanza is set off, as is the one above, italics would only clutter the page. The same seems to me to hold in speaking of the techniques of renga and haikai, including its first stanza or hokku and its last or ageku. The four Japanese words in that sentence are so obviously Japanese, and can be explained so easily that they set themselves off—without disfiguring the page with italics.

A glossary is provided to remind readers of the meaning of a term such as "hokku." Five figures are also given to clarify terms and set forth some matters best given in diagram form.

The annotations are of two kinds. Part One uses both: full citation and abbreviated citation. For the latter, the Abbreviated References gives full citations. In Part One, annotations appear either in footnotes or in the text. In Parts Two and Three they appear in the text.

I HAVE LEFT to this prominent place at the end a particularly important matter. This involves my indebtedness to Konishi Jin'ichi in certain particulars of the utmost significance. (I am indebted to him and many others for much else of value, as the Acknowledgments seek to make clear. But special mention is required of this matter.) The genius of linked poetry involves steady relation and steady variance, with "steady" meaning constant existence and alteration of degree. To existing criteria for explaining linked poetry, Professor Konishi has added two of the utmost importance that will be found nowhere except in his *Sōgi* (see Abbreviated References) and in this book. These two involve estimation of the degree of impressiveness of a given stanza and of its degree of closeness or distance from its predecessor. To the extent that I have followed Professor Konishi in presenting the same sequence (*Three Poets at Minase*), I leave my readers in the best company they can have. But I must warn them that the other five sequences given in this book have the same estimation of impressiveness and relation on the same scale of four I have devised. I have been aided by instruction from Professor Konishi and by the opportunity to teach a class at Princeton in linked poetry that included exceptionally qualified people in language and literature (see the Acknowledgments). I shall be repeating in later pages the warning that estimates of impressiveness and relation are my own. Here I explain that I do not claim mine are right. They are only guides. Some effort is necessary, however, lest two of the most important features of stanza connection be omitted from consideration. I know that such features are crucial to a reader's understanding, and I know no other standards for judging them apart from those I have learned, with whatever misunderstandings, from Professor Konishi. When there seems some doubt, I have tried to indicate other possibilities or evidence for my decision. Just as I owe the reader this warning, so anyone seeking to understand linked poetry is owed an assessment throughout of two of its most important features. For the rest I am happy to rest with confidence in my subject and my readers.

Summer, 1976
Princeton and Briant's Neck, Cape Cod

Acknowledgments

THIS BOOK concerns a subject by no means simple, and it would not have been possible without the aid of many people. If what follows resembles a thirty-six stanza haikai perhaps that fits the subject as well as my gratitude for assistance.

Some twenty years ago this book began, as I now see, in study of Japanese court poetry. Robert H. Brower and I were discussing that tradition with Konishi Jin'ichi, who introduced renga into our studies at a number of points. My Japanese studies have continued to be indebted to his letters and conversation. In the summer of 1974 he made time available in Tokyo for some rigorous discussion of renga and correction of some of my misunderstandings. Since he is one of the last people alive to have had instruction in renga, I am especially fortunate to have been able to consult him.

During 1975-1976, I benefitted from discussion of *Three Poets at Minase* with Tamai Kensuke, who put his encyclopedic knowledge of Japanese diction and his conviviality freely at my disposal.

In the spring of 1976 I taught a course at Princeton devoted to renga and haikai. It involved the two renga and the first three haikai included in this book. The people in that seminar are occasionally referred to in the annotations as "my students." It would be more accurate to style Odagiri Hiroko and Lucy Loh as "my fellow-students" or "collaborators." We also enjoyed the frequent participation of Iwasaki Haruko and Chang Kang-i. Professor Odagiri also later checked through my translation of the fourth haikai sequence here, as well as the annotations on them, making many useful corrections. Our procedure in the course was to translate a unit of renga or haikai into English. This was the more necessary, since the course was conducted in Japanese: the translations ensured that we knew what the poets were up to. We then went through the unit stanza by stanza, specifying topics and sub-topics. Thereafter we dealt with the difficult matters of impressiveness and relation, often debating, often changing our minds. As I have tried to emphasize in the pages that follow, this is very tricky business. To my knowledge, they have been dealt with fully only once in published work in Japanese—by Professor Konishi. The results for this book are therefore to be taken as heuristic suggestions rather than as *obiter dicta*. But not to consider these matters is to deprive linked poetry of two of its most important constituents. Everything that matters involves risk, and I have chosen to run the risk in order to get at what matters. But as here, so later there will be warning signals for the reader.

We also attempted compositions of parts of renga and haikai sequences. These have no claim on anyone's attention. But the result is invaluable for any person seeking to understand the special genius of renga and, in particular, of haikai. An account of our proceedings can be found in a brief article, "Renga to no deai" in *Hon*, 1 (1976), pp. 22-24, which was translated by Professor Odagiri. This seminar was one of the most satisfying courses I have taught. I am deeply grateful to its other members.

In the past two or three years Donald Keene has very generously shared with me essays of his in press. These have assisted me for both renga and haikai and have enabled me to frame an account that would differ from his own. This generosity has been crowned by his authoritative historical account of haikai in his *World Within Walls* (1976), the first volume to appear in his masterly history of Japanese literature. I am deeply grateful that he has shared his work with me so that my own could benefit from it and employ a method that would not conflict with his.

An unusually busy season followed the completion of this study. It was not until March 1977 that I was able to return to the typed manuscript. In the meantime, Matthew Mizenko spent many hours checking my citations and reviewing what I had written. The result of his intelligent work has been many improvements as well as corrections.

I must thank the readers of this study for the Princeton University Press, Professor Makoto Ueda of Stanford University and a second, anonymous person. Both gave numerous suggestions for improvement and correction, providing me with enthusiasm to make yet more changes. As always, I shall welcome any further suggestions from reviewers or remarks that they or others wish to send me privately.

Various people in Japan have assisted my work. Besides the help already mentioned, I shall begin with Mori Haruhide of Kobe University, who sought out materials. Kawasaki Toshihiko and Gotō Shigeo of Nagoya University managed to obtain for me material by Professor Kaneko on renga before it was published in the text I have used for one of the two renga sequences translated here. As the book was in press, an introduction from Fujii Haruhiko put me in touch with Tanaka Yutaka, also at Osaka University, that showed me that the disciples of Masaoka Shiki wrote haikai. This information, demonstrated by a xerox of an important book, has helped me correct certain misimpressions that I and, I believe, others have held. Three of these people are professors of English. So much have I benefitted in Japanese studies from acquaintances in English studies.

This book posed many problems of design that most authors and readers could scarcely be aware of. For the first time I have had the experience of working closely with the designer of the book to try to solve them. Jan Lilly has designed three of my books for the Princeton University Press, and I take pleasure in acknowledging her putting this one right, for her previous assistance, and for her kindness in attending to my problems.

I have saved to this flower-stanza position special mention of R. Miriam Brokaw. Born in Kyoto, she is Associate Director and Editor of the Princeton University Press. She deserves special thanks for her devotion to this study, for numerous personal favors, and for her light but firm touch with an intelligent pencil. I have benefitted from the work of many gifted editors over the years, but I must thank this one for combining enthusiasm, wise care, and friendly consideration.

Linked poetry requires a last stanza. Mine is a hope that readers will participate in my pleasure that, once again, the Princeton University Press has given a book of mine a colophon providing details of its making. My hope is that readers will find as much pleasure in perusing as in holding this book, as also that my poets will be sufficiently served. In visiting the grave of Sōgi at Sōun Temple in Hakone in November 1977 with Professor Odagiri, I felt the centuries melt in the common human fate. I look forward to the assistance of others in bringing these great poets closer to contemporary understanding and to the illumination of our common humanity.

Abbreviated References and
Other Explanations

EDITIONS, studies, and works often cited are referred to in abbreviated form in the pages that follow. Fuller citations are given here, along with the abbreviated forms. When no place of publication is given, Tokyo may be understood.

Court Poetry. Robert H. Brower and Earl Miner, *Japanese Court Poetry* (Stanford: Stanford University Press, 1961).
Hoshika, *Chikurinshō*. Hoshika Sōichi, ed. *Kōhon Chikurinshō* (Iwanami Shoten, 1937).
Ijichi, *Rengashū*. Ijichi Tetsuo, ed. *Rengashū* (Iwanami Shoten, 1960).
Introduction. Earl Miner, *An Introduction to Japanese Court Poetry* (Stanford: Stanford University Press, 1968).
Keene, "The Comic Tradition in Renga." As in John W. Hall and Toyoda Takeshi, *Japan in the Muromachi Age* (Berkeley and Los Angeles: University of California Press, 1977), pp. 241-77. A Japanese version, which includes an account of discussion of the essay, was published in 1976: *Muromachi Jidai—Sono Shakai to Bunka*, under the title "Renga ni Okeru Kokkei no Dentō" (Yoshikawa Kōbunkan), pp. 284-324.
Kidō, *Rengashi*. Kidō Saizō, *Rengashi Ronkō*, 2 vols. (Meiji Shoin, 1973).
Konishi, *Haiku*. Konishi Jin'ichi, *Haiku: Hassei Yori Gendai Made*, 5th printing (Kenkyūsha, 1958).
———, *Image and Ambiguity*. Konishi Jin'ichi, *Image and Ambiguity: The Impact of Zen Buddhism on Japanese Literature* (Tokyo University of Education, 1973).
———, *Sōgi*. Konishi Jin'ichi, *Sōgi* (Chikuma Shobō, 1971).
Kuriyama, *Haikaishi*. Kuriyama Riichi, *Haikaishi* (Hanawa Shobō, 1963).
Namimoto, *Bashō Shichibushū*. Namimoto Sawaichi, *Bashō Shichibushū Renku Kanshō* (Shunjūsha, 1964).

The Narrow Road. Matsuo Bashō, *The Narrow Road Through the Provinces* (*Oku no Hosomichi*), as in *Poetic Diaries* below.

Poetic Diaries. Earl Miner, *Japanese Poetic Diaries* (Berkeley and Los Angeles: University of California Press, 1969).

Renga Haikaishū. Kaneko Kinjirō, Teruoka Yasutaka, and Nakamura Shunjō, ed., *Renga Haikaishū* (Shōgakkan, 1974); with Kaneko editor of the renga section, and Teruoka and Nakamura editors of the haikai.

Sōgi Alone. *One Hundred Stanzas Related to "Person" by Sōgi Alone* (one of the two renga in Part Two).

Three Poets. *One Hundred Stanzas by Three Poets at Minase* (one of the two renga in Part Two).

Ubuginu. A renga treatise, included in Yamada and Hoshika, below.

Yamada, *Renga Gaisetsu*. Yamada Yoshio, *Renga Gaisetsu* (Iwanami Shoten, 1937).

Yamada and Hoshika. Yamada Yoshio and Hoshika Sōichi, ed., *Renga Hōshiki Kōyō* (Iwanami Shoten, 1936), including the invaluable *Ubuginu* with another, similar compilation of renga canons and a section on renga directives (fushimono).

Yunoyama. *A Hundred Stanzas by Three Poets at Yunoyama* (a renga by the same poets participating in *Three Poets*, above). Also pronounced *Yuyama*.

DATES

Whenever possible, I have used *Haikai Daijiten*, ed. Ichiji Tetsuo *et al.*, 6th ed. (Meiji Shōin, 1967) for the dates of poets' lives. Other dates have been taken from standard Japanese sources but are often approximate, even when not so indicated. In the text, dates are given for individuals on their first appearance as important subjects of discussion and sometimes thereafter to assist the reader. They are also given with a person's name in the Index.

NAMES

Individuals are referred to in Japanese fashion. For modern Japanese, the order is surname and then given name: Yamada Yoshio. Some nobility are referred to in full by clan names and their given names or styles as poets: Fujiwara Teika, and in short by the given name or style, Teika. Other members of the nobility are referred to in full by their name of residence and given name: Sanjōnishi Kin'eda, and briefly by given name, Kin'eda. Renga and haikai poets are referred to by their most familiar styles as poets, disregarding earlier or later styles, proper given name, etc. Hence, Shōhaku is so designated, rather than by his noble names or his later style as poet. Such practice will enable readers to consult standard Japanese reference books. Where pronunciations of names vary, I have tried to follow *Haikai Daijiten* (as above, under "Dates").

TRANSLITERATIONS

Transliterations of names and of texts of poems have been normalized, where different, into modern equivalents. Except for titles and occasions of special stress, all Japanese words are given in roman letters. This includes transliterated Japanese texts, which are indented and so set off, as well as the various terms related to linked poetry and defined in the text and the Glossary.

PRONUNCIATION

Japanese names and texts may be pronounced in a manner approximating the original, with attention to a few matters. The language consists of lightly stressed syllables made up of a consonant plus vowel, a vowel, or *n*. In the syllabic prosody, a long vowel constitutes two syllables (*ōno* is a word of three syllables), and an *n* constitutes a syllable (*sen* is a word of two syllables). The vowels are "pure," as in Spanish or Italian. Consonants are pronounced much as in English, with a few exceptions. These include *r*, which involves lightly touching the tongue to the roof of the forepart of the mouth to produce a sound combining features of English *r*, *l*, and *d*. In words with double consonants, both are pronounced. The *h*- series of syllables has somewhat greater aspiration than in English, as with *fu* and particularly *hi*.

For rather more detailed discussion of pronunciation and related matters, see Robert H. Brower and Earl Miner, *Japanese Court Poetry* (Stanford: Stanford University Press, 1961), pp. xv-xvi.

Contents

PART ONE
LINKED POETRY: ITS HISTORY, CANONS,
AND MAJOR POETS

Linked Poetry in Japanese Literature

"She at once capped his verses."
—*Diary of Izumi Shikibu*

FROM ABOUT the thirteenth through the nineteenth centuries, Japanese poets practiced several versions of linked poetry. These include especially renga, which is typically a hundred-stanza sequence (250 lines) composed by perhaps three poets, and haikai, which is best exemplified by the same number of poets and by thirty-six stanza sequences (ninety lines). These sequences have no real counterpart in Western literature: sonnet sequences and unified collections are the best, but rude, approximations. Given the lack of adequate counterparts, we have every reason to wish to know a kind of poetry that extends the boundaries of our experience and of our conceptions of literature.

Any reader unfamiliar with linked poetry will find in it aspects rich and strange. Anyone wishing to introduce it faces the dilemma of making the riches available when the strangeness may make this human coinage seem alien and, at times, nonnegotiable. I can only presume of a reader what I have learned myself: that it is better to have one's patience taxed initially with strange terms and ideas than to have one's intelligence and imagination underestimated. To use a more Japanese metaphor, linked poetry is a very sweet and sustaining fruit with a bitter rind. What follows begins with what may seem some slow peeling.

The fundamental ideas of linked poetry require a terminology to make the strange understandable. The terms are of course Japanese, and what we know of them is often misleading ("we" includes many Japanese). For example, Bashō is usually called a haiku poet, although he never used the word, and spoke always of his haikai. Japanese themselves are often confused by alternative names for the same thing, or the same name for differing things. We can see this from a Japanese explanation for Japanese readers, a bald but useful description by Namimoto Sawaichi: "What is called haiku today was formerly termed hokku. The name haiku came to be widely used in the last decade or so of the nineteenth century as a result of the movement to reform haiku led by Masaoka Shiki. The fundamental importance of the hokku is that it is the first stanza of a haikai. Haikai is an abbreviation of haikai no renga, which nowadays is referred to as renku."[1] These distinctions are of importance but, like so many important distinctions, they are really clear only to those who already know them. Let us therefore posit, with Kuriyama Riichi, certain ages of poetry in Japan, and to that skeletal history add a final age to bring the account up to our own century:[2]

PERIOD	KIND OF POETRY MOST FLOURISHING
Pre-literate to 13th century	Waka or court poetry; the chōka or long poem and tanka or short poem; and some miscellaneous kinds
13th–19th centuries 13th–16th 16th–19th	Linked poetry: renga and haikai Renga; first stanza is hokku Haikai, now called renku; the first stanza is called hokku
Late 19th–20th centuries	Haiku on the model of hokku; subsequently free verse

As everyone knows, the Japanese do not willingly discard literary genres, and, just before the outbreak of war in the Pacific, one could find waka, renga, and haiku practiced, along with free verse. The skeletal history gives too simple an outline, but it will prove serviceable. Let us therefore continue for the moment, content to identify those features which would strike any of us—including modern Japanese—in reading linked poetry.

[1] Namimoto, *Bashō Shichibushū*, p. 48. For full citation of frequently mentioned studies, see Abbreviated References, pp. xvii-xviii.
[2] Kuriyama, *Haikaishi*, pp. 24-26. For reminder of the meaning of these terms, see the Glossary. They are also explained in the text.

Renga and its avatar-successor haikai vary in length. Theoretically speaking, they run from two to ten thousand units or stanzas. Each stanza is a lyric stave, and yet the total effect can be described as plotless narrative, or narrative with many constantly shifting mini-plots. The stanzas are recognizable as part of the five-line tanka, with an upper unit (kami no ku) of three lines in five, seven, and five syllables and a lower (shimo no ku) of two lines of seven syllables each. One of these stanzas is added to another, and in chain renga or long renga (kusari-renga, chōrenga) the hokku opening the sequence is always the upper unit. Then we go through a series of lower-upper-lower until the hundred stanzas of a usual renga or the thirty-six of many haikai are achieved. In joining a new stanza to one written before, a poet uses the old stanza as the first part of the new. The effect is frequently to alter the meaning of the old. The essential fact to understand is the inviolable principle that no stanza has a continuing semantic connection, as a discrete poetic unit, with anything other than its predecessor and successor. We can choose if we like to consider it in itself. We must consider each as a fresh view of its predecessor, which it completes. And we must consider it also as the basis of the next stanza, which alters it in making a new poetic unit. It has no such *connection* beyond.

The principle of constant but strictly limited joining prohibits the development of a plot in any usual sense. By "plot" we mean something that runs integrally through a whole creation. Renga and haikai are linked in a continuity at each point of juncture but are otherwise discontinuous in plot. The same stanza may first be spoken by a man in connection with its predecessor and be altered by its successor to be spoken by a woman. Often the meaning conveyed is changed quite drastically: some development, if not great change, is the point of joining stanzas. Of course linked poetry must qualify for artistic integrity in other ways if not by plot, and, as we shall see, it has numerous practices to give a sequence wholeness and integrity. Once the shifting connections of a given but successive and different two units are understood, something of the special character of linked poetry will be clear. That character compounds response and sequence.

The importance of response and sequence derives from the systematic poetics of classical Japanese literature. If Western poetics originated in the Greek encounter with drama, giving us a crucial interest in mimesis or representation, Japanese poetics (like Chinese) derives from encounter with lyric poetry.[3] The Japanese assumed from lyricism that literataure is distinguished from other human activities by human response in words to something that moves one. This assumption is usually termed "affectivism." Surely there had been some especially interesting situation that led to the response, to an expression? The Japanese also felt that matters do not end there. They believed that another person receiving the first expression would be affected and so be led to a second expression, perhaps a poem of reply. This second assumption is well termed "expressivism." It is altogether appropriate that the two central terms of classical Japanese poetics characterize the affective and expressive axioms. "Kokoro" means heart, mind, or spirit—the human capacity to be affected and to understand. "Kotoba" means words, languages, signs, or techniques—the human capacity to make known to others what has been gained by the kokoro. In a work developing beyond a brief lyric, a series of responses by the kokoro can be said to lead to a sequence of expressive kotoba.

Affective stimulus came from a world conceived in largely Shinto and Buddhist terms. Other people and even spirits were considered to be susceptible, and even birds or animals expressed themselves. One could not keep these affective things simply locked up in one's heart. To a Japanese it comes very naturally to say unhesitatingly something about one's happiness or a misery so great that life would be better ended. In either instance, the "Ureshii!" or suicide has a basis of understanding life that are not always easily translated. The underlying assumptions differ. Once we grasp, however, the importance of affect and expression, we at least have an intellectual hold on what is involved. To use a more poetic example, a person could well be moved by the beauty of a spring dawn to write a poem. Because other people also respond to such things, it would be natural to send the poem to a friend. The friend now has a dual basis for being affected—the thought of the lovely daybreak and the moving words of the poet. So the friend might well send a poem or letter in reply. The original poem could also lead to a poetic response centuries later, when another poet in different circumstances recalled it. Such a se-

[3] I have tried to discuss these matters in "Toward a New Approach to Classical Japanese Poetics," *Studies on Japanese Culture*, 2 vols. (Japan P.E.N. Club, 1973), 1, 99-113.

quence might well go no further. So strong are the affective and expressive axioms, however, that they could lead to such sequences of responses as those of linked poetry.

They were not the sole result. Poetic exchanges have already been mentioned, and those were a special province of waka. As readers of *The Tale of Genji* (*Genji Monogatari*) will recall, it was unthinkable that a poem should get no reply—unless a woman perhaps thought her addresser had no business approaching her in the first place. And a long series of poems might be involved. This practice presumes that proper reply—adequate expression—testifies to proper capacities for being affected. This capacity was described in many contexts as being possessed of kokoro (kokoro aru). Not to possess kokoro was to be barbarian, worse than animals. The warbler among plum blossoms, the frog in summer waters, the stag crying for his mate in autumn—all were poets. All gave voice to experience. Thus being moved and being led to expression defined poetic activity. In addition, these animal singers and criers moved one to respond in poetry, just as would the poem of a friend. Being a poet or singer among poets and singers lends some definition to life, and it also leads to a succession of songs and poems. For such reasons, the essential character of extended literature is assumed to be responsive sequence. Matters such as being subject to an Elizabethan humor or a ruling passion or *idée fixe* do not enter, and being subject to the many "because's" of plot matter even less. The consistency of human character lies in appropriate responsiveness rather than in a dramatic consistency. Spring dawn differs fundamentally from autumn dusk, and the agony of travel in remote areas differs markedly from the yearnings of love in the capital—as everyone (possessed of heart) knows.

The hero of *The Tale of Genji* exemplifies this. Whatever his other characteristics, he is the supreme artist among the important heroes of world literature because in no small measure life had been defined as aesthetic response. His genius often reveals itself in matters akin to linked verse. For example, during his exile in Suma and Akashi he had drawn a sequence of sketches (enikki) of the scenery he beheld, adding to the pictures phrases that further expressed his deep feelings. This record is presented to his friends and dependents at the climax of the chapter entitled "The Picture Match" ("Eawase").

. . . there was no chance of rivaling paintings such as Genji's, painted by a masterly artist working at leisure, his heart fully composed and his thought clear of distractions.

Beginning with Prince Sochi, those who looked at the scrolls found it impossible to restrain their tears. They who had remained in the capital had often thought how very sad, how painful his life in exile must be. Yet how much more than they had realized was revealed here, the nature of his daily life and the very thoughts of his mind being brought as it were before their eyes as present experience.

The contours of that area—its various bays and inlets lying beyond their ken—were here drawn visibly with nothing of that shoreline left obscure. In a cursive hand Genji had added here and there compositions in the native syllabary, producing nothing that resembled a ponderous diary in Chinese, but rather intermittent poems and phrases deep with feeling. Altogether it was of a kind boundlessly appealing. Everyone remained there, thinking of nothing else.

Being moved, responding; being moved, responding—so the process builds into sequence. We may be sure that Genji's pictures made up no plot. But they made a sequence.

The process by which such sequencing eventually produced renga was a long one, but some details may be useful to show how widespread were the assumptions that made linked poetry possible. We can begin with the earliest surviving poetic records, which give us remainders from pre-literate times of poems of joint authorship. Most are dialogues, which, with riddles, are among the commonest kinds of primitive composition in many cultures. Both assume participation. During the eighth century, the oral traditions of some of the early Japanese peoples were set down from reciters and other sources in two collections: *The Records of Ancient Matters (Kojiki)* and *The Records of Japan (Nihon Shoki* or *Nihongi)*. In these overlapping accounts, the deities and other actors commonly get involved in poetic dialogue. Dialogue poems also appear in the great early collection, the *Man'yōshū* (ca. 759). The most distinguished example is Yamanoe Okura's *Dialogue Between the Poor Man and the Destitute Man*.[4] There were also many less sophisticated versions.

As early as the *Man'yōshū*, poems of joint composition exist that are not dialogue poems. This development is crucial for linked poetry, which does not consist of expostulation and reply but of more subtle continuance and of sequence posited on the incompleteness of a poetic process begun with an initial stanza. The tendency of Japanese poems to be short is well known, as is also the tendency for the short to become shorter. It is less well known that a countervailing tendency leads to the integration of shorter into larger wholes.[5] Perhaps the briefest is the so-called short renga (tanrenga), nothing other than a tanka whose upper unit is composed by one person and the lower by another. The example given by early renga critics and followed ever since is the 1635th poem of the *Man'yōshū*, which was composed (so the headnote tells us) by a woman in orders and by Ōtomo Yakamochi (718-85).

Sahogawa no	Whoever it may be
Mizu o sekiagete	Who used the Saho River for its waters
Ueshi ta o—	And tilled the paddy fields—
—Karu wasaii wa	—Should be the one entitled
Hitori naru beshi.	To harvest the ripened grain.

This verse can claim no status higher than a game. But the game takes as its model the most highly respected form of literature.

Linked poetry therefore differs from other kinds of Japanese literature. It does not develop from the merely entertaining or frivolous, as did

[4] See *Man'yōshū* 5: 892-93. A translation of this poem by Okura (?660-733) will be found in *Court Poetry*, pp. 121-23, or *Introduction*, pp. 59-61.

[5] The matter is discussed in a crucial article by Konishi Jin'ichi, "Association and Progression: Principles of Integration in Anthologies and Sequences of Japanese Court Poetry, A.D. 900-1350," *Harvard Journal of Asiatic Studies*, 21 (1958), 67-127. See also *Court Poetry*, pp. 319-29, 403-13, and in the index under "Renga." See also Robert H. Brower, "Introduction," *Fujiwara Teika's Hundred-Poem Sequence of the Shōji Era, 1200* (Sophia University, 1978), which appeared as this book was in proof. Brower assesses impressiveness of the poems in terms corresponding to those here: mon, yaya mon (for monji), yaya ji (for jimon) and ji.

prose fiction (monogatari) and drama (nō, kyōgen, kabuki). On the contrary, it developed as entertainment or frivolity from the serious tanka form. And when renga learned to dress up properly, haikai stepped forth as a barefoot equivalent. Those developments came long after the *Man'yōshū*. There is a passage, however, in *The Diary of Izumi Shikibu* (*Izumi Shikibu Nikki*; date unclear, after 1003) that suggests some of the growing possibilities that would result in linked poetry after some time. The lady is being visited by her lover, Prince Atsumichi, who flusters her by arriving in daylight. Taken aback at being seen, she again puts off his urging that she move into his palace as a concubine. Now that he can see in the daylight what her place looks like, he explores the garden.

He went to a thin place in the hedge at the end of the garden and there broke off a lovely bough of spindletree, its leaves just flecked with autumn color. Thrusting it upright into the railing, he spoke a couple of verses.

Koto no ha fukaku   Like these leaves the words between us
Narinikeru kana—   Take on a truer depth of love—

She at once capped his verses.

—Shiratsuyu no   —Only when you settle
Hakanaku oku to   Like the all-too-transient dew,
Mishi hodo ni.   A moment white, and gone.

The prince is greatly taken by her reply, as well he might be. Leaves are thought to turn in color by the stimulus of dew (or drizzle, or frost), and dew is a long-established metaphor for the fleeting, just as wetness can represent eroticism. By using a lower unit for his opening, the prince suggests that they have been sharing poetry, which is to say response to life, for some time during their intimacy. In fact they have exchanged poems more or less constantly. Her ability to use that assumption and to seize freshly on his leaves-words metaphor (she translates it into leaves-dew, words-heart; leaves-words, and dew-heart) well represents what the sequential character of linked verse basically concerns.

The fifth of the twenty-one imperial collections, the *Kin'yōshū* (ca. 1125), took the radical step of including in its tenth and last book some nineteen examples of such short renga (692-710). These are chiefly to be commended for displays of ready wit, although their inclusion must have confirmed the opinion of many conservatives about the eccentricity of the compiler, Minamoto Shunrai (?1057-1129). This period appears to be the time when short renga reached its height of popularity within waka. For anything further to happen, renga would need to take a second crucial step, developing longer sequences, thereby hoping to achieve a status important enough to distinguish it from waka. The meager evidence shows that the step was taken in the twelfth century, whether or not Shunrai was responsible. It does say something that the highly conservative poet-critic, Fujiwara Kiyosuke (1104-1177), should have set down some rules for renga in his *Fukuro Sōshi* (1159). We might expect a rules-minded conservative to decree that the initial stanza (hokku) must always be the upper unit of a tanka. But, given the prestige of tanka and the practice of most short renga, the rule makes sense. It seems to imply that long renga must have been on his mind. Not much early evidence has been known, but in recent years two long renga have been recovered from the twelfth century. Court poets wrote them as relaxation after the greater rigor of composing waka, or on other occasions when drink and levity prevailed. By the Kamakura period (1185-1382) the distinctive renga form in one hundred stanzas was practiced, and in ensuing Muromachi times (ca. 1392-1568), serious renga achieved true greatness.

The development of long or chain renga was crucial, and it did not so much matter whether its decorum always matched that of waka: we shall be distinguishing kinds of renga subsequently. By extending renga beyond a capping stanza, poets gave it a social reason for existence, and that reason ensured a potential for serious development. Now several people could sit down and compose, taking turns in adding stanza to stanza, making a separate new poetic unit each time. As the length of the chain increased, no single link bore a responsibility to be outstanding. One could have a try and, if the result was nothing exceptional, one knew that someone else would be adding a stanza in two or three minutes, and one could try harder on the next turn. This practice seems to have been well received in the capital and to have been welcomed when it was introduced elsewhere. The dispersion of renga was further promoted by the upheavals around the capital and the political chaos brought by the Ōnin War (1467-1477). On numerous occasions anyone who could do so left

the capital. Among those leaving were the priests and nobles who favored renga. They communicated their fervor to military protectors and
other parties on whom they found themselves relying. Soon commoners
caught the enthusiasm. Japanese like to be up-to-date, and it must have
seemed agreeable to be doing what those arbiters of taste in the capital
had lately thought up.

Those who knew renga sufficiently well found that they could aug-
ment their uncertain incomes with patronage from the houses of powerful warrior chiefs or from well-off commoners. By this time renga had
become an art with highly complex rules, and teachers were much
sought after. Those who took it seriously discovered that they had to
gain something more than mere acquaintance with waka and other court
literature. Where there is a need for instruction, teachers will be found.
So there appeared the renga masters (rengashi). A given master could
count on a serious pupil's requiring a lengthy period of instruction.
Learning and patronage led to a kind of master-pupil relation that was to
continue for haikai and that exists to this day in most Japanese arts.

Many masters were priests, normally in title and ordination, rather
than in practice of temple rites. Or, like Bashō later, they might have the
habits of life by which priests were known. Priests Nōin (998-1050) and
Saigyō (1118-1190) had set examples for poetically gifted clerics in their
pilgrimages around the country, composing poems, and imparting
something of the culture of the court to provincial life. Besides his
poems, Saigyō was esteemed for his knowledge of court football and
love of cherry blossoms (rather than of the then more esteemed plum).
Few traces of Nōin are easily found today, but there are "Saigyō cherries" ("Saigyōzakura") in many places. None of the renga masters became equally beloved, but they were of special importance. When the
political situation became very unstable, they, in their priestly garb, became necessary agents to carry the old culture into a new age and into
new geographical as well as social areas. This was the easier for priests because of their special place in Japanese society, as the example of Saigyō
had shown. Born into a military family at a time when the nobility alone
mattered socially, he had no hope as a soldier of entering into the nobility's social functions and so displaying his great poetic gifts. When he
took orders, however, gates were opened to him and even the imperial

palace was not out of bounds. By the same token, a priest—no matter how highly born or renowned—lost no dignity in associating with soldiers and commoners. He was at once above the world and duty-bound to assist the rest of humanity soiled by its dust.

The special social freedom of a priest does a little to explain how some of the greatest renga masters—Sōgi himself provides a telling example—could come from the humblest or most obscure origins and yet rise to high social esteem. The priest's role as a teacher also makes clear how natural it was for a famous poet like Sōgi or Bashō (1421-1502 and 1644-1694) to walk up and down the country, associating with all ranks of people, teaching linked poetry, participating in its composition, and even lecturing on the Japanese classics. Such exposure brought increased demand. Military bigwigs in Sōgi's sorely tried age sought the aid of people like him, often in terms of a hundred-stanza sequence composed by a single poet. The completed poem might be offered to a shrine to ensure victory in an ensuing engagement. As the nation appeared to settle down, the popularity of renga became a craze. The military authorities who now ruled the state sought in vain to prohibit the excessive spending devoted to it. In time the fever for renga cooled. As the renga masters settled back in the capital, they could reflect that the excitement had confirmed the old idea of the wandering priestly poet and had dyed the literature of their time with a new coloring.

Linked poetry also develops more directly from waka. It has been shown how much the canons of waka mattered to renga, although if only general matters concerned with a lyric poetic system were involved, linked poetry would have developed systematically in China and Korea as well. (See Figure 6.) But more specific matters are also involved. In the twelfth century, court poets brought to mature practice the technique of allusive variation, whereby a poet could greatly increase the resonance and meaningfulness of a poem by incorporating into it elements by allusion to an earlier poem (honkadori) or to a prose classic (honzetsu). The renga poets took up allusion as a matter of course. The first stanza of *Three Poets* alludes to a poem by Emperor Gotoba (1180-1239), as we shall later have cause to appreciate afresh. Allusions might draw on such other sources as court monogatari—almost always *Tales from Ise* (*Ise Monogatari*) and *The Tale of Genji* (*Genji Monogatari*). In addition, there were Chinese legends and poems, and Buddhist lore. Of all these, the court poets were naturally most on the minds of their successors. This is not at all surprising, but it says a good deal that the renga poets do not allude to earlier renga in writing their poems, as a waka poet might allude to earlier waka. (Haikai poets also do not allude to earlier haikai.)

The debt to waka requires larger as well as more detailed accounting. Essentially, it involves a borrowing of sequential and integrative procedures developed by the court poets. As early as the first imperial collection, the *Kokinshū* (905), the compilers of these twenty-one anthologies of various reigns had chosen to organize their poems by principles quite different from those employed in other literatures. Instead of using, for example, chronology and single author canons, the compilers grouped poems according to certain subjects, progressions, and a peculiarly Japanese sense of fitness. The two main groups of books in the usual twenty-book collection were those leading off the first and the second ten. The former were the six books of seasonal poems (including two each on spring and autumn) and the latter the four or so of love poems. Within those categories and others, poems were arranged by natural progression: by the natural and ceremonial sequences of seasonal happenings or by a progression based on the development of a courtly love affair. The non-seasonal, non-love poems were often less rigorously organized and sometimes organized on fresh principles. These presumed lesser books were often shifted about from collection to collection, except that a group that came into increasing prominence tended to be grouped near the end. This group of "zō" poems was thought to be "miscellaneous" in the sense that no single topic such as a season or love predominated. Yet so fine could distinctions become that the books of miscellaneous poems sometimes mirrored the collection at large, beginning with somewhat seasonal poems, picking up with rather love-like poems, and ending with very miscellaneous poems. Such patterns came to be reflected in the highly serious poetry matches (utaawase) and in waka sequences. The latter provide the most direct source of influence of court literature on renga and haikai. These sequences of tanka commonly incorporated one hundred units, just as did renga subsequently. And they were patterned after the large imperial collections, either by mirroring those large wholes or such a unit as spring or love poems. More important still, the compilers or composers of these smaller collections used progressive and associational techniques to integrate the hundred poems into a larger poem of five hundred lines.

The full details of these integrative procedures need not be rehearsed here.[6] Some exemplary details will serve. The love poems in a hundred-poem sequence would use a temporal progression from the man's first yearnings to the woman's last miseries. To that would be added other associations and progressions. The first poem might tell of the man's vague interest in a woman as remote from him as a certain mountain in the provinces. The next might tell how she was hidden from his access as a hill obscured by clouds. The third might develop the image of clouds into the kumoi, the cloudland of the high nobility, implying that she was cut off from him by her high rank. In such fashion the poems could progress from a mountain to hills, and from clouds on hills to metaphorical clouds. Obviously the progressions imply association. The temporal course of the affair might be accompanied by a geographical progression at once highly satisfying and involved in the love progression only as an obligato to the main part. Similarly, some summer poems might have a series on the much-hoped-for song of the wood thrush (hototogisu) in the mountains, foothills, a plain, a named river, and then the capital. Renga owes to the waka sequences the idea that a hundred (or more or fewer) units could be so integrated. It owes to the imperial collections the principle that several people might be involved in the arrangement.

In making use of waka sequences, the renga and haikai masters took over the classifications that made grouping and therefore integration possible. They made matters at once simpler and more complex. The classification in linked poetry is simpler, in the sense that a given stanza has but one of two kinds of main topics: a season or zō, the miscellaneous. In other words, the miscellaneous became a more important category. On the other hand, the old topics that had had separate books devoted to them became sub-topics: love, travel, grievance, Buddhism, etc. (In Parts Two and Three of this book, these topics will be capitalized to emphasize their functions.) Certain other matters such as essential nature (hon'i) will be treated later. For now the basic principles are the important things. If poems or stanzas are to be related, they must be similar;

[6] See the studies mentioned in n. 5.

but they must also differ sufficiently in order to add to what has previously existed. Constant connection in either association or progression requires constant likeness, or the effort would prove unintelligible. Yet without constant alteration, repetition rather than sequence would result. From analogy with connections drawn between upper and lower units of tanka, individual tanka in a sequence were also related more or less closely. Closely related units or poems (shinku) shared more fully such elements as diction, imagery, and conception. Distantly related units or poems (soku) shared much less. It came to be expected that pleasure in reading a progression derived from varying the closeness of relation between constituent units. A few might be connected by obvious resemblances, especially in language. Then two might seem to have no connection at all—none, at least, until one recalled that together they constituted an allusion to some older poem. The allusion may not have been intended by the author of either poem but may have been created solely by the ingenuity of the compilers in their juxtaposing.

The profound debts of linked poetry to waka shade off in matters of decorum. In waka, decorum involved degrees of formality, usually in styles, subjects, diction, and images. Occasionally more was involved, and a given poem might be accepted as waka but be classified as haikai, non-standard. Essentially waka shrank from the non-standard and aspired to be "kokoro aru" (possessed of right heart), for which the more sinified term was "ushin." As renga emerged, it was at first considered to be "mushin" (without right heart), non-standard, "haikai." But a standard version was devised, and for about three or four centuries the renga alternatives were thought to involve choice between the mushin and the ushin, the non-standard and less decorous as opposed to the standard and serious. Among waka poets, renga was by definition non-standard. But, in typical Japanese fashion, what had been born with a grin sobered into dignity. What earlier would have seemed a contradiction—ushin or serious, standard renga—came into being; it is that with which we are chiefly concerned. Mushin renga is sometimes called comic renga, but in truth there are not many examples that would cause laughter. It is rather a matter of a distinctly lower decorum allowing for language (including the sinified), subjects, and conceptions out of bonds in standard renga and of course in waka. Decorum could be violated by introducing two or three words not found in one of the first three or eight imperial anthologies, or by scatology or sex usually managed by word play. Other examples simply seem to play with conceptions (kokoro) or with language (kotoba).

Non-standard renga had perfectly serious objectives, even when frivolous. Among them were an entertainment and naughty fun to exist beside waka seriousness. Both aspects require an understanding as much human as compartmentalized into "literature." Without the waka decorum, departure was neither possible nor desirable. With it eventually came necessity and feasibility. But the departure to lower levels introduced new words, and new words brought valuable new subjects that then could be seen to deserve serious treatment on their own. In the end, the most important and in some ways most difficult thing to understand about renga of the serious kind is its margin of difference from waka. There was no point in the existence of renga if it did not differ. But there could also be no seriousness without profound resemblance.

The later history of renga involves means of preserving what was needed from waka and standard decorum, and of enlarging or making new by admitting what was non-standard in ways that would fuse with the standard. Some of the personalities involved will be concerning us shortly, but since Sōchō is one of the best known of renga poets, it is worth mentioning that he contributed to the development of haikai by writing in the non-standard version of renga. That is, he wrote both the standard kind and what he termed mad jottings, "kyōhitsu."[7] Such poetic madness was a far cry from courtly seriousness. Yet, as so often in human history, the foolishness of one generation became the earnest of a later.

This can be understood best in terms of the evolution from renga to haikai. Haikai is merely an abbreviation of "haikai no renga" (sometimes more simply "haikai renga"), at least as to name. But if it were no more than that, it would have remained simply a relaxed and not very serious version of renga: mushin renga. It took the genius of poets like Bashō to understand that another kind of poetry was needed. His haikai is as much like renga and as much (or rather somewhat more) different from renga as renga resembles and differs from waka. Yet it is not lacking in heart,

[7] See Keene, "The Comic Tradition in Renga."

not mushin. It is a serious version of renga in a lower decorum, much as the novel varies from the prose romance. As we shall see, the lowering of decorum continued to senryū, which developed from a linked kind of still lower decorum into a witty, pungent, and sometimes satiric single stanza, or hokku. These in turn contributed in due course to another rise in seriousness, as the hokku of haikai was gradually separated out as a distinct unit into the modern haiku. In such fashion does the story of renga end in the haiku practiced today after having begun in earliest Japanese literary times. To have affiliations with so much older and so much later is to own something important to the literary genius of the Japanese people. Since a poem is not written by a people, however, but by an individual poet, we may now turn to some of the major renga masters and their concerns.

2

Some Principal Renga Poets

"Renga is not exhausted by the meaning
of the stanza that precedes or of the
stanza that follows."
—Nijō Yoshimoto

THE HISTORY of the development of renga from its short version in antiquity to its successors in haikai and haiku is also necessarily the history
of a line of poets. Their ideals and their practice have given us our subject, which is still far from having been thoroughly studied. Fortunately,
more and more becomes clear not only about the individual poets but
also of how they thought.

It makes good sense to begin with the opinions of the greatest of the
renga masters, Sōgi (1421-1502), who distinguished three periods. The
early one culminated in Nijō Yoshimoto (1320-1388). There followed an
intermediate period, and the modern one began with Sōgi's elder contemporary, Sōzei (d. 1455, apparently over seventy). The modern period
included not just Sōgi but also those who received training from him.
When this period began to close some time in the sixteenth or
seventeenth century, the center of poetic value was shifting from standard renga to haikai no renga (or haikai renga), although the standard kind
continued to be practiced until recent times. We may follow the spirit of
Sōgi's periodizing by beginning with Yoshimoto as a major figure whose
ideas represent a culmination and a point of departure.

Yoshimoto represents a culmination in that he looked on himself, with
good reason, as a representative of the court and of its culture. We shall
be seeing that many of the principal renga poets who came after him
could make no great claims as to their origins. Yoshimoto, however, was
descended from the highest nobility short of the royal house and he
achieved the highest court titles. The power such appointments held had

diminished from earlier days, but they were profoundly respected for
what they implied of legitimacy, culture, and status. Yoshimoto regarded himself primarily as a waka poet and regarded renga as a less
rigorous, less civilized, attainment. He had studied waka with Priest
Ton'a (1289-1372), who compiled the nineteenth of the twenty-one imperial collections, the *Shinshūishū*, about 1364. Yoshimoto himself was to
write the Japanese preface to the next collection, the *Shingoshūishū*, compiled in 1383, and he practiced waka in the manner of the erudite but in-
sipid school of Nijō poets. That group was one of three houses descended from Fujiwara Teika (1162-1241), one of Japan's greatest poets.
His Nijō descendants took on the same place-name as Yoshimoto's but
they were of lower social status. It was typical of Yoshimoto that he
should follow the conservative line of waka poets and yet be flexible for
renga and other kinds of writing not thought so important and less governed by acquired canons. Waka demanded the utmost effort to preserve
old norms. Renga was different. As Kidō Saizō has put it, Yoshimoto felt
one had achieved the aim of renga if one had sufficiently satisfied oneself.[1] By that he may have meant satisfying someone cultivated like himself, but he would have thought such a criterion merely self-indulgent for
waka.

None of this suggests Yoshimoto's importance. He truly understood
poetry and was a versatile writer in waka, renga, and several prose kinds.
Among his principal works connected with renga, pride of place must go
to his *Tsukuba Collection* (*Tsukubashū*), whose representation of major
renga poets of his time no doubt lies behind Sōgi's periodization. So famous was the collection that renga was often called the Tsukuba vocation
("Tsukuba no michi"), and "Tsukuba" came to suggest renga in several
contexts. A few other titles may be mentioned: *The New Rules of Renga*
(*Renga Shinshiki*); *A Secret Treatise of Renga Principles* (*Renri Hishō*, whose
latter part is *The Codified Rules of Renga, Renga no Shikimoku*); *The
Tsukuba Dialogues* (*Tsukuba Mondō*); and *The Kyushu Dialogues* (*Kyūshū
Mondō*). We observe the affiliation with the Nijō poets in Yoshimoto's
willingness to set rules. His contemporaries would have been struck
more forcibly by the ordering principles of *The Tsukuba Collection*

---

[1] This and the next quoted matter are taken from Kidō Saizō, *et al.*, *Rengaronshū, Hairon-
shū* (Iwanami Shoten, 1953), pp. 11-12.

(1356). For, like an imperial anthology of waka, it is organized into twenty books, and its length runs to something over 2,100 stanzas. Renga had thrived sufficiently to be worthy the treatment accorded waka. For this unprecedented action to have been taken by an unimpeachably civilized nobleman suggests that renga had gained true prestige.

Yoshimoto's most famous pronouncement adorns a very simple, important point with what looks like the faded brocade of images and sentiments from waka: "Renga is not exhausted by the meaning of the stanza that precedes or of the stanza that follows, nor yet by prosperity or decline, grief or happiness; for just as we set boundaries only to have them shift away, so there is nothing in this transient world. As we consider it today, it has grown tomorrow. As we consider it spring, it has become autumn. As we consider the flowers, they have faded to yellow leaves. Is it not all summed up in 'whirling petals and falling leaves'?"

The commonplaces associate renga with waka, and their series well emphasizes the shifting meanings at each link of the renga chain. What follows recalls Tsurayuki's affective-expressive poetics in the preface to the *Kokinshū* four and a half centuries earlier: "When the moon shines on the snow or when the flowers brighten the trees, we yield to time's presence and observe its manifestation—so our hearts work within us and express themselves in words."

Many critics have remarked on Yoshimoto's greater liberalism toward renga than toward waka. The novel or original meant more for him in linked poetry, as we can see from his dictum that the opening stanza should be rich with a profound conception, pleasing in diction, elevated, and fresh. The first and last of these requirements do not enter his conception of waka. He did not require the diction of renga to be restricted to the first three imperial collections of waka. Two of his other principles were to have a profound effect, not just on subsequent linked verse, but also on nō. He defined the yūgen of renga as beauty rather than as mysterious or suffering profundity. And he established the basic sequential pattern of renga, haikai, and nō when, in his *Tsukuba Dialogues*, he required for renga as from music earlier the jo-ha-kyū rhythm: introduction-development-rapid close.

Yoshimoto gave currency to other crucial ideas. He called for a mixture of superior (umon) and ordinary (mumon) stanzas. These are nothing less than the design and ground (mon and ji) degrees of impressiveness that will be crucial to our analysis. He did tend to place more emphasis on words than on total effect. But he also said that in renga the listener should be startled by some brilliance or novelty of subject, so departing from his waka conservativism. Among numerous sayings, one that most deserves attending to is his stress on connectedness or dependence (his word is "kakari"). "In renga," he wrote, "connection comes first. Connection is its poetry. Its poetry is connection." This important principle appears to be indebted to his study of renga with Kyūzai (or Kyūsei, Kusei, Gusai; d. 1376 or 1378), who touches on such matters in one of the first (*Kenji Shinshiki*) of the renga formularies that began to appear in the 1370's.

Yoshimoto complained, perhaps from snobbishness, of the lack of connectedness in the renga by commoners. If connection was all he desired, he must have liked Kyūzai's style in stanzas like these:

Mononofu no	Mount Tonami
tate o naraburu	standing like shields aligned
Tonamiyama—	by warrior hands—
nami ni katabuku	into the waves there slowly slips
yumihari no tsuki	the moon curved like a full drawn bow[2]

The stanzas are well connected by the assonance and consonance of "*Tonamiyama / nami* ni." But the court poets would have been jarred by the military imagery. The difference in diction derives from different realms of experience and helps to account for Yoshimoto's uneasiness with renga by commoners. He aimed at a waka-like courtly beauty, whereas most of the commoners in his day aimed at pleasure, wit, and delight. His sympathies with them are therefore more significant than his complaints. In particular, his devoted study of renga gave it a prestige it had not had. Here was a very high-born nobleman to whom linked poetry

---

[2] Kidō, *Rengashi*, 1, 19-24. This study will be cited chiefly for poetic examples and quotations from renga critics, but my debt is greater than that alone suggests. For full citations of titles frequently referred to, see Abbreviated References, pp. xvii-xviii.

had dignity. It was worthy of rules-making like waka, worthy of selection for an anthology resembling the imperial collections, and above all worthy of practice. Yoshimoto was the last of the major court renga poets, if by that we mean a person not only born to the upper ranks of the old nobility but also a bearer of its titles and definer of its highest art, waka. Linked poetry now mattered and so would be worthy of dispute and change as well as of practice.

Most of the poets of the middle period designated by Sōgi differ from Yoshimoto and resemble Sōgi himself in their possessing priestly or otherwise sinified names. We can select three who resemble Yoshimoto in being distinguished for waka but in whose practice renga more and more assumes the central place. These three are Imagawa Ryōshun (1325-1420), Priest Shōtetsu (1381-1459), and Bishop Shinkei (1406-1475). My very strong preference would lead to naming this the period of Shinkei, except that he was but fifteen years senior to Sōgi. How long most renga masters lived! We are therefore dealing with development typified by major individual styles rather than with dates pure and simple.

It was Ryōshun to whom Yoshimoto had written his *Kyushu Dialogues* complaining about commoners. Ryōshun was not one of the careless ones, and in fact was a man of many parts. Besides mastering linked poetry, he showed real abilities as a warrior and an administrator. He also wrote waka, wisely choosing the style of the Reizei line, which, like the similarly liberal Kyōgoku line, was also descended from Teika and opposed to the Nijō house.[3] His advocacy of Reizei ideas in renga might have had important effect, but he was apparently not widely attended to as a renga critic. Such lasting effect as those ideas may have exerted came indirectly from his being the waka teacher of Shōtetsu.

Renga may appear to have attracted those born to live to advanced years: Shōtetsu died in 1459 at seventy-eight. But other matters are involved. The disturbances in the kingdom, the complexities of the art, and the requirement of long apprenticeship meant that one had best not die in middle age if one wished to exercise influence in linked poetry. From about 1430 (when Shōtetsu was nearing fifty), renga was largely

[3] For samples of his waka and more on his preferences, see *Introduction*, pp. 137-43.

the possession of warriors or of priests. Shōtetsu had a priest's social freedom, but it was his rank as one of the few most important waka poets of
the time that drew people to study renga with him.[4] Knowledge of court
literature was required for prestige, for a range of allusion, and for aesthetic canons. It was to such ends in those unsettled times leading up to
the havoc of the Ōnin War that warriors, priests, and some of the nobility were meeting to discuss their court inheritance. Shōtetsu was not
himself a dominant renga poet as were Shinkei, Sōzei (d. 1455), and
Chiun (d. 1448). The last two were, however, his disciples in waka and
from him imbibed something of those Reizei principles that had meant
so much to Ryōshun. Shōtetsu was also one of the first to offer renga
poets instruction in *The Tale of Genji* and *Tales from Ise*.

What Sōzei and Chiun learned from Shōtetsu and their study of the
classics gives their renga a courtly aura not to be found in the typical
compositions of warriors and commoners before them. A few stanzas
will serve to show their new style, especially in contrast with Kyūzai's
stanzas on the shield mountain and bowed moon.[5]

yumizue furitate	waving their bows on high
kaeru karibito	the hunters set off for home
★	★
saoshika no	at Irino
Irino no tomoshi	the torches of the stag hunt
kiyuru no ni	go out on the moor
★	★
mukaeba tsuki zo	as one turns about the moon
kokoro o mo shiru	understands one's very heart
★	★
nishi o nomi	only in the west
negau io no	does one long to claim one's hut
yowa no aki	at autumn midnight

Or again:

---

[4] For waka by Shōtetsu, see *Introduction*, pp. 138-40.
[5] Kidō, *Rengashi*, 1, 28. I do not specify poets here or give each stanza twice as for more
important examples below; the purpose here is purely illustrative.

furusato wa	oh for the capital
no ni fuku kaze no	over the moors there blows the wind
yadori nite	where one spends the night
★	★
tabine no yume wa	the dream the traveler beholds
yasuku samekeri	easily yields to waking hours

The first two stanzas rather resemble Kyūzai's, except that he sought to impose warrior experience on the court world, whereas these stanzas do the reverse. The remaining stanzas, as a glance at the last two will reveal, show how their authors understood court poetry, both as to sensibility and as to the waka-like strong continuity between individual stanzas.

Shōtetsu was at one with Yoshimoto and with many later critics in advocating the ideal of yūgen. So various were the meanings given the term that one must always inquire what an individual means. Shōtetsu meant the ethereal beauty (yōen) and richness (yojō) that distinguish much of Teika's poetry. To those who studied with him he imparted the ideal of such beauty, especially for seasonal stanzas. To this heritage poets like Sōzei imparted something of the warrior's sensibility, as was perfectly natural.. But Shōtetsu's greatest waka student—Shinkei—transcended his teaching and his teacher by intensifying and enlarging experience, and by the most brilliant style of all renga poets.

Shinkei was one of the most difficult of Japanese poets, in waka and renga alike. This difficulty is epitomized in his remark that renga and waka are the same thing (something Bashō was also to insist on, in somewhat different terms). That means that the best of Ryōshun's and Shōtetsu's ideals for waka were brilliantly adapted to renga, but he also seems to have taken from renga back to waka an intensity then all too lacking in that flagging art.[6] In fact, Shinkei is a poet of real genius, not studied as he deserves, perhaps because of the difficulties he presents. But we also lack information about the person or persons with whom he studied renga, although he does record that he studied it from about 1420. In 1447 he participated with Shōtetsu in a sequence designated, like so many, "A Hundred Stanzas Relating to 'Person.' " The older poet wrote the opening stanza:

[6] For examples of Shinkei's waka, see *Introduction*, pp. 140-42.

> Na mo shiranu   Their name unknown
> kogusa hana saku   the little plants color with flowers
> kawabe kana   the banks of the river

To this Shinkei added a highly admired stanza:

> shibafugakure no   the marsh waters of autumn
> aki no sawamizu   cover over the wild grasses

Many poets could have written the opening stanza. Few would have continued its beauty in the very firm and more austere autumnal scene. The difference lies in artistic intelligence.

With Shinkei's practice and criticism, a new sense of kokoro or human presence seems to enter renga (and waka), along with a renewal of the expressive elements of poetry. One of his pronouncements shows the freshness and indeed the truth of his ideas. He is speaking of an ideal of poetic beauty, "en," for which the usual translation, "charm," is inadequate. It is rendered "meaningful beauty" in the following translation: "The element of meaningful beauty cannot be found except superficially in the outlines (sugata) of a stanza or in simplified language. It is found in a stanza that derives from deep concern with the passions of the human heart and the manifold transient things of the world; it proceeds from the heart, as without forgetting human feelings, one delicately considers a whole life in the blessing of being human."[7] The concern with human passion and suffering differs widely from Yoshimoto's fine language. The same concern often appears in his renga. For example, to the following—

> Aware ni mo   It is with anguish
> mashiba oritaku   that the plucked twigs are kindled
> yūkeburi—   into evening smoke—

Shinkei added—

---

[7] Kidō Rengashi, 1, 406; his discussion of Shinkei will be found in 1, 405–13. Selections from Sasamegoto have been translated by Dennis Hirota, Chanoyu Quarterly, no. 19 (1978), pp. 23–46, appearing while this book was in press.

sumi uru ichi no   selling charcoal at the market
kaeru Sanoyama   he returns to Mount Sano

Shinkei alters the rather routine stanza before his, which suggests some elegant recluse in his hut, by taking the imagery as a real possibility. His charcoal vendor may sell his (or her?) ware to townspeople but is so poor that to cook what passes for an evening meal he must gather and burn twigs, not being able to afford to use that on which so humble a livelihood depends. With his sure eye, Sōgi praised this stanza for being especially characteristic of Shinkei's poetic merits.

Another stanza added to an upper stanza shows how Shinkei's seem to leap from the sequence in which they appear. To

Waga kokoro   My heart is full
tare ni kataran   to whom can I unburden
aki no sora   the autumn sky

he added

ogi ni yūkaze   to the reeds the evening breeze
kumo ni karigane   to the clouds the cries of geese

The routine sequence of personal noun and particle in the earlier stanza, "tare ni" (to whom) is picked up and given exciting life by Shinkei's emphatic parallelism: "ogi ni" (to the reeds) . . . "kumo ni" (to the clouds). By itself, his stanza suggests only that the wind is in the reeds and the geese cry in the clouds, but he uses the earlier stanza to add to that sense another. The wind and the geese become burdened in heart, like the person speaking the previous stanza. "One should tell the breeze and geese" is what the earlier stanza leads us to anticipate, and that meaning is the ordinary one and is also present. One cries out to the wind and geese about one's deepest feelings. They have already told theirs to the reeds and clouds. Looking and hearing, Shinkei's speaker has his own heart filled over twice more.

Not all his stanzas are so complex, as one or two more opening stanzas (hokku) show.

Hana ochite	The flowers fall
ozasa tsuyukeki	and the bamboo grasses lade with dew
yamaji kana	the mountain path
★	★
Kiku hodo wa	While I listen
tsuki o wasururu	I forget about the moon
shigure kana	as drizzle falls

The first stanza is nice, and it is simple. As the translation has attempted to show, the adjective at the end of the second line governs a noun before and after it, so that "tsuyukeki" ("lade with dew") describes both the bamboo grass and the path. The second hokku is much more difficult. Moon and drizzle are not thought of together in poetry, for the good reason that when one can hear that kind of rain from heavy low clouds one cannot see the moon. Of course to mention that the moon is forgotten is to recall it. The most natural way of interpreting this stanza syntactically would go another way, taking "wasururu" not as the verb for the topic phrase "kiku hodo wa" but as an attributive governing "shigure."

> While one listens
> the drizzle has forgotten
> about the moon

On this reading, the speaker remembers and criticizes the drizzle for depriving him of the moon. This meaning is present, but it merges with the other and principal meaning, because the drizzle is a metaphor for the speaker's tears as well as being meant literally.

Shinkei can be more difficult still, as in this hokku.

Minu shima wa	The unseen island
sazona yomogi ga	must resemble spring in a garden
niwa no haru	rampant with overgrowth

The words are not difficult, but the meaning could not possibly be clear today without Shinkei's note (his adding it shows that his contemporaries were not expected to understand it either). He remarks that his overgrown and negligible garden reminds him of the isle of Mount

Hōrai, a place of eternal youth: that is, when spring returns to make his humble scene beautiful.

Shinkei's brilliance makes his predecessors look tame. His cultivation and intelligence make others look amateurish. Sōgi had a high opinion of him and included his stanzas in *The New Tsukuba Collection* (*Shintsukubashū*). As Konishi Jin'ichi puts it about that anthology, if one concealed the authors' names, only Shinkei's stanzas are sufficiently distinctive to stand forth and claim their author. Konishi goes much further: "I believe that Shinkei's stanzas are of unmatched greatness. Sōgi also writes outstanding stanzas, but if one considers stanzas alone, it is Shinkei's that one would judge to excel by the profound effect they have on us."[8] That is very high praise. But for linked poetry it is not the highest. Renga is not an art of isolated stanzas but of relation—what Yoshimoto termed connection. Those who think hokku or opening stanzas to be the same thing as haiku would have to rank Shinkei the greatest haiku poet, with Bashō second. But Shinkei wrote renga and Bashō haikai. In Shinkei's failure to excel in the art of relation he must yield to the greater renga genius of Sōgi.

The place of Sōgi (1421-1502) in the history of renga can be appreciated in terms of his relation to other major poets and to the background of the times. What he termed the present or modern age of renga began, it will be remembered, with Sōzei. Sōzei died in 1455, when Sōgi was in his renga nonage, a mere thirty-four years old. Many of the other important renga poets perished in the Ōnin War or in the tribulations that followed. These include Gyōjo (1405-1469); Nōa (1397-1471), who was also a painter; Senjun (1411-1476), who survived most of the war by moving to the province of Bizen; and Shinkei. All who could do so fled at some point to the provinces, taking their culture with them, and since they often took little else, profits from it became their means of survival. Shinkei's *Sasamegoto* (or *Whisperings*) shows, as do other accounts, that renga was often composed orally by commoners unable to write. The dispersed nobility and priests aided in the education of the people with whom they came in touch.

Sōgi played a major role in such transmission, perhaps because he seemed able to meet with anyone on easy terms. In his *Eastern Dialogues*

[8] Konishi, *Sōgi*, p. 52.

(*Azuma Mondō*), he writes feelingly about those who gathered around him in Kadotagawa in the province of Musashi: "Their inquiries into the vocation (michi) of poetry and their conduct are gratifying. We have also thought that we might hope to be together in the next world."[9] After the Ōnin War, poets like him could take something of the sturdy provincial spirit back to the capital. And there, especially at court, particularly under the aegis of Gotsuchimikado (r. 1465-1500), linked verse became popular. The nobility linked stanzas in Japanese or by turns in Japanese and Chinese (wakan renku). Sōgi found himself able to join that exalted world. The reasons are somewhat complex, but clearly when he returned from the east he had a conception of renga that suited the times. Poetry was no longer the easy possession of a small group, nor the vocation of a few dedicated poets, nor yet simply a pastime. It had become a profession.

Sōgi was well endowed—especially by the absence of some qualifications necessary earlier—to desire to make renga a livelihood. Among the many masters whose origins were low, his are unknown, and his incentives to excel had to be correspondingly strong. His disciple, Sōchō, confessed to being the son of a smith. Sōgi does not speak of the house from which he came. Even the province of his origin is unknown, although some have argued for Ōmi near Lake Biwa and others for Kii to the south. The first certain date comes from Sōgi's own account late in life: he turned to renga about 1450, or at least when he was twenty-nine. It is generally assumed from scraps of evidence that he turned to renga after training in Buddhism of the Zen kind at Shōkoku Temple in the capital.[10] He is one of the many men at this time and somewhat later who took orders as a way of establishing themselves in the world and, having gained a place, practiced a vocation in poetry rather than in priestly rites. Training in the priesthood became for people like Sōgi a means for an otherwise inconceivable rise in the world. Material motives were surely involved, but so was that high culture which in Japan and elsewhere may require money but which earns respect apart from it. The evidence is scarce, but it may have been from his Zen Buddhist training that Sōgi received his knowledge of Sung aesthetics; it may also be that such knowledge was part of later training.[11]

[9] Kidō, *Rengashi*, 1, 434.   [10] *Ibid.*, 1, 436; but the evidence is not conclusive.
[11] On Sōgi and Sung aesthetics, see Konishi, *Sōgi*, p. 44.

Sōgi reminds one of Priest Saigyō before him and of Bashō after when he speaks of himself in his *Record of a Journey in Kyushu (Tsukushi Dōki)*. For all the sense of inadequacy, he clearly knew what he was up to: "From my youth to my present age of sixty I have been preoccupied with the single-mindedness of a fool, losing myself in the reedy marsh of good and evil and, like a waterplant overwhelmed by waters, ceaselessly overcome by grief. Immersed in the transhifting of dream and reality, I could scarcely reject the moving appeal [aware] of spring and have yielded to time, longing to see in the provinces those places of famous name."[12]

Sōgi did find time to pursue his renga studies. His manner of doing so perhaps suggests something of the agitation of those times or perhaps a restlessness in wishing to know the best poets of the time as well as places famous in verse. For whatever reason, he studied less than five years with Sōzei, and rather longer with Senjun until that master's death in 1476. At the same time he was also working with Shinkei, and in the sequences they wrote together his stanzas take on the intensity of that brilliant poet. Sōgi did refer to the other two teachers more often, but as one example will show, he was generous in praise of many: "To see into renga one should, then, compile a collection of the deep conceptions and lovely diction found in the stanzas of such poets as Sōzei, Chikamasa, Shinkei, Senjun, and others like them." Because he had the genius to create his own way, he took what he needed wherever he could find it.

In 1473 Sōgi returned to the capital. Although the war lasted another three years, the capital apparently had acquired some of its former calm. The following year he composed a thirty-stanza renga at the behest of Gotsuchimikado, an event clearly implying his having gained prestige. Besides the sovereign, numerous of the high nobility patronized the poet. He sometimes wrote renga with them, and sometimes for them. At other times he participated with them in renga matches (rengaawase). The reasons for this rise to greatness are not wholly clear. Kidō Saizō speculates that Sōgi had powerful recommendations from major figures in noble or military circles, that he had met some before going to the provinces, and others while there. Kidō also speculates that his connection with the Nijō line of waka poets may have given access to the nobility. Another, simpler, explanation (that does not necessarily rule out the

---

[12] Kidō, *Rengashi*, 1, 437; his discussion of Sōgi is in 1, 433-58.

others) may be that the deaths and dispersal of older renga masters helped to bring someone with Sōgi's gifts into eminence with unusual speed. Perhaps his talents were required. Whatever the explanation, he rose rapidly on returning to the capital. There is great significance in the fact that during this period he was showing his stature as a scholar by bringing out his commentary on *The Tale of Genji*. Since he did this in 1475, he had obviously prepared most of it in the provinces. In the next century, the master Satomura Jōha (the last major figure in this chapter) wrote that Sōgi had taken instruction in the *Genji* from one Shidara in the Kamakura military government and later from Ichijō Kanera (1402-1481). The developing scholar appears to have taken his papers with him wherever he went—whether to Musashi, Bizen, Nara, or back to the capital. He was writing renga all the time but preparing himself to make that mark as a classical scholar that was required for the highest respect of his contemporaries. As all this demonstrates, in those chaotic times culture seemed to matter the more. And then, as at no time we know of before or after until the last century, a person of genius from the lowliest, most obscure origins could become respected as poet and arbiter of learning.

In Japan as in other countries, the rise to eminence is normally accompanied by a certain symbolism by which the established order fits the new person into what it comfortably recognizes. Sōgi understood this. He studied the classics. He went on poetic travels to celebrated places. Later he defined his style of living in terms of a grass-thatched hut (sōan). Poetic travel and the hut were important symbols to many poets, but the three everyone thinks of are Saigyō, Sōgi, and Bashō. Bashō refers to "Sōgi's drizzle" and to "Sōgi's dwelling."[13] One of Bashō's hokku strikingly demonstrates his sense of continuity with Sōgi.

Yo ni furu wa	In the world of time
sara ni Sōgi no	it falls and yet the more in Sōgi's
yadori kana	grass-thatched hut

Contrary to the most important rule about an opening stanza, Bashō here includes no seasonal word. He presumes it to be unnecessary be-

---

[13] What follows on Sōgi is chiefly indebted to Konishi, *Sōgi*, pp. 9-59.

cause of his allusion to the fourth stanza in Sōgi's *Grasses of Forgetfulness* (*Wasuregusa*).

Yo ni furu mo	Even as time falls
sara ni shigure no	so the more in this world falls drizzle
yadori kana	at a grass-thatched hut

Shinkei also has a stanza from about that time.

Kumo wa nao	It is to the clouds
sadame aru yo no	one looks for a world of certainty
shigure kana	in the cold drizzle

The world of drizzle represents the privations of the Ōnin War as well as of the hermitage. These facts merge in their poetry, however, for, as has been well said, the literature of the hermits was born in the grass-thatched huts.

No easy road lay open. Sōgi could not realize what seems so bucolic without years of preparation and the good fortune not to be swallowed up by the chaos of the times. We might think that his success would lead him anywhere but to a thatched hut. But the hut was a symbol of refined taste and comfortable status.

The prestige of renga in the provinces, and its possible benefits to the poet, can be glimpsed in the superstitious awe in which it was held by some. Sōgi was beseeched to compose sequences on behalf of others. Somewhat later Sōchō composed his *Thousand Stanzas on Call to Battle* (*Shutsujin Senku*, 1504) to assist Imagawa Ujichika. About half a century before, Sōgi had written his *Thousand Stanzas at Mishima* (*Mishima Senku*) to alleviate attacks of sexual desire in the son of one of his most constant patrons, Tō no Tsuneyori. The success must have made him seem an almost miraculous physician, but it is obvious that success in battle or in efforts to cure depend not on the poetry so much as on the belief in its efficacy.

For his part, Sōgi was not only prospering but traveling, experiencing what generations of poetic travelers had led him to expect. Travelers carried writing kits then rather than cameras, as his *Journal of Travel to Shirakawa* (*Shirakawa Kikō*) well shows: "Along the way to the

Shirakawa Barrier one discovers brooks in the valleys, winds in the pines on the peaks, and other things of unusual appeal. To this side and that leaves had fallen from the boughs, traces appeared of huts of mountain-dwellers, and in the marshes at the foothills frost-withered reeds were broken over. The field wardens were gone from the paddies by the hill-sides where the stag cried out for his mate, and by the hut about to tip over, the bird-clapper with its all but rotted rope-pull made a sound whose loneliness swelled within me."

The prose does not have the intensity of Shinkei's. The images are mostly standard. But Sōgi clearly had to experience what he had been reading about. He was not born to a social position where these matters were a natural inheritance, known for longer than he could remember. More than that, the whole renga-flow of images has a greater power than any single image suggests. He did not walk about aimlessly. As with Saigyō going to Yoshino because it was best for cherry blossoms, so much more at this later date did poets seek out those places where flowers seemed essentially to be flowers, the moon characteristically the moon, and the dew to be especially dew-like. This is the idea of essence (hon'i) that we shall see meant so much to linked poetry.

Sōgi's devotion, expressed in travel, his ease with people, and his native genius, led him to the success symbolized by his elegant "hut," which he named Shugyokuan. That edifice—let it be said plainly—lasted twenty-seven years before being destroyed by fire and in it he had poetry parties, with more than a dozen participants and their attendants. It was no "hut about to tip over," as he reports from his trip to Shirakawa. In fact, he seems to have been well off since he was about fifty. If that is an achievement for any poet, it must be thought remarkable in traditional Japanese society for a person with no distinction of birth and whose only attractions were his abilities and personality.

Without depreciating his attractions, we can see that his success involved other things. Good luck, good friends, and a knack for doing the right thing at the right time seem to have been involved. After his initial period as a priest living on alms, he appears to have made his place in the world less as a poet than as a scholar of classical literature. His reputation for classical learning gave him status in itself and made him attractive in the potentially profitable business of teaching renga. His profession as poet was legitimized by the otherwise far less profitable authority of savant in the classics. To the man, all these things must have seemed nothing other than features of his single life, or at least difficult to sort out. Konishi Jin'ichi has evaluated them best, and without the usual solemnity. He writes of Sōgi's effectiveness in teaching the classics in terms of a Sōgi University with a College of Renga (Renga Gakubu).

Some consideration must also go to the high value placed on such learning during the Muromachi period. So many important sectors had much to gain from it. To many of the nobility, learning was one of the few avenues they could pursue for family livelihood. To the military, it was a way of achieving some of the prestige that would confer an air of legitimacy on the power they had newly gained—or presently sought. To the priests, it was a means of consolidating their educational position, inculcating their precepts, and transmitting new ideas from China as well as from their native culture. To lay commoners, it represented a way of entering into the highest traditions of the nation, much like taking the first few Buddhist vows. Learning must also have given to all concerned some sense of order and continuity in those contentious, warlike generations. In all this, linked poetry was a solvent of social distinctions. People from various groups could sit together on common terms, gaining an easy access that was probably otherwise infeasible. (Even today a taxi driver and a corporation director can and do belong to the same haiku society and attend the same parties.) The renga masters were probably no more than symptoms or perhaps catalysts in such developments. Sōgi certainly represents them particularly well.

His connection with Tō no Tsuneyori was probably his most important. From Tsuneyori, Sōgi received instruction in the first of the imperial collections, the *Kokinshū*. After that his fortunes rapidly improved. And if before he had to live off the back country, Tsuneyori's instruction and influence enabled him to get on in the capital itself. By 1474, when he was fifty-three, he was teaching the classics to others in addition to his disciples. One of the other poets of the Minase sequence, Shōhaku, records hearing him elucidate *The Tale of Genji* about this time. For generations, much of the teaching of the classics had been grammatical and syntactic, and the well-esteemed, well-paying disciple might be taught secrets of little importance—some minor textual variation or small gloss on a word in an old poem. Sōgi was enough of a newcomer *and* a scholar to treat the classics far more seriously, making their study a profession, just as renga had become. Konishi attributes to him the first thorough analysis of *The Tale of Genji*. By 1477 well-placed people were visiting the Shugyokuan to hear him discuss that masterpiece. A decade later he was discussing *Tales from Ise* before one prince and, a bit later, before another, the future emperor Gokashiwabara (r. 1500-1526). Also in 1487, he taught the classics at Shōkoku Temple to an audience made up of the nobility as well as of his disciples. It appears reasonably certain that he had his priestly training in that very temple. He had arrived at the temple from no one knows where, and from it he walked around to beg alms. Now he was revered. Only such a person could have achieved so much. But such a person could have done so only during the flux and openness of those years of upheaval. He could provide what many important people in his age desired.

In 1488 Sōgi received his most important official appointment. The Kamakura authorities gave him office as shogunal administrator of the Bureau of Renga Contests at the Kitano Shrine in the capital. The position was little more than an academic deanship—head of what Konishi calls the College of Renga. It did, however, signify his primacy among renga poets. It also honored his learning. A decade earlier he had been lecturing on *Tales from Ise* in the provinces. Two weeks after his appointment, he was called to the shogun's encampment to lecture on the same subject. A little later he was discussing the same work before a provincial magnate. He seems to have been willing or eager to master any subject related to his renga profession. Doing so, he retained his connections of many years' standing with people of various rank.

Sōgi no doubt thought more apparent than we the connection between these matters and his poetry. Learning had long been esteemed in Japan and considered a requisite for a poet. For that matter, there were and had been in Japan as elsewhere poets hidebound with learning and costive with pedantry. We can be sure that the revival of learning in the Muromachi period produced a number of dry-as-dust droners with little sense of a living past. Sōgi excelled because he was very different. He wished to relate the past to the present and to see a classic whole rather than in minute parts. This cannot have been unrelated to his putting great

value on Teika's prescription to seek out original conception in literature.[14] In Sōgi's mistaken view, that was the great secret of Nijō poetics.
Konishi believes the misconception derived from his study of the *Kokinshū* under Tsuneyori. It was a happy error that enabled a practicing poet
and teacher to bring his learning to fruit in his poetry and his creative
sense to bear on his learning. The learned but fussy Nijō poets went
through a poem word by word. Notes survive from Sōgi's disciples to
show his holistic approach. This method had emerged among priests of
the Zen persuasion, who had inculcated it from about 1400, following
certain Sung critics. In this Sōgi was not so much original as right.

It will be recalled that it is Shinkei rather than Sōgi who excels the
other renga poets in the quality of his stanzas. For that matter, he is also a
better waka poet. Yet Sōgi is the greatest of renga poets precisely because
of his holistic sense of a sequence, whether that be of thirty or a thousand
stanzas. He understood that the genius of linked poetry lay in the integrity of the whole, not in the brilliance of parts. Only a person who taught
the classics in his way could have conceived of renga as he did, although
perhaps the direction of influence went the other way. In any event, once
these matters become clear, it is very simple to observe how his many
interests fitted into a single approach. It is therefore also appropriate that
Sōgi's manner of teaching renga itself should have taken on a corporate
character as a Sōgi University, and that for his College of Renga he
should compile collections of stanzas, in order that his disciples might
have their textbooks. Such holism and relevance as he propounded will
need to be borne in mind in the liveliest possible way when we come to
consider some of the manifold canons of renga composition.

Mastery of that composition involves three arts: of the whole, of stanzaic connection, and of stanza style. Sōgi's conception of the second obviously relates to the first, but something must be said of his stylistic
ideal. He postulated resplendent grace (yūbi) as the quality to be sought.
This idea connects rather closely (although not in written characters)
with the chief aesthetic ideal of his time, yūgen. Many poets of the court
had regarded yūgen in terms of grace tinged by sadness, deprivation, and
mystery. Sōgi composed stanzas with such elements, when decorum so

---

[14] See *Court Poetry*, pp. 259-60.

required. But he shared with Yoshimoto and others a greater emphasis on the beautiful, and more and more he came to set as his ideal the resplendent (hanayakana). He might have followed tradition, which was by now second nature to him, and cultivated the ethereal beauty of a spring dawn or the poignant sadness of autumn dusk. Again it must be said that he wrote lovely stanzas on just such subjects. But he had the independence of mind to set his heart on a humbler flower than others, a gaudier or less elegant thing, the wild yellow rose (yamabuki). It is impossible to tell where that preference came from. But Shōhaku recognized the preference as something particular, something that distinguished his old master far more than did those elegant verses on drizzle falling about a grass-thatched hut that so captivated Bashō. So it is that in his collection, *Plants of a Spring Dream* (*Shummusō*), Shōhaku has the following waka with the headnote, "Thinking how Sōgi liked this flower."

Someokishi	Dyed with moisture,
Kokoro no iro o	It is the color of the heart
Katami tote	Left as a keepsake,
Miru mo tsuyukeki	For even a look reveals the dew
Yamabuki no hana.	Tearful on the yellow roses.

Sōgi has not lacked tributes, but one test of poets and readers alike involves the availability of a poet's works to readers. By this test, he has not measured up to such perennial favorites as Saigyō and Bashō. There have been signs of change, however, One recent book gives sixty sequences by him alone or with others. These include fifty-four of one hundred stanzas and six of one thousand stanzas.[15] There is some paradox that interest in renga should be widening so rapidly now that it has ceased to be practiced as a living art. The paradox can be accepted if it will bring

[15] See Etō Yoshitada, *Sōgi no Kenkyū* (Kazama Shobō, 1967). *Three Poets* (*Minase Sangin Hyakuin*) appears on pp. 257 ff.; *Yunoyama* (*Yunoyama Sangin Hyakuin*) on pp. 283 ff.; and *Sōgi Alone* (*Sōgi Dokugin Nanihito Hyakuin*) on pp. 329 ff. (all pages referring to the second pagination). Translations of the first and third are given in Part Two. For a translation of the second with introduction and commentary, see Steven D. Carter, "Three Poets at Yuyama," *Monumenta Nipponica*, 33 (1978), 119-49 and 241-83. Only the former had appeared when this book was in proof, but through the kindness of Michael Cooper, editor of *Monumenta Nipponica*, I was able to see proof sheets of the latter half. Carter's fine work well represents the freshening American interest in renga.

renewed knowledge of Sōgi, Shinkei, and other renga poets. The same conventional wisdom that prefers Saigyō and Bashō to Sōgi has chosen *Three Poets at Minase* for highest favor. Anyone who knows renga knows that sequence. The best critics prefer *Three Poets at Yunoyama* (or *Yuyama*) to the Minase sequence, however, and Konishi Jin'ichi declares with confidence that the highest beauty of renga will be found in Sōgi's late *Hundred Stanzas Relating to Person*. Such reasons have led to the selection of *Three Poets* and the late sequence as examples for translation in the next part of this book. Of the second, one can say without equivocation that it exemplifies Sōgi's dictum: "The essence of renga is to give a mind (kokoro) to that which lacks a mind, to give speech to that which cannot speak."[16]

Sōgi also wrote the nonstandard version—mushin or haikai no renga. Using the central terms of classical poetics, kokoro and kotoba, he distinguished between haikai of words and haikai of thought. Any example of the former, kotoba no haikai, will almost certainly prove untranslatable because of word-plays. One such example has the headnote, "On a trip, he stopped at Goi no Shō, where the master of the place was wearing a high-cut hakama." Sōgi produced an upper or opening stanza (5, 7, 5 syllables) to which the man of the house replied with a lower (7, 7). The point of each involves a series of syllables in the Japanese syllabary, as if Sōgi had said something like, "This place is U V W X Y Z," and the reply had been, "If so you are A B C D E."[17] A haikai in thought (kokoro no haikai) is much more translatable, and again our example is a short renga.

Namida oba	The tears let fall
oni mo oto su to	show that even demons weep
kiku mono o—	by the sound one hears—
—kawara no ame no	—upon the roof tiles the rain
akatsuki no koe.	gives forth the voice of dawn.[18]

---

[16] Quoted by Ichiji Tetsuo, *Renga no Sekai* (Yoshikawa Kōbunkan, 1967), p. 386.

[17] See Araki Yasusada, *Sōgi* (Sōgensha, 1941), p. 95. To Sōgi's "Kon ka kikukeko," the man replies, "Ai Ueo kite." I heard a version of that word-play in Sapporo in 1961. In some surprise, a man says to his wife, "You know, I am Ai Ueo." She laughs and says, "Well, then I am Kaki Kukeko."

[18] *Ibid.*, p. 100.

These performances would not guarantee Sōgi a claim on our esteem. They do reveal a lighter touch in him, and they represent something important to understanding the ushin or standard renga. With the existence of a nonstandard form, it was easier to keep the standard one to its own ways. As every true, or prudent, conservative knows, order can best be maintained when some license is allowed. And the existence of the nonstandard form also gave scope to the later genius of Bashō. It is good that Sōgi could relax, that on occasion at least he should give thought, as it were, to the thoughtless and find a language not of the language of renga.

The next two masters requiring attention are those who joined Sōgi at Minase: Shōhaku and Sōchō. It says something favorable about both Sōgi and renga—and perhaps also tells us something about the chaotic situation of the times—that two people so very different should have assisted him both at Minase in 1488 and at Yunoyama in 1491. Of the two, Shōhaku is the more unusual in the limited sense that he came from a background that formerly produced the waka poets. He was of noble family, and his taking of vows was obviously not a means of getting ahead in the world in the same sense that Sōgi's action was. Like so many other renga masters, however, Shōhaku did not take orders to become a practicing priest. He became a nominal priest, it seems, to lead a cultivated life as a poet and aesthete. He is now best known for his renga, but he was also a scholar of classical literature, a waka poet, and a composer of Chinese verse. Some modern Japanese scholars seem to find Shōhaku to be a bit precious, perhaps because of his statement of his three loves: flowers (possibly plums, possibly cherries), fragrances, and sake. Yet those preferences were traditional and had counterparts in Chinese poetry. Also, like the next person, he had to try to survive those dangerous years, and following his aesthetic, semi-priestly way was not the worst method of doing so.

Less effort has been devoted to study of Shōhaku than of the more racy Sōchō. Given his social status, his dates are certain and, like most other renga masters, he lived long: 1448-1528. The best-studied part of his life is that from 1488 to the year of Sōgi's death, 1502. During these years Shōhaku participated in three very important renga, including those at Minase and Yunoyama. He also was one of the poets of the *Thousand Stanzas at Shugyoku Hermitage* (*Shugyokuan Senku*), which was composed at Sōgi's residence. During these years he was also involved in matches of Chinese and Japanese verse, in connected waka, in illustrations for *The Tale of Genji*, and in a joint or competitive discussion of *The Tale of Genji*. The discussion involved Sōgi, Sōchō, and four others.

Studies of the classics had assisted Sōgi's rise. As a son of a minister of state in the old hierarchy, Shōhaku did not need such assistance; he had ample access to court and high military people. Since such connections were no guarantee of security during the bad times, Shōhaku moved for reasons of safety to a place near modern Kobe when the Ōnin War made life so dangerous in the capital. He seems to have moved back and forth between it and the capital, according to conditions and need. The interest in renga during the reign of Gokashiwabara led to some demand for his presence, and on one occasion he wrote the opening stanza for a renga in which the emperor participated. It is very revealing that such records show that women participated in renga composition at court, where they had always had a higher place as writers than in any other culture. But Japan was rapidly becoming more of a man's world. Later in his life, as the country calmed down somewhat, Shōhaku spent much of his time making extracts from the classics and taking those walking trips so much favored by renga poets. In all this, because he was a priest, he led a freer life than did his fellow aristocrats. His connections with the court distinguished him, on the other hand, from most other major renga poets.

Shōhaku's style and achievement have not been thoroughly studied. One contemporary said, not very flatteringly, "Shōhaku's is a simple style."[19] Sōgi's anthology, *The New Tsukuba Collection* (*Shinsen Tsukubashū*) includes thirty-one of Shōhaku's stanzas to Sōchō's thirty-eight, which would seem to express a preference, although, as we shall see, Sōchō's appeal compounds personal elements with a lesser talent. Kidō Saizō offers somewhat measured praise. He finds Shōhaku's stanzas limpid and easy, "with just a touch of aware" or heightened feeling. On the whole he thinks him best with the style of tranquil beauty (yūen). He concludes by offering two stanzas that he justly terms outstanding.

Tsuki izuku	The moon is elsewhere
sora wa kasumi no	as the sky is overspread with haze
hikari kana	glimmering with light

[19] Kidō, *Rengashi*, 2, 554; his discussion of Shōhaku is in 2, 545-57.

Hitogoe ni	With a single cry
sumu ya kari naku	the geese in flight clear the form
yowa no tsuki	of the midnight moon

The former, obviously an opening stanza, offers a scene in which the moon cannot be seen because of the warm spring haze. However thick that may be, the moon suffuses it with its glow. In the latter, the geese returning south in autumn cry out in one voice as they fly across the face of the moon. As if by that sound, the autumn moon suddenly clears of its clouds, revealing them and it.

Shōhaku composed the following stanza to open *One Hundred Stanzas by Three Poets at Yunoyama.*

Usuyuki ni	Beneath thin snow
ko no ha iro koki	the fallen leaves deepen in hue
yamaji kana	the path on the hill

The leaves have fallen long since, but their color has not yet faded. Since an agent like dew or frost or snow was thought to change the color of leaves, even these fallen ones are altered. Under the light scattering of white, they appear the darker, giving a chiaroscuro of beauty to the little path leading up the hill. We may look at two other stanzas in connection with those before his. (In each case the other poet is Sōgi at top form.) Here are the twenty-fourth and twenty-fifth stanzas from the Yunoyama sequence.

Izumi o kikeba	Listening to a cold summer well-head
tada aki no koe	I hear only the voice of autumn
hotaru tobu	and till late at night
sora ni yobukaku	I sit on the verandah watching
hashii shite	fireflies trace the sky

Both summer stanzas suggest autumn. Sōgi does so explicitly. Shōhaku does so by directing attention to light in the night sky, which in renga immediately suggests the moon, as it also does autumn. In addition, the second chapter of *The Tale of Genji* has talk of the attraction of fireflies and the voices of insects, suggesting that summer really is over. As a last example, we may take the closing stanzas from *Yunoyama*.

Tsuyu no ma o	Do not think misery
uki furusato to	is all life offers in the brief moment
omou na yo	dew lasts at the old house
hitomurasame ni	how the moon seems to have waned
tsuki zo isayou	with just one sudden rainstorm

Sōgi's stanza (the first three lines) recalls the episode in *The Tale of Genji* in which Kaoru thinks of Prince Hachi's palace at Uji. Now that Ukifune has disappeared and is presumed dead by drowning herself in the Uji River, who will look after the place? He believes that he has himself lost two women to death there, and he certainly has given a third to Prince Niou. Again and again there are plays on *uki-ushi-Uji* (miserable, misery, and the place-name) in the Uji chapters of *The Tale of Genji*. Sōgi generalizes. Just as Ukifune will find more than misery, so may others. "Furusato" came to mean one's native place, but it had wider application earlier, meaning a place where one had lived formerly, or even a place where one had experienced important things. Shōhaku's last stanza is quite unusual in avoiding the affirmative or celebratory tone usual to closing stanzas. Instead he talks of the sudden rains that can come up in autumn and winter. During one, when of course the sky was overcast, and the moon invisible, it seemed that the moon had waned a great deal. Actually the clouds probably lasted only a day or two, but the moon seemed to have diminished in so short a time. To introduce the moon (even at so very late a point in a renga) lends some affirmation to the stanza, and that it should seem to have waned even more than it did suggests a person refined in feeling about it. Also, rain falls heavily after Ukifune's disappearance, and the world grows dimmer for some of the characters. Shōhaku has caught all of this in his stanza.

The four stanzas given as examples of Shōhaku's style exemplify two related but distinct qualities: his best stanza style and his skill in stanza-joining (tsukeku). In this second, which is essential to renga, he is quite superior, as we shall have cause to appreciate in *Three Poets at Minase*. Again and again he manages to do the unexpected with great naturalness, and to catch what is essential in what the poet before him has written and yet to move things on most interestingly. If his usual stanza style is relatively plain, as no doubt it is, then that is a quality he shares with Sōgi himself. On the other hand, Shōhaku seldom drops below his own standard, being remarkably trustworthy in working with Sōgi. At this remove in time, analysis of personality is impossible about someone of whom so little is presently known. But we may concede that he would have become a greater poet if he had tried harder, and that he would likely have tried harder if his social circumstances had been less comfortable. We may concede these things because they are true of us all. But we may also guess that as more becomes known about Shōhaku and his work he will have an increasingly important place in the history of Japanese poetry. Our greatest loss—at least a loss suffered by those of us who wish to have an idea of the personality of our poets—is lack of information about him as an individual. It would be good to know as much about him as about the third poet at Minase, Sōchō.

As Shōhaku was the son of a minister of state, Sōchō, five years his junior (1448-1532), was the son of a blacksmith. He wrote about such personal matters with a highly engaging candor. Because of his rather eccentric character, he attracted the comments of others. Because of such comments and his personality, he has attracted the attention of many people. He became a priest at seventeen, probably in the old Shingon sect, and when the Ōnin War broke out before he turned twenty, he went off to the provinces for six or seven years. He appears to have met Sōgi a year or two before going down from the capital, but their close ties seem to date from about 1476. In 1480-1481 he returned from his own peregrinations, and sometime about the next year he began to accompany Sōgi on his journeys. It was at the end of that first decade of their association that they and Shōhaku wrote the Minase and Yunoyama sequences. Sōchō was one of the busiest of travelers among the renga poets, which is saying rather a good deal. He kept returning to the capital and leaving it, spending time with commoners in the provinces, with warriors of like inclination in outlying districts of the capital, and with the highly eccentric priest Ikkyū, who lived near the capital.

Sōchō enjoyed patronage from many sources, but his closest ties were with the Imagawa family, and particularly with Imagawa Ujichika. As with Sōgi, such connections developed more from a knowledge of the classics than of renga, at least as to initial respect. All three of the poets who sat down at Minase knew more about the classics than did most of the nobility. For Sōgi and Sōchō such learning was essential to give them the connections that Shōhaku could enjoy by his family rank. But it was not just learning that benefitted the blacksmith's son. He appeared to have had special adeptness in negotiating treaties and other matters in the service of the Imagawa family. At a time of war and constant betrayal, an agent one could trust and whom others trusted must have been of the utmost value. In some of this employment, Sōchō may have acted as an intelligence agent, a role for which a priest was in some ways better suited than a lay person.[20] For all his obligations to the Imagawa house, he seems to have been a free agent. He travelled at will with Sōgi and to visit patrons in places other than the Imagawa territory of Suruga, modern Shizuoka: "from his fifties or before until he was about eighty, Sōchō more or less spent his life in travel."[21]

The other principal influence on Sōchō was that even greater eccentric, Priest Ikkyū.[22] He it was who drew Sōchō back to the capital. Although both of them belonged to celibate Buddhist sects, both formed connections with women. (Perhaps the reason Sōgi included more of Sōchō's stanzas than Shōhaku's in his collection was Sōchō's personality. Sōgi could have recalled Ananda, the Buddha's favorite disciple for three decades, in spite of certain sexual lapses.) Ikkyū was promiscuous. Sōchō was frank enough to write about the woman with whom he lived and to report that he had two children by her. Such matters may have been cause for some small scandal, but the most criticized episode in his life occurred at the death of Imagawa Ujichika. News of his patron's death was sent on purpose to him at Ikkyū's dwelling, where he nonetheless chose to remain rather than to go to Suruga. The fact that he was then seventy-eight appears to have been thought no excuse. The "numerous small differences" between Sōgi and Sōchō as renga poets are said to be attributable to Ikkyū and, as Kidō Saizō also says mildly, Sōchō shared

---

[20] The suggestion is Donald Keene's in "The Comic Tradition in Renga."

[21] Kidō, *Rengashi*, 2, 580; his discussion of Sōchō is in 2, 576-98.

[22] A fascinating sketch of Ikkyū is given by Donald Keene, *Landscapes and Portraits* (Tokyo and Palo Alto: Kōdansha, 1971), pp. 226-41.

with the eccentric priest a number of human weaknesses not possessed by Sōgi.[23]

It is not easy to account for Sōchō's prominence in the history of renga. One can only presume that his personality is the reason. His stanza style and his stanzaic connections were certainly criticized by his contemporaries and pose us some problems of appreciation today. Whatever the standards of setting canons of judgment for renga, the agreement of past with present is disquieting. Yet people liked him, even people as different as Sōgi, Ujichika, and Ikkyū. The streak of oddness in him seems to have increased his appeal. His skill in negotiations also suggests that he was a good judge of people and that he enjoyed their trust in his good faith. And one other thing: he had a curiosity about himself, with the ability to arouse it in others, qualities rare and welcome.

Any criticism of Sōchō's poetry involves those high standards that we bring from Sōgi and Shōhaku. The troublesome fact is that Shōhaku and such others as Sanjōnishi Sanetaka (1455-1537) could be so specific in their criticism. They faulted him, particularly, for his opening stanzas. Kidō Saizō considers the three in Sōgi's *New Tsukuba Collection* to be insubstantial, thus confirming the adverse criticism of centuries ago. Sōchō's technique of joining stanzas was also faulted, and that is a more serious matter. To this stanza—

Sakura zo wakanu	The cherry flowers cannot be told
mine no shirakumo	from the white clouds on the peak

he added

aoyagi no	among new willows
Kazuraki shiruki	the hill of Kazuraki is distinct
hana sakite	with flowers blooming

Sanetaka wrote, "It is an attractive thing to add to those white clouds on the hill of Kazuraki some flowers blooming. But to say that Kazuraki is distinct with flowers blooming is extremely odd."[24] If there are both

---

[23] Kidō, *Rengashi*, 2, 583, 585.   [24] *Ibid.*, 2, 586.

clouds and flowers, how could the hill's outlines be distinct? Kidō remarks that Sōchō tends to relate his stanzas insufficiently to those which precede, with only the general character (sugata) of the two stanzas being harmonious. This is not a matter of his writing stanzas of distant relationship. In *Three Poets* for example, there are five stanzas distantly related from their predecessors, and of these four are by Sōgi and one by Shōhaku. Sōchō's fault is rather a degree of muddle that often derives from a tendency to vague and subjective writing. On some occasions, however, his virtues and faults seem the very contrary of those named.

Mireba yuki	What is seen is snow
kikeba shigure	what is heard is winter drizzle
yamaji kana	on the mountain path

Here the syntax is mannered and rigorous to no purpose. The exertion seems to be rather useless. Yet Sōchō also wrote some splendid stanzas, as we shall see in *Three Poets*. And his importance is such that a couple of other examples must also be given.

Shigureki ya	It was drizzling
yūhi o nokosu	the evening sun is left to shine
aki no ame	by the autumn rain
★	★
Kaigane wa	On Mount Kaigane
yuki ni shigururu	with the snow winter drizzle chills
yamaji kana	the mountain path

In the second example, the images resemble those of the mannered stanza but possess far greater naturalness and force.

Sōchō wrought no changes of importance in the Sōgi styles and often composed quite ordinary stanzas. Yet the attraction he held for his contemporaries still somewhat holds. In his later years he kept journals that have survived. They are often sketchy, but their strong personal element conveys something of their author's irrepressible engagement with the world and his concern with himself. The journals also give glimpses of what life was like in the troubled times, particularly for a man of letters.

Travel is often the subject. Such accounts are well flavored with poetry in varying hues. The concern with world and self makes a comparison with Samuel Pepys less than far-fetched, but the native tradition of poetic and other diaries gave him all the models he needed. There is also in such writing a prophecy of Bashō, the more so because many of the verses are haikai rather than standard renga.

Takano hijiri no	At Takano the holy sage
yado o kou koe—	voices his longing to be lodged—
—chihayaburu	—mighty he is
Miwa yamamoto no	at the foot of Miwa Mountain
chayabōzu.	the teahouse priest.

The sage turns out to be as inclined to comfort as the rest of us. The old pillow word (chihayaburu) is ascribed to a priest impressed by his own powers at a wayside teashop. The mighty gods have associations with Miwa Mountain that go back to the *Records of Ancient Matters* (*Kojiki*)— and one might go on with such nice details. But, more importantly, the humor conveys genuine insight into our fallible human nature.

Such haikai or mushin renga, the nonstandard kind that really was first born of linked kinds, clearly shows Sōchō to be a more adept hand than Sōgi. We may say that Sōchō had a fundamentally haikai mind— just as we can say that his nonstandard kind is very much haikai of thought (kokoro no haikai) rather than mere verbal play. Donald Keene has made a related case for Sōchō's contribution to a central feature of haikai, stanzaic connection.[25] The two major early schools of haikai differed on the use of verbal or conceptual relation between stanzas. The added stanzas (tsukeku) of Yamazaki Sōkan (dates uncertain) tend to employ verbal connection (kotobazuke), and his conception came to dominate the school of Matsunaga Teitoku (1571-1653) as well. Sōchō's technique of conceptual connection (kokorozuke) adumbrated the other major haikai school, the Danrin line initiated by Nishiyama Sōin (1605-1682). Some of those well-related stanzas by Sōchō were in fact indecent or scabrous, even those written at an advanced age.[26] He seems to have

[25] Donald Keene makes this point at the end of "The Comic Tradition in Renga."
[26] In "The Comic Tradition," Donald Keene gives some examples of such poems and discusses their place in Sōchō's life.

been a rumpled genius, but the blacksmith's son had come a long way.

Satomura Jōha (1524–1602) appears in this rehearsal as the last principal renga poet. Others followed him, and a little will be said of some of them, but by the seventeenth century the haikai version of renga begins to assume greater prominence than the standard kind. Jōha claims our attention for the intrinsic worth of his poetry. My own understanding of linked poetry, such as it is, derives chiefly from the Jōha school in which the family of Yamada Yoshio (1873–1958) was hereditarily trained. Konishi Jin'ichi was one of the last to study with Yamada, and from Konishi's books and advice I have derived my standards. Others exist, as must be insisted on, but it can be seen that Jōha has a special place.

Neither the exact year of his birth nor its place is certain. Like so many other early renga masters, he was essentially a nobody who came to matter by luck, longevity, hard work, and genius. Unlike most others, he appears not to have had a long poetic apprenticeship. The first certain thing about him is that, about seventeen or eighteen years of age, he became a disciple of Shūkei, who died a couple of years later (1544). Thereafter he worked under Shōkyū (1510–1552) for a period of not more than eight years, which makes his whole apprenticeship a matter of only a decade. After that, he appears to have been on his own.[27]

The haikai poet Teitoku and others have left some unflattering descriptions of Jōha. Much the most interesting is Teitoku's remark that Jōha chose renga as a way to get ahead in the world, as an enterprise in which artisans and merchants could meet with the nobility. Because that is such an evident fact with so many people before Jōha, the important thing is that Teitoku should say it about this one of many examples. It seems reasonable to infer that the old social rigidities are coming back, and this is confirmed by other evidence in Jōha's lifetime. We also possess a malicious verbal portrait of him, which can be offered as "a caricature of a face," a sense of what was ugly at that time. His face was said to be large and without eyebrows, to have bright but indistinct eyes, rounded and thick ears, with somewhat else including a loud voice. One would be

[27] This account of Jōha draws on Kidō, *Rengashi*, 2, 775–92. Donald Keene has written a biographical essay, "Jōha, A Sixteenth-Century Poet of Linked Verse," a copy of which he kindly sent me. When published, it will give full details of Jōha's life with examples of his art. Jōha has only lately received close attention and only recently have literary dictionaries and histories mentioned him at all.

hard-pressed to draw a picture of the characters in *The Tale of Genji*, except perhaps for the red-nosed Suetsumuhana. There is of course also the rapid-fire talk of the Lady of Ōmi. But here we have a full-scale satiric portrait of the kind that the newly emerging society would relish. Haikai and even less idealistic writing cannot be far off. Some of the description probably is ill-natured exaggeration. But we have seen with Sōchō (if we did not know it from our own times) that poets can have warts of personality as well as of appearance. We must consider Jōha to have been a homely, ill-favored person. That was another disadvantage he overcame.

Ill looks were as nothing compared to his great asset—apart from his talents: he was able to ride the crest of the wave. There was a great boom for renga during the Momoyama period (variously dated, but the usual earliest and last dates are 1568 and 1615). In terms of expense, the craze for renga resembles the tulip mania of Europe in the seventeenth and eighteenth centuries. In terms of literary emphasis, it resembles the cult of Byronism in the nineteenth century. Money was lavished on the masters, and no costs were spared for the celebrations accompanying renga contests, including lavish banquets and expensive prizes. Matters reached the point where satire (we see this again) had grown feasible. Among the kyōgen that laugh at the craze is *Night Is Good for Renga and Thieves* (*Renga to Nusubito wa Yoru ga Yoi*). It seems that some who impoverished themselves by the one turned to the other to satisfy their addiction.

So the stakes were high. As Jōha began on his own, he and Sōyō (1526-1563) saw the possibilities and promoted the status of renga among common people. Sōyō was the son of the renga master Sōboku (d. 1545), a phenomenon of poetic inheritance that was becoming more common. Sōyō did not lack ambition. He proposed to become the indisputably first renga master of the land. He had a rival in Jōha's second teacher, Shōkyū, with whom he had to share acclaim and a place at important renga sittings. When Shōkyū died, his son Shōshitsu (1541-1603) was only thirteen, far too young to continue at once the renga practice of the house. He obviously required instruction, and Jōha was brought in as poetic regent of the house. In time, two lines of Satomura renga emerged from this coalition, with Jōha head of the northern and Shōshitsu of the southern. We have seen with earlier renga masters that good fortune like Jōha's was usually necessary. We have also seen that poetic genius was insufficient in another set of terms: study of the classics was also necessary for a poet to earn full respect.

Jōha's good fortune did not desert him in this matter. He managed to succeed his first teacher, Shūkei, as renga master of the Sanjōnishi household. Such an appointment after such short training suggests remarkable talents and personality. (Perhaps he was not quite so ill-favored after all.) The Sanjōnishi family was one of the houses of the Fujiwara clan entitled to ministerial appointment, and so held immense prestige. By this time their fortune and power had greatly declined, but they still carried high court rank, and acquaintance with them was dearly coveted. Shōkyū had been the foremost classical scholar of his time and a waka as well as a renga poet, much like Shinkei and Sōgi before him. Jōha's acquaintance with both Shūkei and Shōkyū no doubt explains how he became acquainted with his teacher in the Japanese classics, Sanjōnishi Kin'eda (1487-1563). In his *Account of a Pilgrimage to Yoshino (Yoshino Keiki)*, Kin'eda reports that Jōha frequently visited him and showed a profound attachment to the art of renga ("Tsukuba no michi"). Jōha made rapid progress in his classical studies, composed waka with Kin'eda on their travels and no doubt at other times. They became close friends. Before long the pupil became a teacher in the classics and was one of the poets invited to compose an important sequence, *A Thousand Stanzas by Four Poets at Ishiyama (Ishiyama Yongin Senku)*. In 1554 he and two others composed a hundred-stanza sequence so well received that contemporaries thought the future of renga had never been brighter. Although as a student of the classics Jōha excelled other poets rather than people who specialized in such study, there is no doubt of his knowledge or of his poetic gifts. Recognition came, and it must have been sweet. He spent a total of about six months at intervals between 1555 and 1558 discussing the classics before two members of the nobility who had formerly held the highest civil title, Chancellor (kampaku). It is not always clear what sources Jōha enjoyed for his learning, but Kidō Saizō is no doubt right in thinking that Kin'eda is most likely. Certainly Jōha learned quickly.

A proper renga master might also be expected to travel a good deal. Jōha preferred to stay put, and apparently had no great financial inducement to travel. He did make some trips, especially with Kin'eda. In 1553 he went with his friend to Yoshino, Ise, and Yamato to see places familiar in poems and stories, what Japanese call the poetic pillows (utama-kura), which are of such comfort to help novices fill a line. Fourteen years later he made a trip to Ise and from there up the eastern coast to what is now Shizuoka, combining visits to famous places with writing of renga. He fulfilled his wish to see Mount Fuji. In 1569 he set out once again with the aim of seeing another of the most famous beauty spots, Amanohashidate, composing poems along the way. Like many travelers before and since, however, he found his object of visit caught in a long spell of rain. He dutifully wrote a stanza, putting the best face on it before moving on.

Kaze ya hikari	Is it the breeze or light
kasumi ni ukabu	where upon the haze there floats
Tamazujima	the Island of Tamazu[28]

In spite of such moving about, Jōha was really not much of a traveler. The daimyos and others who wished to study renga with him had to go up to the capital.

Such settled residence appears to testify to changes in the nation and in the social circumstances of renga. Jōha's major predecessors had travelled frequently, partly to preserve their lives, partly to obtain patronage, and partly for the pleasures of following the tradition of priestly poets. The Momoyama period certainly had its upheavals, but the capital itself was safer for residence than it had been in Sōgi's time. The widespread craze for renga also testified to an economic demand that made the suppliers able to stay in the capital and be approached there. Another development that we have glimpsed was assisted by both the increased safety and demand. "Houses" of renga could now be founded, as they had been earlier for waka. Jōha was born into an age when a nobody from nowhere might still become the leading renga master of the day. He died at a time when houses of renga had started their dynasties. So was brought to an end that social mobility for poets and others that characterized the sixteenth century. About the time of his death—that is, at the beginning of the seventeenth century—there began the new political order in Japan represented by the Tokugawa military family and its location in Edo.

[28] Kidō, *Rengashi*, 2, 786.

More will be said of this in connection with haikai, but clearly the new stability was premised on rigid social divisions and hierarchies. This is not to say that social mobility ended entirely. The Japanese, like other peoples, have always found ways of accommodating true talent. In Yamada Yoshio we have an example of someone born in the provinces and rising to high estimation for his prodigious scholarship. He came from a good enough family, but he failed to attend Tokyo or Kyoto University, which in modern times some have thought an even greater calamity than poor social origin.

Jōha's status as a poet is quite secure. Like Sōgi and Shōhaku before him, and unlike Shinkei, his stanza style does not earn highest marks. Relative to the possibilities of renga, his is usually simple, and his most important contribution is of another kind. He brought a special concern to numerous features in the progression of the whole sequence. In particular, he stressed what has been termed fluctuations in the tempo of the sequence.[29] It is quite true that a sequence requires at least some stanzas that stand out for quality, and much is expected in particular from an opening stanza. It is also true that linked poetry requires varying and yet meaningful stanzaic relation. Jōha practiced both of these aspects of renga well, but he developed Sōgi's insight into the need for wholeness in the sequence, a developing integrity that used and transcended individual stanzas. Jōha took the matter further, varying the relationship among the parts. It is true that "speed" in renga is a metaphor for a cognitive entity. Eight stanzas are eight stanzas, and so do not really go faster or slower. But by dwelling for more or fewer stanzas on seasons and subtopics, by the use or nonuse of transitional stanzas, by the following or not following the natural chronology of the seasons, and by the use of such other devices as locality and place-name—by many such means a sequence may *seem* to be retarded or accelerated. The third section of a hundred stanza sequence (the kyū, stanzas 93-100) was designated a fast finale. But Jōha manipulated "speed" throughout the sequence, giving a heightening to the various kinds of relation of stanzas that had been perfected before him.

By such token, only a whole sequence fully discussed can show the distinction of Jōha's art. That being infeasible, we may take the first eight

[29] Kidō, *Rengashi*, 2, 787-88, a very important point.

stanzas, the introductory first part (jo) of a sequence written by him
alone in memorial of the death of his good friend, Kin'eda. These stanzas
start off the third century of a thousand-stanza renga from 1563 (and may
be compared with Sōchō's apparent lack of response on the death of
Ujichika). The opening stanza alludes to a poem in the *Shinkokinshū*
(1:114), making clear that the flowers mentioned are cherry blossoms
about to go before a mountain breeze.

1   Semete sa wa   Above all else I long
    wasuregatami no   never to forget for his keepsake
      hana mo gana   the flowers lately past

    Semete sa wa   Above all else I long
    wasuregatami no   never to forget for his keepsake
      hana mo gana   the flowers lately past
2   tsumu ni sumire no in being picked the violets
    tsuyu moroki sode   weaken my sleeve with fragile dew

    Tsumu ni sumire no In being picked the violets
    tsuyu moroki sode   weaken the sleeve with fragile dew
3   kururu no no   on a darkening field
    kochō mo yadori   the butterfly also cannot settle
    sadamarade   on a place of rest

    Kururu no no   On a darkening field
    kochō mo yadori   the butterfly also cannot settle
    sadamarade   on a place of rest
4   tori no naku ne ya   are not the calls of crying birds
    haru shitau ran   longing for a vanished spring

    Tori no naku ne ya   Do not the calls of crying birds
    haru shitau ran   long for a vanished spring
5   seki no to no   at the barrier gate
    yama no ha kasumu   the mountain rim hazes over
    yowa no tsuki   the moon at midnight

    Seki no to no   At the barrier gate
    yama no ha kasumu   the mountain rim hazes over
    yowa no tsuki   the moon at midnight

6	ato to oku shi mo wakarekinikeri	though we left remembrances we parted as if for good

| | Ato to oku shi mo
wakarekinikeri | Though they left remembrances
they parted as if for good |
| 7 | honoka ni mo
ukaberu oki no
ama obune | if but faintly
and borne upon the ocean swells
the little fisherboat |

| | Honoka ni mo
ukaberu oki no
ama obune | If but faintly
and borne upon the ocean swells
the little fisherboat |
| 8 | ochiba wa mizu no
hayakawa no sue | waters take the fallen leaves
off to the end of the swift river |

This sequence differs from those by Johā's contemporaries. That difference will be more strongly felt if, after reading through *Three Poets* and its commentary, the reader will read its first eight stanzas again and thereupon return to this opening. It will be found that Stanzas 6 and 7 have the kind of relation more typical of *Three Poets*, and that the connection in the others is one of rapid and constant progression.

Like all other renga masters, Jōha was expected to write opening stanzas and be judged, to some extent, by them. It appears that not even Japanese scholars can categorize the art of his opening stanzas very easily. Here are a few of which Kidō says rather vaguely that they seem to have been born with unsteadied ease and to treat what is seen as what is felt.[30]

Haru yo tada hana ni yokogumo mine no matsu	The entire spring night a cloud stretches among the flowers the pine on the peak
★	★
Hana hitoki ochikochi hito no sekiji kana	One tree in flower along the road to the barrier people here and there

[30] *Ibid.*, 2, 790, also the source of the stanzas.

Toshi o heba   As the years pass on
mihaten hana no   I wish to see all that Mount Yoshino
Yoshinoyama   offers of cherry flowers

★   ★

Tsuki ya fune   The moon or a ship
yūgiri wataru   fording across the evening mist
aki no umi   and the autumn sea

We might spend pages appreciating these opening stanzas, but there are others finer yet.[31]

Ametsuchi mo   Heaven and earth
hito ni yuki no   are joined as one with snow
hikari kana   radiating all

★   ★

Mozu nakite   The shrike cries out
yamazatobitaru   and the mountain hamlet floods
kozue kana   with dripping branches

If we consider that Jōha's genius lies less with individual stanzas and more with the progressions of sequences, these hokku will suggest how remarkable his highest talent is.

This brief history of the development of renga in terms of important poets does not bring the full story to its close. But there is a real sense that it reached its last time of greatness in Jōha's age. The usual conservative urge to establish poetic houses grew stronger, abetted by a government that wished everyone to have a place and to stay in it. Such houses made teaching renga easier and criticism more exact. But they also militated against the constant infusion of obscure talent that so marks the great period of renga. The genius of linked poetry gradually passes to haikai, especially as it came to be practiced by Bashō. A lower decorum and a wider horizon became necessary. In its standard version, renga always maintained much of what was central to waka. In fact, in most important respects one need adjust less in going from waka to standard

[31] *Ibid.*

renga than in moving from standard renga to haikai renga. For this reason, Japanese critics who divide their literature into the elevated or elegant arts (ga no bungei) and the common or vulgar arts (zoku no bungei) have unhesitatingly placed renga among the elegant. We shall have to ask how to place haikai subsequently, but our next stage requires attention to those conventions which enabled renga to make entities of poems composed of stanzas usually written in rapid succession by more than one poet. The same canons, with some alterations, hold for haikai as well.

3

Some Canons of Renga

> "The word 'dream' should be used
> at intervals of at least seven
> stanzas. Generally speaking it
> implies love."—*Ubuginu*

IT WILL BE clear that renga is no single thing. It has been practiced in short versions of two stanzas and in long versions up to ten thousand. There are some *ad hoc* units (iisute), but the usual lengths are from eight to one thousand stanzas, with one hundred being thought the norm, from which fifty was one variant, and of which a thousand was basically a variant ten times over. Let us assume such variety, because it certainly existed. The cousin of variety, multiplicity, exists in the renga canons, and it is very hard to describe both cousins at once. What follows will take the one-hundred-stanza (hyakuin) version as the norm.[1]

Two central features distinguish renga. Together they distinguish it from such Western genres as sonnet sequences, which have sometimes been proposed as counterparts. The first involves the fact and consequences of composition in rapid succession by one or more poets. The point of the succession under such conditions must be emphasized: a given stanza (after the first and before the last) shall form a poem both with its predecessor and its successor. Each stanza is therefore a part of two poetic units of continuous and discrete sense, first as second part, next as first. The lack of further connection is not absolute, in the sense that a few stanzas in succession may concern the same topic or be part of a unit like that of the fast finale (93-100). But no stanza makes integral and *continuous sense* with any other stanza except that immediately before

---

[1] The Japanese names for the most common sets of stanzas are: senku, 1000; hyakuin, 100; gojūin, 50; yoyoshi, 44; kasen, 36; iisute, a few or some odd number. The same names hold for haikai.

it or immediately after it. That is why this art has the name of a chain (kusari): each stanza "links" with the one before and after but with no other. It is as though two adjacent quatrains in Gray's *Elegy* make sense with each other but never with noncontiguous quatrains. Or it is like a novella in which each sentence (or paragraph) makes sense with the one before and the one after, but with no other. A corollary of this is that the meaning of a single stanza varies as it forms a linked poem, first with its predecessor and then with its successor. More accurately, the art of linked poetry involves adding stanzas in such a fashion as to keep something but to change the meaning of what might be called the stanza itself and the stanza in connection with its predecessor. In such fashion, the sequence is truly sequential and a sustained plot is impossible. Only when we have fully grasped the implications of such an unusual procedure do we understand the special import of linked poetry with its connectedness and disconnectedness.

The second important feature of renga is its rules. These are what take decades to learn in order for them to become second nature, in order for several poets to create at a sitting really important poems while working in quick succession, a stanza every few minutes, written down and checked. These rules are the counterpart saving renga from being a fundamentally meaningless game or anarchic "serial" poetry. And these rules are a headache for us. Two considerations prevent their all being set down here. One is that no one, certainly including myself, knows them all. The other is that if I were to set down all I have encountered (I shall not say remember), this book would concern nothing else. Since they cannot all be set down, selection is desirable, and selection requires exercise of judgment.[2] Some that will find their way into these pages may seem arbitrary, and others may seem natural. The aim is to present

---

[2] My selection is based on knowledge gained from Konishi Jin'ichi directly or indirectly from his *Sōgi* and from the renga treatises that will be mentioned subsequently. The *Haikai Daijiten*, ed. Ichiji Tetsuo *et al.*: 6th ed. (Meiji Shōin, 1967), is also of considerable use for renga. For a rather different selection, involving translation and abridgment of Konishi's *Sōgi*, see Konishi Jin'ichi, "The Art of Renga," translated with an Introduction by Karen Brazell and Lewis Cook, *The Journal of Japanese Studies*, 2 (1975), 29-61. This is a most useful essay. In studying and teaching renga, I have found the treatise *Ubuginu* essential. This manual is said to have been compiled by one Konkū, of whom I have been able to learn nothing.

those which seem central to an understanding of linked poetry without so cluttering the discussion as to overburden the reader. As one example of the kind of information we do not need to know first, let us take the Japanese word for frog used in renga: kawazu. In classifying that particular well-voiced species, we must set it down not as an animal but as an insect. The reason is that the written character employs the insect radical (no. 142) rather than the animal (no. 94). It should be evident that the so-called renga that have become a pastime once more with Japanese in the last quarter of this century have little to do with rules. They vary widely as to interest, but they are an amusement rather than an art.

The distinction is necessary but not moral. After all, renga began and long continued to have sport of such kind as its end. It was only when it became more serious in the minds of Yoshimoto and his predecessors that rules seemed necessary. Renga resembles all major kinds of Japanese literature except one in having begun as entertainment and ending in seriousness. The one exception is waka. Lyric poetry composed by a single individual defined what literature was thought to be about. For a some time, in fact, only it *was* literature. As we have seen, linked poetry has close ties with court poetry. If indeed no one could have predicted renga from the existence and practice of waka, no one could have invented and practiced renga without waka. There is no cause for surprise that the poets of linked verse should also have written waka, and written it well. Similarly, it is also not fortuitous that they spent so much time studying *Tales from Ise* and *The Tale of Genji*. For in their different ways, these two are concerned with integrating the lyric into narrative.

Such connections must be drawn in the very spirit of renga. And so must some disconnections. Renga is after all its own form, strictly related to nothing else but its haikai variant and its mutant with linked Chinese verses. It is also by far the most complicated kind of Japanese poetry. If there exists what seems a parallel elsewhere in the world, the law of stanzaic continuity-discontinuity and the matters that follow will quickly deny it. The complexity—and the necessity of coming to terms with it—can be glimpsed in two remarks reported by Konishi Jin'ichi from his renga teacher. Yamada Yoshio said that the art had to be practiced for twenty years to gain mastery and that only thereafter did it become apparent whether one had talent. We recall the advanced ages of most renga masters and feel a sinking of heart. Yamada also said that one cannot understand the rest of medieval Japanese literataure without knowledge of renga. He had in mind particularly nō and haikai but also the general aesthetic of medieval Japan. That is also dispiriting, especially after the former remark. It is like having to learn Japanese all over again, and the discouragement one feels is augmented by the fact that Yamada was the last person who knew renga thoroughly enough to practice it easily. How melancholy it seems that no one can write proper renga any more! Yet how happy the situation really is. After all, renga ceased to be practiced as a continuous art only in this century. We can therefore learn more about it at closer remove than we can, for example, about all Western classical literature combined. We can learn more about renga canons than those of any European vernacular literature before the last century, and even later. It is little short of amazing that the criticism of Nijō Yoshimoto (1320-1388) still has pertinence to renga written in this century. Yoshimoto was born about a decade before Geoffrey Chaucer. Even if we had an art of poetic narrative left us by a contemporary of Chaucer, it would have no connection with narrative practiced in this century. And if our uninterrupted tradition of renga criteria goes back from our time only to Jōha, that is as if Sir Philip Sidney had bequeathed us an art of poetry relevant to T. S. Eliot. Much of what passes for scholarship and criticism of Western literature—or in Japanese monogatari—amounts to mere guesswork by comparison with what can be known about the practice of renga. Which is not to suggest that possessing the knowledge obviates problems.

In what follows, the reader will discover a description of some of the rules and other features of renga. Each is set off by an initial word or phrase in capital letters. I hope that this method will enable a person new to linked poetry to relocate something that has slipped the mind, or someone well acquainted with such poetry to hop over what is sufficiently well known.

STANZA NAMES. In a given renga certain stanzas have special names.

first stanza	—	hokku
second stanza	—	waki or wakiku
third stanza	—	daisan
last stanza	—	ageku

All other stanzas are ordinary ones, hiraku. (The Glossary provides any reminders that may be needed.) Since each stanza except the first is added to a predecessor, each is also an attached or joined stanza, tsukeku, a word also used in an abstracted sense to refer to the fact or art of attaching. The same terms apply to haikai, although Bashō favored the kasen in thirty-six stanzas (named after the sanjūrokkasen, or thirty-six famous waka poets); the hankasen or half kasen in eighteen appears to have been used solely in haikai.

POETS AND COMPOSITION OF SEQUENCES. A hundred-stanza renga was commonly begun at evening, as the opening stanza of *Three Poets* shows. A hyakuin like that took about two to four hours, which means that a new stanza was produced on the average of every three minutes. On a formal occasion, the composer would recite the composition and a judge would consider it for any corrections. If it passed, it would be set down with a designation of the poet's name, the first time in full and thereafter only by its second character. Sōgi thereby became Gi; Shōhaku, Haku; and Sōchō, Chō. Poets tended to derive the first character of their artistic name, or style, from the first character in their master's style. One's individuality came with the second. Each of the poets might keep a copy of their poem. *Three Poets* would also have been copied in a fair copy on fine paper subsequently, because it was a presentation for the memory of Emperor Gotoba and the Minase Shrine. When composed for contests, each stanza received two, one, or no points. The person whose total was highest received the prize. A thousand-stanza unit usually took five days, with the poets composing a certain number of stanzas each day:

1st	2nd	3rd	4th	5th
100	300	300	300	50

The excess fifty stanzas (zuiga) composed on the last day would not be published but would provide an interlude of some two and a half hours before the banquet. Not all sequences are composed by several poets. The names for a sequence composed by one or two are a bit special; thereafter one can use one system of Japanese numbering.

One Poet	Two Poets	Three Poets	Four Poets
dokugin	ryōgin	sangin	yongin

Except for corrections insisted on by a judge or for the making of fair copies, renga were not subject to revision. The essence was composing at a sitting. Yet there are exceptions, including one of the highest importance in the sequence composed by Sōgi alone late in life (see the head-note to it in Part Two). There must have been others. After all, Bashō is unlikely to have been the first compulsive reviser in Japan. Yet the assumptions and the circumstances—of presentation, of evaluation for a prize, or of an entertainment before a banquet—ordinarily precluded revision.

PARTS OF A RENGA—SHEETS AND SIDES. A renga was set down on paper according to certain set ways. For a hyakuin such as the two examples in Part Two, four sheets of paper were used. Each paper was folded to make two outsides and two insides, with only the two outsides being written on. Holes might be made at one end to tie the four together, but, in any event, each sheet had a front and a back side. The poets wrote a certain number of stanzas on the eight available sides. (See also Figure 1.)

1st Sheet (22 stanzas)
    Front Side 1-8   (8 stanzas)
    Back Side 9-22   (14 stanzas)
2nd Sheet (28 stanzas)
    Front Side 23-36   (14 stanzas)
    Back Side 37-50   (14 stanzas)
3rd Sheet (28 stanzas)
    Front Side 51-64   (14 stanzas)
    Back Side 65-78   (14 stanzas)
4th Sheet (22 stanzas)
    Front Side 79-92   (14 stanzas)
    Back side 93-100   (8 stanzas)

Anyone acquainted with Japanese aesthetics knows that such an arrangement is peculiarly symmetrical. Perhaps the symmetry is a way of poising order against the shifting authorship. In any event, other things make the symmetry less prominent. There is, for example, a shift in the order of alternating composition, as will be discussed in the introductory comments to *Three Poets*. It can be said that no single order was required, but poets had to choose an order for a given sequence.

THE JO-HA-KYŪ RHYTHM. As has been mentioned, each sequence also has what may be termed a rhythm of development that, to mix metaphors, imposes another grid on the sheet-side distinctions given above. (See also Figure 2.)

1-8	Introduction or Preface (jo)
9-92	Development (ha)
93-100	Fast Finale (kyū)

This rhythm is taken over from court music (gagaku), in which tempo could in fact be changed. It can be seen that the Introduction is dealt with by the front of the first sheet, and the Fast Finale with the back of the fourth. The long Development requires the other six sides. (The pattern for the thirty-six-stanza kasen will be discussed with haikai.) It was thought that the Preface might spill over into the Development and the Fast Finale might well begin a stanza or two before its sanctioned place. Rigid symmetry was no more welcome in renga than elsewhere in Japanese aesthetics. To put it another way: the last stanza or two on the front of the fourth side of a hundred-stanza renga will begin to take on "speed." This rhythm is certainly a feature in which renga influences other medieval literature, as Yamada declared. In Figure 2 will be seen a design of the jo-ha-kyū rhythm in a nō play as well.

FUSHIMONO CLASSIFICATIONS. We must now consider to some extent the remarkable system of classification in renga. In the title or at the head of a renga is a directive. For *Three Poets* it is a heading: "A renga relating to 'person' " (*Nanibito* [or *nanihito*] *o fusuru renga*). By the time of Sōgi this directive or fushimono had become little more than a sign, a mark that ordinarily gave a sequence its title. For example, *Three Poets* was originally known as *One Hundred Stanzas Relating to "Person"* (*Nanibito Hyakuin*). We may surmise that it took on its present name when it became famous, so that it might be distinguished from the numerous other hyakuin with the same very popular directive. No such change was necessary for that sequence which Sōgi wrote for himself late in life: *A Hundred Stanzas Relating to "Person" Composed by Sōgi Alone* (*Sōgi Dokugin Nanibito Hyakuin*), although in fact it was also known by the fushimono "Relating to China" (*Nanikara*). Other titles often have the era and era-year of their composition. Fushimono must have been part of the game in early renga, but later they might even be added as an after-thought. In any event, it was originally a conception that provided a focus for a sequence. If *Three Poets* were an early renga, we would have to think of joining "person" to the appropriate word in stanzas or, in other words, the poet would have to give it recognition somehow. Here is the first stanza of *Three Poets*:

Yuki nagara	Despite some snow
yamamoto kasumu	the base of hills spreads with haze
yūbe kana	the twilight scene

The connection here would clearly have to be with "yama-," thus giving us "yamabito," "person of the hills." The categories of appropriate words can still be found and studied.[3] But the fushimono provides a rare instance in renga, and Japanese poetry more generally, in which a feature of art gets simpler rather than more complex in the course of time.

STANZA ENDINGS. Other conventions continued to be honored more rigorously. The hokku or opening verse must be a unit capable of being separate, discrete. The third must end with a participle, "-te." The fourth usually ends with a noun (as does Sōgi's in *Three Poets*). But there are also three possible verbal endings. The most frequent of these is "nari" (a copula also used as an auxiliary). In addition, renga has some eighteen cutting words (kireji), such as Sōgi's "kana" at the end of the first stanza of *Three Poets*. Others include the presumptive auxiliary verb "ran," which sometimes seems to be devoid of meaning, and the perfective inflection, "-keri," which also loses some of its semantic force. Renga poets were expected to use "-keri" only in the 7-7 syllable stanzas, except that it might be used in the opening stanza. All this seems far removed from Romantic ideas about art, and indeed it is.

RECURRENT WORDS; SPECIAL STANZAS. In order to ensure various kinds of continuance and discontinuance and to honor certain ideas about things that had begun in waka, certain words and topics had to appear

[3] See Yamada and Hoshika, p. 14. Pages 13-20 are concerned with *fushimono*, along with appropriate diction and images. See Abbreviated References, pp xvii-xviii, for full citation of studies frequently referred to.

with stipulated frequency, or no more often than at stipulated intervals. Others were governed by rules about minimum or maximum numbers of stanzas for continuance. The most important such rule involves moon stanzas and flower stanzas. In a one-hundred-stanza sequence we expect there to be eight moon stanzas and four flower stanzas. That is, there should be one moon stanza on each side of each sheet, and one flower stanza on each sheet. The last moon stanza was the one most likely to be omitted, if there was an omission, as is the case in *Three Poets*:

1st Sheet	1-22	
Front	1-8	5 Moon
Back	9-22	13 Flower; 18 Moon
2nd Sheet	23-50	
Front	23-36	25 Flower; 27 Moon
Back	37-50	48 Moon
3rd Sheet	51-78	
Front	51-64	55 Flower; 58 Moon
Back	65-78	66 Moon
4th Sheet	79-100	
Front	79-92	81 Flower; 90 Moon
Back	93-100	[Moon omitted]

From this it can be seen that the placing of these stanzas determines a good deal of our sense of the whole sequence. Placing also involves the parts, because a flower stanza is always a spring stanza, and a moon stanza is usually an autumn stanza. If the moon belongs to another season, special designation is necessary, such as "natsu no tsuki," the summer moon. Or sometimes a moon stanza was also a flower stanza, in which case it is a spring moon. The flower stanza is superior in that it appears less often. A stanza qualifies for being a flower or moon stanza only by having the word "hana" (flower) or "tsuki" (moon) in it. On the other hand, "tsukihi," "months and days," does not mean moon, and hence Stanza 42 in *Three Poets* is not a moon stanza. Similarly, a stanza is not a flower stanza even with the word "hana," if that is part of the name of a flower (tachibana, ume no hana, sakurabana, etc.). Named flowers (na no hana) do not qualify for flower-stanza status, and we observe that there are four such in *Three Poets* (2, 68, 80, 91). In general, any such stanzas beyond the minimum required involve the moons and not the flowers. They are too precious for that. It should also be said that it is never made clear what flower is designated by "hana" in renga. At the time of Sōgi, opinions were in flux as to the finest flower of spring. Earlier poets would have known that it was the plum (ume). Later poets would know it was the cherry (sakura). It seemed more evocative not to specify. The same principle holds with insects. Those with names (na no mushi) might come with appropriate seasons. Those without (tada no mushi, mushi) always went with autumn but were felt to be so evocative as to be allowable only once in one hundred stanzas.

STANZA TOPICS, SUBTOPICS, AND MOTIFS. The handling of topics and subtopics does not follow the rule that the more impressive deserves least mention. Topics are of two kinds and are adapted from the classifications of waka. The two are Seasonal and Miscellaneous, giving us a total of five, but in the practice of renga and haikai alike the four seasons account together for about half the stanzas and Miscellaneous (zō) for the rest. In waka, Miscellaneous means not dominated by any one topic, which might include, besides the four seasons, Love, Travel, and so on. In renga a stanza belongs to Miscellaneous simply if it has no seasonal topic. The other topics of waka (Love, Travel, Lament, Grievance, Buddhism, Shinto, etc.) therefore become subtopics in renga and haikai, so that we may have Spring Love (Haru no Koi) or Miscellaneous Love (Zō no Koi). We know that we have spring if certain phenomena belonging to that season appear. For reasons to be explained, however, some images and words designate a topic or subtopic by convention. For example, although the first stanza of *Three Poets* has snow, it is a spring stanza, because kasumi (haze) and its verbal forms always designate spring. It is strong enough to overcome, as it were, the power of snow. Similarly, the felt or actual presence of a concealed house (kakurega) implied reclusion and Grievance. The practice of renga differs somewhat from waka in terms of the frequency with which certain topics are treated. There is a higher proportion of stanzas with Grievance and Buddhism subtopics in many renga. The greatest negative change is with Love. In waka, it had been the second principal subject, after the seasons. Now it is a subtopic and appears on balance less (with the exception of sequences devoted to Love). And the number drops further in most haikai.

Seasonal stanzas predominate in the Introduction section of a renga (jo, 1-8 of a hundred), as *Three Poets* exemplifies.

1-3	Spring (3)
4	Miscellaneous (1)
5-7	Autumn (3)
8	Miscellaneous (1)

In the long development section (ha, 9-92) numerous nonseasonal concerns are introduced, which means both that such a subtopic as Travel may be added to an Autumn stanza and also that Miscellaneous stanzas become more frequent. It is very often the case that a topic ending one side or one sheet is carried over to the beginning of the next. Perhaps some of these facts can be shown in rude outline by continuing after stanza 8 in *Three Poets*, stopping with 92: that is, by considering the lengthy Development section (ha).

1st Sheet
back

9-12	Miscellaneous (4: con. from 8)
13-15	Spring (3)
16	Miscellaneous (1)
17	Winter (1)
18-20	Autumn (3)
21-22	Miscellaneous (2)

2nd Sheet
front

23-24	Miscellaneous (2)
25-27	Spring (3)
28-31	Autumn (4)
32-36	Miscellaneous (5)

2nd Sheet
back

37-44	Miscellaneous (8)
45-48	Autumn (4)

49	Miscellaneous (1)
50	Winter (1)

3rd Sheet
back

51	Winter (1)
52	Miscellaneous (1)
53-55	Spring (3)
56-58	Autumn (3)
59-61	Miscellaneous (3)
62-63	Winter (2)
64	Miscellaneous (1)

3rd Sheet
back

65	Miscellaneous (1)
66-69	Autumn (4)
70-76	Miscellaneous (7)
77-78	Spring (2)

4th Sheet
front

79-81	Spring (3)
82-88	Miscellaneous (7)
89-91	Autumn (3)
92	Miscellaneous (1)

It can be seen that as soon as we get into the Development section, the peace of the Introduction is altered. The back of the front sheet starts off with three Miscellaneous stanzas (making 4 with 8), a run that is new. We then settle back into Spring (13-15). Then there is great fluctuation: one on Miscellaneous, one on Winter, and then suddenly three on Autumn right after Winter. Later, the poets work with series of longer and shorter runs, the longest being those thirteen Miscellaneous stanzas stretching from the front to the back of the second sheet. The purely topical emphasis eases toward the end of the Development. We have four Autumn, seven Miscellaneous, five Spring, another seven Miscellaneous. If this easy pace were to last, we would have another long run of seasonal stanzas. Instead we have the usual minimum number of Autumn, three, and the front of the fourth sheet ends with one Miscellaneous. That combination assists in giving us a head start on the Fast Finale of 93-100. Its character of "speed" cannot be understood by topics alone, however, and we shall have to consider other matters.

Before doing so, we must observe how important Spring and Autumn are in *Three Poets*. We get no Summer stanzas at all. Twice we have a pair of Winter stanzas (50-51, 62-63) and once a single instance (17). It is considered odd or wrong to have fewer than three successive Spring or Autumn stanzas, and often one sees five. Three is the usual maximum for Summer and Winter, and one the obvious minimum. Miscellaneous stanzas vary from one to several, usually upwards of about seven or eight. The run of thirteen (32-44) in *Three Poets* is so long as to be worthy of comment.

The art of relating stanzas also entails the possible use of subtopics. These are what in waka are topics for books not either Seasonal or Miscellaneous: Travel, Grievance, etc. To show how those add to the pacing and enriching of a sequence, let us classify the fourteen poems of the back of the first sheet (9-22) according to topic and subtopic, if any. If no subtopic is involved, only the topic is given.

```
 9 Miscellaneous
10 Miscellaneous
11 Miscellaneous; Grievance (jukkai)
12 Miscellaneous; Grievance
13 Spring; Transience (mujō)
14 Spring
15 Spring
16 Miscellaneous; Travel (tabi)
17 Winter; Travel
18 Autumn; Travel
19 Autumn; Love (koi)
20 Autumn; Love
21 Miscellaneous
22 Miscellaneous; Grievance
```

This little sample shows how inadequate it is to consider topics alone. The agitated passage spoken of before (stanzas 16-18) is somewhat smoothed or harmonized by the use of Travel subtopics. On the other hand, the subtopics are deployed with topics in 18 to 22 in ways more agitated than the topics alone suggest.

The topics and subtopics show the adapting to renga of elements in waka. In what follows we must consider matters adumbrated by, or extracted from, waka by the renga poets. The one such subject treated most naturally after subtopics are motifs, what might be termed sub-subtopics. In setting these forth, we shall have to sacrifice some things, but surely there will be enough left to leave us feeling unneglected. My account continues to be indebted to Yamada Yoshio and Konishi Jin'ichi.[4] It will be found that the categories are neither parallel nor exclusive, but we are interested in clarity and utility. The motifs distinguished here can be grouped into six sets, which may as well be set out all at once and then commented on.

1. Persons, Birds, Insects (Living Things)
2. Residences, Clothes (Signs of Persons)
3. Plants, Trees, Cultivation (Growing Things)
4. Night, Radiance
5. Falling Things, Rising Things
6. Peaks, Waters

A given stanza may have none of these motifs, or it may have several. For example, a moon stanza will inevitably be assigned Night and Radiance motifs. Often the proper topic is not so obvious. For example, one brought up with English is likely to think of dawn in connection with day. But Japanese speak of nightbreak ("yoake") rather than daybreak, so that the Night classification is used. The third category is especially difficult, since in Japanese "kusa," here given as Plants, covers a variety of objects from small grasses to substantial plants. Also, a tree may be cultivated in a garden or left to grow in the wild as a tree. (This matter has particularly troubled my own efforts to classify.) Falling Things include such as rain, snow, dew, and frost. Rising Things include

---

[4] See Konishi, Sōgi, pp. 236–43 for his chartlike analysis of the stanzas of Three Poets (and pp. 86–95 for his discussion of motifs). Much of the analysis is taken from Yamada Yoshio, Renga Gaisetsu (Iwanami, 1937), pp. 233–40, but in the most difficult and important particulars of stanza impressiveness and connection, Konishi's work is an innovation.

clouds, haze, mist, smoke. If there seems to be something arbitrary about these assignments, the explanation will have to wait for a discussion of essence "essential nature" (hon'i). I shall pass by certain other simplifications inherent in my method.[5]

STANZA IMPRESSIVENESS AND RELATION. We must now consider two last matters of classification. They are in some ways the most important of all for renga as an art of related stanzas, and both involve estimation of successive variance. Degree of impressiveness, the first of these, is special, because it relates to the stanza on its own. Closeness of connection is also special, because it relates the stanza to its predecessor. We have had to wait until Konishi Jin'ichi's *Sōgi* before anyone chose to reveal the importance of these facts to us, and I shall be following his method, with some slight adaptation for haikai. In each of these classifications there are four degrees. For impressiveness the highest is "mon," the lowest "ji." For relation, the closest is "shin," the most remote "so."

These can be grouped and translated as follows.

Impressiveness		Relation	
mon	Design	shin	Close
monji	Design-Ground	shinso	Close-Distant
jimon	Ground-Design	soshin	Distant-Close
ji	Ground	so	Distant

The most important statement that can be made about the impressiveness or relationship of stanzas is this: in a renga no one category of either is absolutely better than another. A Design-Close stanza is not in itself better than a Ground-Distant stanza. There is one exception. The hokku is independent of relation (there being none before it) and it should be a Design stanza and therefore a renga collection often has a special hokku

[5] One of my omissions is the tai-yū classifications for residences, peaks, and waters. This distinguishes between what is primary, fixed (tai) and what is incidental or mobile (yū). Examples of tai include: for Residence, gate (mon); for Peaks, hill (oka); for Waters, sea (umi). Examples of yū include: for Residence, garden (sono); for Peaks, suspended bridge (kakehashi); for Waters, waves (nami). See Brazell and Cook's translation (as in n. 2), p. 44; they render "tai" as "essence" and "yū" as "attribute," and show that a sequence had certain usages allowable and disallowable in a succession of verses ("kuzari" to be discussed later).

section. The important consideration, however, is that we have gradation in the course of the sequence. With four variables in two categories, there is a possibility of forty-eight different combinations. With four Seasonal topics and the Miscellaneous topic, and with the fourteen motifs distinguished in this simplified account, the range of variation is incalculable, especially since the number of words that could justify the Trees motif, for example, is by no means small.

Something must be said about determining the degree of impressiveness and closeness of relation. Numerous factors influence impressiveness, and some can only be learned, not taught. The quality of language is involved, as is the handling of a topic. Something too familiar or too strange might lower the impressiveness of a stanza. In short, there are no scientific rules whatsoever. As critics everywhere have discovered, evaluation is no simple matter. Yet some statements can be made. In the absence of other considerations, a Seasonal stanza is more likely to be more impressive than a Miscellaneous stanza, and a Spring or Autumn stanza more impressive than a Summer or Winter. By the same kind of token and with the same kind of reservation, a Flower stanza or a Moon stanza will be impressive. The stanzas in the jo or introduction are expected to look good, and the first one or two must be Design. As was said earlier, plain, unnamed insects (mushi) are deemed more impressive than named ones such as bell crickets (suzumushi). Sōgi shows a relatively greater liking for Ground stanzas than his contemporaries. But even while being Ground, they are far more interesting than some of the Ground-Design or even Design-Ground stanzas by Sōchō in *Three Poets*.

It will be recalled (see p. 22, above) that Yoshimoto had set forth the rule that there should be variety of impressiveness, and his terms are nearly the same as those used here. His criteria derive from the arrangement of waka in an imperial collection or in a hundred-poem sequence. The compilers or the poet, seeking to integrate thousands or a hundred poems into a sequence, came to feel that it would be more satisfying if there were fluctuation in the impressiveness of poems on summer, let us say. Western anthologists seek the best or the representative. The Japanese have sought the best, and the most representative, but they have also included some poems not so good in order to make it a pleasure to read through a collection. They seek, as it were, an irregular landscape for traversing, not a level high plateau. This principle was taken over by renga poets from court poets and made central to their linking.[6] The idea of closely and distantly related stanzas also derives from court poetry. Shinku and soku originally referred not to renga or haikai but to the relation between the two parts of a tanka: its 5, 7, 5 syllable upper part (kami no ku) and 7, 7 syllable lower part (shimo no ku). When the parts were clearly and intimately related, the whole poem was "shin." When one had to work at discovering a connection, the whole poem was "so." This distinction went into renga because in late classical court poetry (ca. 1241-1500), the compilers of anthologies and sequences recognized that one could also relate one poem to the next closely or distantly.[7] There was some disagreement about what was most desirable, but all later waka poets recognized the possibilities.

Closeness or remoteness of relation can sometimes be distinguished more easily than impressiveness. Frequently, however, we shall disagree. In general, two criteria are involved, as we have seen in another connection: relation by words and phrasing (kotobazuke) and relation by conception (kokorozuke). Everyone is in some sense a beginner with linked poetry, and everyone is well advised to consider words and diction before moving to conception. Conception may be the subtler and the more interesting, but, as I have learned with some effort, it is also the most fraught with problems. After all, if two adjacent stanzas have the same topic and subtopic, if they share very similar words, if both begin with a negatively inflected verb and end with three nouns joined by the possessive particle, one's task is not to arraign subtleties in the critical court but to call it Close and move on. When there is difference in all such matters, then one may hesitate to ask whether there is enough in the conception to require a Distant-Close rating rather than a simple Distant. The injunction implied has been simplified somewhat, but there is no substitute for attending to the words of the Japanese.

On the other hand, words often involve conceptions, since it is in the semiotic systems we call languages that we express and understand conceptions. This overlapping or interrelation can be exemplified by the

---

[6] For the liveliness of this issue among some waka poets, see *Court Poetry*, pp. 322-29; see also n. 7.

[7] See *Court Poetry*, pp. 403-13 for a discussion; also the preceding note.

formalized word-associations to be found in renga, as in waka before it. Word-association (engo) will often be found in a single stanza, as when with a travel subtopic the traveler is said to lie down on a pillow made of cuttings. The word "lie down" (fushi-) can also be taken as "stalk" or "joint" for bamboo or other things cut. The same associations can also draw two stanzas together, although of course the composer of the first would have had no idea that the composer of the second would affect such a connection. In one stanza we may have dew (tsuyu), frost (shimo), drizzle (shigure), or other such cold moisture that the Japanese associate with the changing of color of leaves and the withering of plants. Such an image of moisture in one stanza can therefore readily be developed in the next. In such a case, the closeness of connection affected varies. If word-association alone is involved, a very small degree of closeness results. But if explicit use is made, and especially if a strong causal development is meant, then indeed the stanzas will enter into Close or Close-Distant relation. Other uses of words that may have a varying effect in this regard involve the kind of real or apparent juncture between stanzas. One common way of ending a stanza is with a noun, although any complete Japanese syntax requires ending with a finite verb. One stanza might end with "haru no yo no tsuki," or "haru no yo no hana": "spring's night's moon" or "flowers." The next stanza could begin with an attributive verb (modifying an ensuing noun) that yet might seem to look back on the noun concluding the previous stanza, as, for example (to continue with our moon or flowers), "mihatenu yume no," which one could translate something like "of an unfinished dream." But "mihatenu" means something more like "seen not through to its end," with the "mi-" being the word "to see." The explanation may be rather tiresome, but by using "see" at the beginning of a stanza following "moon" or "flowers" at the end of a preceding stanza, a natural connection is effected—as if "moon / seen not through to its end"—even though it may not be fully involved in the syntax or even be a feature of the main predication of the stanza. There would not be, then, by such means alone any closeness of connection. On the other hand, poets sensing the need for a Close connection after some rather Distant can assist each other. A Love stanza could be written in such a way that its syntax could easily be extended to make what almost looks like a waka.

This little excursus makes another point. Word-association (engo) may or may not be involved in continuous syntactic predication. The chances are that it will not. This important feature of Japanese poetry greatly assists renga in its special feature. At least engo illustrates the distinction between continuous meaning and continuous features. As has been said, two and only two stanzas connect in continuous meaning. This does not, however, prevent continuity in *topics*, which may go on for several stanzas. Perhaps it is true to say that a continuity of topic (for perhaps three stanzas) or engo (for only two) cannot but possess cognitive significance. With a continuity of three stanzas, one cannot say that a given stanza "means" only in terms of its predecessor and successor. But the elements of a stanza and its wholeness "mean" rather differently. As simple, full predication, a stanza is restricted to connection with its neighbor before and after. As part of an evolving sequence, the elements and wholeness of a stanza contribute to a whole realized only as we reach its end. Editors sometimes comment critically, as for example at the end of the fiftieth stanza, that a unit there ending—which would be either all the second sheet (ni no ori) or just its back (ura)—is marked by a large number of poems on Grievance and other human affairs.

STANZA FUNCTIONS. We are now at a point where some at least of the systems of classification can be brought together. We discover that we have been considering matters related to a sequence as a whole: sheets, sides, flowers, moons, and so forth. And that we have been considering matters that can be understood in terms of the function of an individual stanza. These functions can be understood in a multiplicity of ways, but for the sake of clarity let us consider that they are of four kinds:

Impressiveness	Design, Design-Ground, etc.
Relation	Close, Close-Distant, etc.
Topics, Subtopics	Seasons, Miscellaneous, Love, etc.
Motifs	Living Things, Radiance, Peaks, etc.

For a fuller version, Figure 3 may be consulted. It is the kind of chart my students and I have used to help us to appreciate the art of linked poetry. It will be observed that of the four kinds given above, all but Relation involve the stanza by itself. Such being the case, one might infer that the other matters assist in judging Relation. In any event, a little practice soon makes one skilled with topics, subtopics, and motifs. And one can consult with a treatise like *Ubuginu* when there is doubt. One can then complete the matters about the stanza by judging its impressiveness. Whereupon one is as well prepared as possible to assess the closeness of Relation, and by consolidating the categories at this point we can clarify the previous discussion.[8]

SELECTION AND EMPHASIS. We must now consider a different set of canons involving means by which renga selects and intensifies. All literature, perhaps all expression, selects and intensifies because all cannot be known at once and because some degree of importance in certain things rather than others is assumed to justify expression. Traditional Western poetry drew on the resources of the art of rhetoric to a greater degree than Japanese poetry has ever done, because there was no tradition of public speaking in Japan to develop oratory. On the other hand, all literatures make much of imagery, comparisons, and metaphor. Renga has a special category of the assumed or dissembled (nise-) that is its own kind of classified metaphor, which exists alongside such aspects as imagery, simile, personification, metonomy, synecdoche, and other figures.

One feature of the selection-emphasis of linked poetry involves the language and therefore is also characteristic of other Japanese poetic and literary kinds to lesser or greater degree. By comparison, English is very much a pronoun language. Japanese have means of specifying the person imagined to be speaking, thinking, or doing, as well as the person of whom that first person may be speaking. Among the means we must include a very large number of personal nouns for first and second persons and some for third persons. But these are seldom used in poetry except as an occasional possessive (e.g., "waga," "my"; "taga," "whose"). Usually indication of place or direction will assist us in knowing who is meant. And certainly verbs play a very important role. In speech as well as in writing, the verb chosen and the kind of inflection or auxiliary will make clear whether a person is speaking of self, of the person addressed, or of a third person. But in poetry the range of deferentiality, formality, and intimacy of verbs is very greatly reduced. It will be in the headnote, if at all, that we find a haberu, tatematsuru, owasu, and other such verbs

[8] For further details, see my brief piece, "Renga to no Deai" ("An Encounter with Renga"), *Hon*, 1, no. 4 (1976), 22-24.

that signal the person meant in *The Tale of Genji*, for example. It would take unusual fortitude to say that waka and linked poetry are more ambiguous than the language of *The Tale of Genji*, but the ambiguity is different. Our poetic verbs lack the range of selection for formality. Verbs are, however, inflected. The inflections may include aspect (e.g., the perfect), negation, and mood (e.g., the imperative). But they do not indicate person and number. Nouns can be given attachments to insist on plurality, but in their usual state they are singular-plural rather than singular or plural. (Of course a word like "sun" is normally presumed to be singular.)

Such lack of stress on person and number allows for selection and emphasis that differ even while using the same lexical materials, the same "text," as some critics are fond of calling it. If I write a love stanza in which, by various means, I suggest pretty evidently that the speaker is a woman, you, writing next, can use other means to make your and my stanza both be spoken by a man. Perhaps the next one of us will take your man and make it humankind in order to generalize on experience. Each renga stanza is, then, subject to constant reinterpretation by its successor, and the same "text" may yield quite different results. In fact, commentators sometimes almost suggest that a given stanza has, as it were, three distinguishable meanings: what it means as it were by itself (ikku to shite), what it means in the context given by its predecessor, and what it is made to mean by its successor.

It is worth stressing these matters. The stress indicates that Japanese poetry is not the same as our own in every respect. It also shows how linked poetry may glide from stanza to stanza, making alterations of sense that really are infeasible in *natural* English. As a final reason for this stress, it gives us, on the one hand, a sense of the almost giddy possibility that exists in any language and that is taken over for resource by literary versions of a particular language. Selection and emphasis imply wide ranges of ambiguity and of non-sense out of which order and sense and clarity can be made to emerge. In what follows the concern will fall on rigor, order, clarity—on the arbitrary elements of a particular literary language.

One aspect of selection and emphasis in renga involves the kind of preferences that have been spoken of in passing earlier. Two of the brief and cryptic phrases in the treatise *Renga Shinshiki* say a great deal by implication. Looking up "autumn," one discovers "spring, autumn, love." Looking up "summer," one reads, "summer, winter, travel, Shintoism, Buddhism, grievance." In addition summer has added to it elevations and watersides, as well as residences.[9] This telegraphic expression means that the various topics or subtopics are conceived to be on a par with each other. Spring, autumn, and love are of outstanding importance, which is why we never expect to see but one stanza devoted to them, and usually find three or more. Summer and those other topics or subtopics belong to a multitude that have importance, but only such as one stanza can satisfy and that would be exaggerated by more than about three.

Sōgi makes such preferences clear in his collection, *Chikurinshō* (*Bamboo Forest Miscellany*). Following Chinese example, he gathered stanzas from seven earlier renga masters. But how was he to arrange them? He could arrange them under their authors' names. But a Japanese could hardly be expected to do that. He might integrate them into a sequence of his own devising. But he really had to have at least one section devoted to famous opening stanzas (hokku), which would be lost or look odd with their separating devices (cutting words such as "kana") in a sequence. And, after all, there were 3,382 stanzas. Sōgi had a real problem, one that had troubled him from his first collection, *Wasuregusa*. He tried this and that system of classifying stanzas. Not surprisingly, they all bore some resemblance to an imperial anthology. The stanzas in *Wasuregusa* were grouped under the heads of the four seasons, Love and Miscellaneous, precisely the three major groups of the later imperial collections and in their order. This early arrangement involved the awkward inclusion of hokku at the beginning of each of the seasonal books. But at last he came up with a series of ten books, a miniature imperial collection.[10]

1.	Spring	6.	Love
2.	Summer	7.	Love
3.	Autumn	8.	Miscellaneous
4.	Winter	9.	Miscellaneous
5.	Travel	10.	Opening Stanzas

[9] See Yamada and Hoshika, pp. 25 and 69.

[10] See Hoshika, pp. 44-45, whose version is not quite the final one but is chosen, apparently, for textual reasons. Most imperial anthologies have twenty books in such order, but there are precedents for ten.

As in an imperial anthology, so here in *Chikurinshō*, seasonal poems lead off the first half, love poems the second. Sōgi goes further, grouping the opening stanzas in an order like the first four books—that is, they follow the court model even more closely.

The number of stanzas in the various categories will also suggest renga preferences.[11]

1.	Spring	466
2.	Summer	166
3.	Autumn	502
4.	Winter	226
5.	Travel	238 (1-5: 1598)
6-7.	Love	518
8-9.	Miscellaneous	980
10.	Opening Stanzas	286 (6-10: 1784)
		(1-10: 3382)

It is particularly striking that Sōgi's classifications follow the distinctions of waka rather than of renga. As we have seen, renga has but two kinds of topics: a Season and Miscellaneous (meaning simply not a season). For renga purposes, Sōgi should have considered Travel and Love as subtopics of a Season or Miscellaneous. Instead, he begins the second half of his collection, as imperial collections of waka had begun, with Love as a category parallel to the Seasons and to Miscellaneous, and he devotes a book to Travel as if it were as important as Summer. In *Chikurinshō*, Miscellaneous therefore means any non-seasonal stanza except those with the subtopics of Travel or Love. From this we can see two seemingly different things. We can see that renga differs from waka in what could only have been thought some serious, important ways. Yet we also see that the differences are, so to speak, those accounted for by waka in the first place.

SUSPENSIONS. The canons of renga include two further principles, each of great importance, although one is largely technical and the other very conceptual. The technical one is the principle of sari or sarikirai, of omission or suspension of a given word, image, or topic for some number of stanzas. This is the counterpart to the principle of continuance of spring

[11] *Ibid.*, pp. 55 ff.

stanzas for three or more in succession. The most obvious example is a word like "dream" (yume), which is thought precious enough to be used only at seven-stanza intervals. It is in fact used only four times in *Three Poets*. "Mushi," unnamed insects, is allowed only once in one hundred stanzas. Certain other words are allowed but once in 10,000 stanzas—not at all in a hyakuin. The principle of omission extends to minute details. If one stanza treats certain features of night, in the next one does not use various words that might indicate daybreak, because that would be too obvious a progression.

HON'I-ESSENTIAL NATURE. The conceptual principle is that of hon'i, or essential nature.[12] Essential nature implies that diction, topics, and imagery have a special emphasis. They are not devoid of stress or selection. The idea is not entirely Asian. Traditional literatures, indeed all literatures, tend to reject the neutral, the ungraded. If nothing else, fashion intervenes, so that, for example, a senator is dignified in one season and absurd in the next. In the West, the mimetic theory did not involve simple replication of "nature" or reality. From Aristotle's version onward, mimesis involved representation of universals and of contingent or causal elements in reality. These are matters very different from a neutral version. Similarly, in East Asia the dominant affective-expressive theory operated in terms of very qualitative selection and emphasis. What was thought to be low or comic seldom had a place in high literature, unless it could be introduced in some special, sophisticated way, like pastoralism in the West. We have seen that poetry possessed of such elements was thought to be haikai or mushin, non-standard.

In court literature anyone who has taste or recognizes the essential character of things is kokoro aru, possessed of heart (or in its sinified version "ushin"), directly opposite to mushin. Such a person recognizes certain essential *poetic* truths. These may not seem to accord with our notions of poetic truth, because we may come with different senses of an all-encompassing Truth. The most famous and concise expression is probably that by Sei Shōnagon (late 10th-11th century) at the beginning

---

[12] For the background in waka, see *Court Poetry*, pp. 252-55, 263, 275, 396, and 505. For hon'i in renga, see Yamada Yoshio, pp. 87, 129-37, 174, and 219-20. In particular, see Konishi, *Sōgi*, pp. 136-49, for a very cogent presentation (omitted by Brazell and Cook). For a classification by a major renga poet, see Jōha's *Shihōshō* or *Renga Hon'ishō*.

of her *Pillow Book* (*Makura no Sōshi*). In her opening words she advances four propositions about which time of day is the most characteristic and finest in each of the seasons (I omit her descriptions): "For spring, the dawn. . . . For summer, the night. . . . For autumn, the dusk. . . . For winter, the first light."[13] Obviously there are lovely winter evenings and summer sunrises. But, essentially, summer is best for its nights, when the heat of the day yields to some degree of coolness. One sometimes can give such reasons why the hon'i for something is as it is, but often the choice is arbitrary. It is as though poetry requires that a choice be made, and it *was* made—not randomly but aesthetically, arbitrarily, to give some essential truth that would probably not cover all circumstances and possible exceptions.

Such a point must often be read into poetry, as with the famous poem by Fujiwara Teika (1162-1241; *Shinkokinshū*, 1: 38).

Haru no yo no	The bridge of dreams
Yume no ukihashi	Floating on the brief spring night
Todae shite	Soon breaks apart;
Mine ni wakaruru	And from the mountaintop a cloud
Yokogumo no sora.	Takes leave into the open sky.

Whatever else might be said of this poem, the assumption that spring is essentially the season of dawn makes clear what time of day it is when the dream breaks off so that the scene can be made out in the light. The same poetic logic makes clear why it is that among the autumn poems of the *Shinkokinshū* the most famous are its "Three Evenings."[14] This way of thought, so obviously present in court literature, was intensified and codified by the renga poets, so much so that a modern critic like Hoshika Sōichi can casually refer to the four seasons as "flower-bird, moon-snow" ("kachō, gessetsu").[15] Obviously we do not expect snow in

[13] See Ikeda Kikan *et al.*, ed., *Makura no Sōshi*, etc. (Iwanami Shoten, 1958), p. 43. Ikeda's lengthy note on p. 333 shows that these preferences were particularly Japanese. The Chinese had the concept of pen-i (hon'i) but were less certain about times and seasons. This gave Japanese freedom to have their own system and to appeal to Chinese precedent for convenient exceptions.

[14] They are *Shinkokinshū*, 4: 361-63, poems by Priest Jakuren (d. 1201), Priest Saigyō (1118-1190), and Teika. For translations, see *Introduction*, pp. 117, 103, and 104.

[15] Hoshika, *Chikurinshō*, p. 50.

summer, but there are lovely flowers in summer and autumn, and the moon shines the year around. But essentially, as it were—by the doctrine of hon'i—spring is the time for flowers and autumn for the moon.

Such preferences were so well known that adaptation was possible. One could always find a different precedent in the Chinese poets, who were less categorical, in at least this respect. More often a poet would show a new kind of heart (kokoro) and create an adapted hon'i. The first stanza of *Three Poets* implies such an alteration.

Yuki nagara	Despite some snow
yamamoto kasumu	the base of hills spreads with haze
yūbe kana	the twilight scene

We have noticed that kasumi and its variants, "haze," essentially imply spring. In fact kasumi can appear at any season in Japan. Poetically, however, it is so vernal that no one says "*spring* haze" ("haru no kasumi") and so essential that it overcomes the snow image to give us a spring stanza. Haze alone of vernal phenomena may appear at any stage in a progression of spring waka. By coupling it with remaining snow, Sōgi obviously designates the season as early spring. But, contrary to custom and to Sei Shōnagon, he made this beautiful spring an evening beauty. He took his precedent from Emperor Gotoba (1180-1239). Gotoba apparently liked spring evenings at his Minase palace. Certainly his most famous poem (*Shinkokinshū*, 1: 36) suggests as much.

Miwataseba	As I look about
Yamamoto kasumu	Where the haze drifts below the hills
Minasegawa	Along Minase River,
Yūbe wa aki to	I wonder why it was I felt
Nani omoiken.	That autumn was the time for dusk?

Conceptions of hon'i feature in renga criticism. Yamada Yoshio quotes an earlier treatise: "Again, in renga there is that which is termed hon'i. For example, although the wind may blow high and the rain fall heavily in spring, essentially spring rains and winds work with great gentleness."[16] To take another example, for renga love is essentially one-

---

[16] Yamada, p. 130. The passage is paraphrased at large in modern Japanese by Konishi, *Sōgi*, pp. 137-38.

sided, loving or longing without having the affection returned. (Sometimes a brief time of happiness is presumed or allowed, so that subsequent change may have the greater effect.) A passage from the treatise *Ubuginu* makes this explicit: "The essential meaning of love is to love a person passionately, but unsuccessfully, unrequitedly. The essential character involves the expiration of the loving person in body and spirit. It holds the same meaning for men and women alike. To write of being loved by somebody is neither love nor the essential character of love. This matter is the same as longing in vain to hear the wood thrush sing."[17] As Konishi Jin'ichi has put it, the principle of essential nature gave the imagery and ideas of renga a mold or idealized usage.[18]

Not all essentials were fully molded. Another passage in *Ubuginu* discusses the handling of one of the most powerful concepts in all Japanese literature, dream (yume): "The word 'dream' should be used at intervals of at least seven stanzas. Generally speaking it implies love. If it is used in travel stanzas, it intensifies the sense of travel. From its very conception a dream in temporary sleeping conditions implies travel. . . . But when dream is used with words for spring or autumn [e.g., 'haru no yume,' a dream in spring; or 'yume no aki,' an autumn of dreams], love is not meant. Another opinion holds that 'dream' does not always mean love."[19]

Such allowance is in fact permitted even in matters that supposedly have more restricted "mold." According to *Ubuginu* and other accounts, love cannot be had with joy. (The two main verbs, "kou" and "omou," might often be better translated "yearn for.") And one does discover over and over the man longing toward the beginning of an affair, and the woman suffering after the morning that he parts from her. This can be discovered in the 518 love stanzas that Sōgi included in his *Chikurinshō*. The male point of view is quickly exhausted, at least in terms of the early stages of love. In the twenty-third stanza (no. 1383) we discover what a waka poet might have called the compound topic (*musubidai*) of "love in the spring" ("haru no koi").

[17] Yamada and Hoshika, p. 175.   [18] Konishi, *Sōgi*, pp. 141-48.

[19] Yamada and Hoshika, p. 299. Professor Konishi directed my attention to this passage in a letter some years ago (16 May 1966) and to another in the *Utsuho Monogatari* (3 vols. [Iwanami Shoten, 1959-62], 1, 67): "After that dream the Lady was in an unaccustomed state." That is, sexual relations got her pregnant.

au wa ureshiki   to meet is to be happy
haru ni koso are   in a springtime that we share

("Ureshiki" yokes both "au wa" [to meet] and "haru" [springtime].) It
is as though a double joy is derived by the fulfillment of love at such a
season. This stanza violates *Ubuginu*'s draconian stipulation about love
being always miserable. But it makes the woman's misery soon entered
into thereafter that much more miserable.[20]

Such matters of convention and practice show how renga was developed naturally but distinctly from court poetry. Teika had composed
renga, and Sōgi composed waka. There is significance in the fact that it is
very difficult to discover examples of Teika's linked poetry but easy to
discover Sōgi's tanka. So great did the prestige of the older poetry remain, and so little seriously had renga once been taken. Yet by Sōgi's
time there was no question that the genius of Japanese poetry had passed
from the waka of the court to the renga of the priests, the commoners,
and the soldiers, with the interested nobility participating. Neither Japanese literature nor linked poetry stops with renga, however, and we can
therefore now attend to later developments. In various ways, renga exercises on them just that fundamental degree of influence that waka had on
it. Equally certainly, change led to at least as great a differentiation from
renga as renga shows from waka.

[20] Hoshika, *Chikurinshō*, p. 164.

4

From Renga to Haikai
and Haiku

> "If one does not understand such
> things naturally, it is hard for one to
> understand them at all."—Bashō

THE GROWTH of renga into a serious art entailed avoidance of what was felt to be simply amusing. What was only amusing was mushin, without proper heart, idea, or conception. By the middle of the fourteenth century, the words tell of the growing reputation of ushin renga, the serious, standard kind. This was now called "good renga" ("yoki renga"). It was also called "beautiful" or "skillful" ("uruwashiki," "jōzu"). The other kind is now "bad renga" ("waroki renga") or even "mad renga" ("kyō renga," "kyōku").[1] Yet such renga masters as Yoshimoto and Sōgi considered that there was such a thing as a distinct haikai style (haikaitai or haikaitei), even if it was not very admirable. Perhaps with court poetry on his mind, Nijō Yoshimoto wrote in his *Renri Hishō* that "This art is entirely an amusement."[2] The art (michi) he speaks of is renga as a whole, not merely haikai no renga. An explanation requires that we go backward a bit before we proceed from renga to its successors.

Certain poems in the nineteenth book of the *Kokinshū*, ca. 905, are termed haikai poems (haikaika; for reasons unknown its first character uses radical 149 rather than 9). There was speculation as to the meaning of that classification, and subsequent compilers of imperial collections were not eager to emulate this feature of the first. One such compiler,

---

[1] Kuriyama, *Haikaishi*, p. 45. I shall cite this account when quoting, but I am indebted to it for other information as well, as will be apparent.

[2] *Ibid.*, 47.

Minamoto Shunrai, wrote: "There are also poems called haikai. Nobody understands this very well."[3] Fujiwara Kiyosuke (1104-1177) explained, however, that such writing was basically humorous. He does not mean that it is joking or intentionally funny, but that there is something absurd, unnatural, or indecorous. His explanation is as good as any, and would explain at least why Komachi's poem (*Kokinshū*, 19: 1030) might be so classified just because she used too many pivot-words. But the exact tone of haikai varies and is quite difficult to explain out of context.

Haikai renga became seriously practiced in time, and as linked poetry its fundamental art remained the same as the standard kind. It too used ever-varying alteration in quality and in closeness of relation, topics and subtopics, and motifs. As Yoshimoto put it in his *Kyūshū Mondō*, "In waka poetry and renga poetry alike, there are design [umon] poems and non-design [mumon] poems. . . . A design stanza should be mixed in as every fourth or fifth."[4] Or again, in his *Tsukuba Mondō*: "People of the past have told us that in a hundred-poem sequence also we should compose ground poems and also mix in outstanding ones."[5] One of the difficulties of dealing with ideas of haikai and renga in this early period is that only a few examples have survived, and those which have make it difficult to distinguish the two. In his same *Tsukuba Dialogues*, Yoshimoto has a revealing description of renga in the early thirteenth century. "From about 1215, the Cloistered Emperor Go-Toba set as fushimono white, black, red, and other colors for solo renga by Lords Teika, Karyū, and others." Teika wrote a stanza about a carter with a great beard (Ōhige no / mikurumazoi). That produced something black, but one can hardly infer from this by so gifted a poet that he was taking his commission seriously.[6]

One of the important factors required for linked poetry to be taken seriously was a sorting-out of social groups interested in such arts. It seems most improbable that linked poetry would ever have developed into a serious art if the court society had continued to hold power. Surely, its waka would have been poetry, and linked poetry mere verse. As we have seen, renga were sometimes composed by people who could not read or write, and they belonged, with many others, to the lower

[3] *Ibid.*, p. 13. [4] *Ibid.*, p. 48.
[5] *Ibid.* [6] Kuriyama gives the quotation on p. 40, the stanza on p. 44.

classes or commoners (jige) rather than to those higher classes (uezama) that had dominated literature for so long. Yoshimoto and Shinkei are transitional figures, and although both were not comfortable with the lower classes who were writing the new kind of poetry, they acknowledged their existence. By the time kyōgen came to parody linked verse, it had become widespread and was no longer the property of a single social group, not even of those quasi-priestly masters. For example, in *The Winnow User* (*Mikazuki*), a husband bids his wife (a renga-widow) good-by with three lines of verse.

Mikazuki no	It is sad keepsake
izuru mo oshiki	that I bear in this departure
nagori kana—	under the new moon—

and she at once replies with her own two verses:

aki no katami ni	whereas the souvenir of autumn
kurete yuku sora.	is the growing darkness of the sky.

Both stanzas of this short renga—for that is what these are supposed to be—sound rather pompously serious, but their word-plays render them haikai. The husband's departure under the thin crescent moon ("mikazuki"—hence the title of the piece) is sad because he poses as a lover leaving his lady at dawn. It is also sad because his keepsake from this romantic tryst is a winnow (the "mi" of "mikazuki"). The keepsake or "nagori" is also the word for the fourth sheet of a one-hundred-stanza linked poem. The wife's reply plays on "katami." This is another word for keepsake or souvenir, and it also means seeing his shape. Her "kurete" plays upon Kure as the Wu dynasty (her husband is off on a long trip in time) and to grow dark, just as her "aki" plays on the season of autumn and his growing tired of her. If that great poet Komachi wrote haikaika because of word-plays, then this is haikai style with a vengeance. It differs from Teika's great-bearded carter in that it has the façade of being a waka, whereas Teika made no pretense. The most interesting thing about this episode—apart from its picture of the renga epidemic—is that it shows a woman composing. We seldom have a chance to see women writing after the court period. The point must surely be that *even* women are writing during this craze.

The necessary conditions for haikai as great poetry were grasped only slowly and took hold for only two brief periods. The reason may be suggested by one of Konishi Jin'ichi's remarks. In that common division of Japanese arts into the elegant or refined (ga) and low or vulgar (zoku), most critics would assign renga to the refined arts and haikai to the low. Konishi protests, saying that haikai has one refined leg and one vulgar leg.[7] To walk comfortably with such dissimilar legs is no small art. That is to say, it has to use meaningfully and aesthetically a language extended to include low images, sinicisms, and other techniques banned from both waka and renga. At the same time, this fresh, widened, lowered world had to be treated with mature art if what language implies—thought, values, and other aspects of our understanding of life—was to be more than a game. It is very worthwhile to attempt to write renga and haikai for one's own edification. The effort reveals that haikai is the more difficult. In truth, one leg does seem to be walking off toward renga and waka while the other slouches mischievously off toward senryū and low comedy. Matsuo Bashō (1644-1694) makes the same point. In his *Essay from a Traveller's Book-Satchel* (*Oi no Kobumi*), he remarks: "High art is all one in nature, whether in Saigyō's waka, in Sōgi's renga, in Sesshū's painting, or in Rikyū's tea ceremonial."[8] He would no doubt have also included the author of *The Tale of Genji*, Po Chü-i, and Tu Fu among those who had perfected their own version of the artistic Way (michi, which also has Buddhist associations in many usages). For that matter, he would have included such a phrase as "and in the haikai of Bashō," for what was said of him seems to be nothing other than he felt himself, indeed really nothing less than the truth: "He had composed haikai for over thirty years and was the first to do it truly. His haikai was the same in name as that of former times. Yet it was not of that old kind but the genuine thing."[9]

Normative standards such as those in the last two quotations differ

[7] Konishi, *Haiku*, p. 6.

[8] Kuriyama, *Haikaishi*, p. 20; *Bashō Bunshū*, ed. Sugiura Shōichirō *et al*. (Iwanami, 1959), p. 52. "High art" (fūga) is the subject of the next sentence and is implicit here.

[9] *Ibid*., p. 51.

from descriptive ones, and the founders of a true haikai have generally been taken to be Yamazaki Sōkan and Arakida Moritake. Sōkan's dates are especially uncertain. A standard reference book, *Haikai Daijiten* (*A Haikai Dictionary*), cites sources saying that he died in five different years between 1534 and 1577, at ages varying between seventy-two and eighty-nine. He is most famous for a collection usually referred to as *Inu Tsukubashū* (compiled ca. 1523-1532), that is, *The Dog Tsukubashū* or *The Dog Tsukuba Collection*, after Yoshimoto's renga collection. It should be said that dogs were no object of sentimentality at the time (although there was a later shogun who doted on them), and in fact warriors would use them for live archery practice. That is the hairy, crooked leg of haikai, muddied a bit more. But most manuscripts call the collection *Haikai Renga* or *Haikai Rengashō*. These hardly win a prize for snappy titles, but they and the other one do show how difficult Sōkan was finding it to define haikai as something both serious and distinct from earlier renga. He and Moritake (1473-1549) reflect their times and training by holding to many features of standard renga, but their contemporaries and successors agreed that these founders opened poetry to less restricted language and subject matter, while aiming at pleasure and amusement. Such had been something like the origins of renga and such, as Kiyosuke recognized, was pretty much the meaning of "haikai." Whatever its title, Sōkan's collection does not seem very revolutionary today. He does not include that many stanzas of his own, and he does include examples by Shinkei, Sōgi, and Sōchō. In the text before me (*Kōhon Inu Tsukubashū*, 1934), there are the following divisions and proportions.

The Seasons	pp.	1-39
Love		40-50
Miscellaneous		50-130
Opening stanzas (on seasonal topics)		131-156

These categories and the dimensions allotted each should be compared with their counterparts in Sōgi's *Chikurinshō* (see above, p. 79. We see very clearly the ancestry back from haikai to renga to waka.

The schools of haikai developing at the time suggest at a minimum the aspirations of those who were taking haikai seriously, even when it was generally thought an amusement. Only a cynic would think that profit alone or feudal "housing" of all occupations explained away the apparent seriousness. Matsunaga Teitoku (1571-1653) reacted to earlier styles and began one of the first distinct schools of haikai.[10] In other words, this contemporary of Jōha's was consolidating haikai socially, much as Jōha was doing for standard renga. Teitoku perhaps went further than others for haikai. His *Gosan* set forth rules. In reaction to what seemed the license after Sōkan and Moritake, he propounded renga-like rules and criteria. Teitoku was a learned person, and to an obvious command of haikai he could add knowledge of renga, waka, and the prose classics. It is only natural that he gathered followers. Among them were one of the greatest scholars of waka, Kitamura Kigin (1624-1705), and the best poet in the new style, Yasuhara Teishitsu (1610-1673). Some idea of the mixture of the common and the refined in the Teitoku style is conveyed by one of his best known hokku.

Mina hito no	For all alike
hirune no tane ya	the cause of noontime napping
natsu no tsuki	is the summer moon

The idea of sleepyheads taking a nap in the middle of a summer's day would not be allowed in renga or waka. Perhaps the moon should be the autumn moon. But the cause—their staying up at night to appreciate the moon—is something that Lord Narihira or Prince Genji would have thought wholly proper for any person pretending to refinement.

The other major early school of haikai, and one that lasted longer than any other, was established by Nishiyama Sōin (1605-1682). He gave it the name of Danrin, some say after the name of a place owned by a friend (itself taken from a name for a place for Buddhist studies). Sōin studied Satomura style renga and until his late years regarded haikai as little more than a pastime. Like Sōchō with mushin renga, he seems to have taken more and more seriously what is now properly called haikai.

---

[10] See Donald Keene, "Matsunaga Teitoku and the Beginning of *Haikai*," in *Landscapes and Portraits* (Tokyo and Palo Alto: Kōdansha, 1971), pp. 71-93. More recently he has given us an authoritative history of haikai in *World Within Walls* (Holt, Rinehart and Winston, 1976), chs. 3-6 and 14-15.

Later in life both seem to have thought the non-standard linked poetry a special means of broadening subject matter and including more of life as well as of certain matters very important and otherwise untreatable. The great freedom in diction allowed by the Danrin school appears to have had behind it as one motive just this desire to enlarge possible subject matter. In terms of stanzaic connection, however, words were less important than conception, something owed in part to Sōchō, as we have seen. The fact that the Danrin style is special in its conceptual connections (kokorozuke) makes one thing abundantly clear: it is a linked poetry that we mean when we say haikai. There is no need to link discrete haiku.

Sōin had many followers. Among the best known there is an author more famous for prose fiction, Ihara Saikaku (1642-1693), and there is also a gifted poet in Chinese as well as Japanese, Arai Hakuseki (1657-1725).[11] Many of those who followed the Danrin style seem to have looked on Sōin more as one who authorized great freedom of language rather than for anything more serious. Naturally there was a degree of reaction. Kamijima Onitsura (1660-1738) is among those sometimes credited with revising lax ideas of the Danrin school by stressing the seriousness of haikai as literature. I find his most famous opening stanzas rather sentimental, limp. Yet with Onitsura coming after so many explorers of possibilities thitherto unglimpsed, it may be fairly said that all haikai required further was Bashō.

Literary genius is always rare, and yet it seems to create an age of writers. Few people would be interested in haikai today if someone like Bashō had not appeared. During his lifetime and afterward, the Danrin styles held sway, and although they produced some important writing, they produced nothing on the order of excellence of Bashō's poetry.

Along with Danrin haikai, there flourished a pastime called maekuzuke for which Bashō felt contempt, but which tells us not a little about the poetic world in which he lived. This enterprise has been described in quite inconsistent terms. But the usual explanation holds that separate, unlinked stanzas were attached to a foundation stanza that was not of the hokku kind (kami no ku) but of the two-line kind (shimo no

[11] On Saikaku as a haikai poet, see Howard S. Hibbett, "The Japanese Comic Linked-Verse Tradition," *Harvard Journal of Asiatic Studies*, 23 (1960-1961), 76-92. Saikaku and Bashō are almost exact contemporaries.

ku). For a fee one could obtain a foundation stanza from, say, a respected teacher in the capital. Then one could gather with three or four fellow provincials, each taking turns adding a three-line stanza (kami no ku) unrelated to each other. The fee would include marking or correction by the master. In the maekuzuke we see an amusement leading to stanza detachment, proto-haiku. About this time there also came into use tanzaku, stiffened strips of paper, often beautiful, on which individual hokku could be written. Here is another sign of change leading toward haiku.

Other pastimes existed, and among them was oriku. Each stanza produced a single syllable, which when written out in sequence above the stanzas produced a word. The game seems to be a kind of acrostic resembling the "names of things" (mono no na) in court poetry (see *Kokinshū*, 10). Bashō was not lacking in wit, but he had far more to offer than such games allowed. Yet his kind of poetry was not as popular during his lifetime as these amusements and the flourishing Danrin styles.

We are fortunate in having a number of accounts of Bashō easily available in English, and most of them deal with his life in the context of the art or the times or both.[12] They show that his writings can be divided into three overlapping categories. They include: haikai sequences, nowadays called renku; prose writings in which hokku are scattered; and hokku written as such or for his disciples to extend into sequences. The hokku mingled with prose make a kind of writing referred to as haibun, and in a sense resemble the inclusions of poetry in prose such as we find in *The Tale of Genji*. But many of Bashō's haibun belong to a category termed travel records, kikō, or what we may more generally term poetic diaries. The evidence shows that the hokku scattered in his prose often were used by those he traveled with, or visited, to write a longer or shorter sequence.[13] Bashō was a slow writer, producing in his lifetime

[12] In the introduction to *Bashō: The Narrow Road to the Deep North and Other Travel Sketches* (Harmondsworth, Mddx.: Penguin, 1966), Nobuyuki Yuasa gives a cogent summary. His translations are of works to a considerable extent autobiographical. Some of these concerns are shared by my *Poetic Diaries*. But *Matsuo Bashō* (New York: Twayne, 1970) by Makoto Ueda will surely remain the standard account in English for years to come.

[13] See *Poetic Diaries*, p. 166 and note, for an example. Since his fellow traveler, Iwanami (or Kawai) Sora (1649-1710) was keeping his own very factual diary, comparison shows when Bashō fictionalizes and when individual hokku interspersed in the prose were actually used for sequences during travel.

fewer stanzas than Saikaku dashed off in a single day.[14] He would fuss over a single stanza for a long time, working on this or that line until what he sought was finally gained. He also took literary conventions seriously enough to ignore them when the purpose they were designed to serve could be better served by something else.

Such matters have been put in terms distinguishing Bashō-style haikai or renku from renga: "The chief instances of the renku–form include the hyakuin in one hundred stanzas, the gojūin in fifty, and the kasen in thirty-six. These forms were inherited from renga, with the hundred-stanza form termed normal and the other two abnormal. In Bashō's school [or style, shōfu], the hundred-stanza form seldom appears and the thirty-six stanza form is the norm. Of the forty-two renku sequences in his *Seven-Part Collection* [*Shichibushū*], forty-one are the thirty-six stanza kasen and only one is in a hundred stanzas. The use of the kasen form derives from Bashō's insight, and his thinking is clear enough: new sake will not prosper in old casks. By comparison with such other schools of renku as the Teitoku and the Danrin, Bashō's had developed into something substantially finer. . . . [For this higher undertaking] the hundred-stanza form was too extensive, where as the kasen was neither too long nor too short, a more suitable form to use."[15] The nonstandard kind of haikai is at last acquiring its own standardness in a less lengthy, less formal-seeming, but essentially broader and indeed more difficult kind of sequence.

This must still seem rather vague. Let us consider Bashō's handling of the hokku. Opening stanzas in renga, it will be recalled, specify the season and possibly other details of the occasion when the poets sat; they also had terminations called "hokkugire," hokku-cuttings, and of these the cutting-word "kana" was much the most common. In Bashō's school, one encounters an occasional hokku that is nonseasonal, miscellaneous, a fact that tells us the tendency toward haiku has still a long way to go. And as for the termination of the hokku, Bashō felt that there could be cuttings by virtue of the stanza's integrity, so rendering a

[14] Ueda's estimate (*Matsuo Bashō*, p. 36) of one thousand stanzas seems low, but he may have in mind only *hokku*, and there are problems of canon and of counting variants. On Saikaku's prodigious feats in mass production, see Hibbett, as in n. 11.

[15] Namimoto, *Bashō no Shichibushū*, p. 46.

"kana" or a "-keri" superfluous. As this was put by the master who liked his students to call him The Old Man, "There are cut stanzas without cutting words. This kind of cutting is the best of all. If one does not understand such things naturally, it is hard for one to understand them at all."[16] That last remark is a very daunting one. In the end, one knows how to get things right, and explanation is only tedious. Bashō is discriminating between real poetry and mere versifying. Of the maekuzuke he said that all it took to connect stanza to stanza was something "that a peasant could enjoy hoe in hand." It is ironic in view of Bashō's later popularity throughout Japan that this movement of "haikai fit for common people" should have earned his displeasure.[17] He has been so sentimentalized (especially by those who fail to distinguish between haikai and haiku) that one welcomes the real Bashō, warts and all.

A kasen was written in haikai just as in renga, using two sheets of paper, with six stanzas on the front of the first and the back of the second, and with twelve stanzas on the other two sides. (See Figure 4 for more detail.) The waki or second stanza was always to be of the same season as the first. This condition, and the desire for a rather quiet opening, gives the first side, the "jo," a preparatory cast. (This is generalization. As in renga, the jo section of a given haikai might last beyond the sixth stanza, and so on.) The stanzas on the back of the first sheet (7-18) and on the front of the second (19-30) constitute two-thirds of the kasen. This is the "ha" or Development section, and it is in it that variety is chiefly to be found. The last unit comprises the final six stanzas (31-36), the Fast Finale or "kyū" which work up to a kind of climax, so giving a sense of "speed." They also tend to be less humorous, more elevated. In particular, the closing two are usually positive, affirmative. We see therefore the jo-ha-kyū (Introduction-Development-Fast Finale) of renga and nō. Within a free conception of this rhythm, Bashō and his followers worked with great ease, producing sequences markedly different in effect.[18] For example, the moon and flower stanzas get shifted from their supposed fixed locations with great freedom, although the thirty-fifth is

[16] *Ibid.*, p. 49.   [17] Kuriyama, *Haikaishi*, p. 174.

[18] The three kasen by him and others in Part Three have been chosen partly to give a conservative sequence, a radical sequence, and a sequence happily combining convention with departure.

usually a flower stanza as "required." One of the sequences in *Fuyu no Hi* (*The Winter Sun*) ends in wretchedness.[19] Spring and autumn stanzas do not always appear at least three in a row in the Development section. And other irregularities can quickly be found. More positively, Bashō and his followers made a great deal of love stanzas, because they tend to greatly agitate a sequence. The art of stirring up at the right time requires great skill. No doubt that too is, as The Old Man said, a matter that one will hardly know at all if one does not know it naturally.

By making the conventions more flexible, Bashō also made them more difficult to use. It is of great interest that he not only derived them from renga, which is natural enough, but that he also adapted them in his haibun such as travel diaries with interspersed hokku.[20] In his effort to get at the essence of his heart—or of a single stanza—he was willing to adapt, and change, and polish. His most famous stanza, the torture of critics and the plague of translators, runs as follows in the established version:

Furuike ya	The still old pond
kawazu tobikomu	and as a frog leaps in it
mizu no oto	the sound of a splash

In what seems to have been the earliest extant version, Bashō had a different second line, "kawazu tondaru," "and when the frog leapt in it." The use of the preterite makes the scene more remote in some unspecified past. In a subsequent version, he got the present tense that we know but started off with a brighter image: "Yamabuki ya," "Yellow roses bloom." He must have decided that image was too lovely in a conventional sense and at last chose the version we know.

[19] This is commented on by Namimoto, *Bashō no Shichibushū*, p. 47.

[20] Konishi Jin'ichi remarks on the haikai no renga features of the episode with the prostitutes at Ichiburi in *The Narrow Road Through the Provinces* (see *Poetic Diaries*, pp. 43-44). His point is that love stanzas would be expected at this point, and I now understand far better what he meant. Since then a similar reading of *The Narrow Road* as a hundred-stanza haikai has been given by Andō Tsuguo in *Oku no Hosomichi* (Senkōsha, 1974), pp. 179-95. See also his *Bashō*, 2nd ed. particularly (Chikama Shobo, 1971), which has excellent criticism. (The second edition is worth separate mention for the added, and moving, chapter on the visit to Hiraizumi.)

Another illustration of his slow progress toward full satisfaction involves the poem which was said to have initiated the shōfū, the Bashō style or school.

Kareeda ni	On a withered bough
karasu no tomaritaru ya	has not a crow stopped for its perch
aki no kure	in autumn dusk

After that 1680 version, Bashō revised the second line to the one we know: *karasu no tomarikeri*, "a crow has stopped for its perch." The line still is too long (jiamari), with nine syllables rather than the expected seven, but it is at least down from ten and in fact reads very well. Later versions of this well-known hokku are only orthographical, but Bashō once used it as the first part a hokku-waki, or a two-stanza haikai. There are a number of instances of this in his collected poems, and one sees in it something like a return to the tanrenga that had been written nine centuries earlier.[21]

Bashō's early stanzas are often irregular, in having supernumerary syllables, and he would keep them so long as they sounded right. This typifies his desire to get things right, even if the rules had to be bent or broken. He was quoted as having defended the supernumerary syllables in the crow stanza and another. "To appreciate stanzas with a supernumerary line, you must be acquainted with the whole business, or you will hardly ever understand it." He was also indulgent with the rules-breaking of others. In the important thirty-fifth, last flower stanza of the *Aku oke no* sequence (see below, p. 333), Kyorai violates convention. Instead of writing a proper hana no ku, a stanza using simply "hana," "flower," he introduces a specific one by name.

Itozakura	The drooping cherries
hara ippai no	have flowered in such loveliness
sakinikeri	as fills me to the top

[21] One is able to follow Bashō as reviser in *Teihon Bashō Taisei*, ed. Ogata Tsutomu *et al.* (Sanseidō, 1962). The hokku-waki will be found on p. 185, and the quotation on p. 636. On p. 6 the various versions of this stanza are set forth.

When Bashō heard that, he said, "Your stanza is self-indulgent," and laughed. He was apparently taken by the phrase hara ippai, as if one could have one's bellyful of flowers (a phrase more positive than in English but still vulgar).[22] He was always willing to sacrifice one thing to gain a better, just as he sought to realize the utmost from any stanza or sequence that he wrote.

The Old Man was clearly the essential poet in this great period of haikai. When he died in 1694, the art went into sudden decline. It seems extraordinary that such talented poets as Bonchō, Kyorai, and Kikaku should have suddenly seemed to lapse in their art. They had worked closely with Bashō in many sequences and had had long conversations with him about his poetic ideals and his practice. No single explanation will account for the decline. Its suddenness and degree are baffling. One clear fact is that there had been disagreements about the best kind of poetry. The special problems of Bashō's late style will be discussed later. But he was concerned with what he termed the "swaggering elegance" of Kikaku's writing, suggesting that the interesting qualities of his writing were showy rather than ultimately satisfying. From the other camp came this dismissal of Bashō: "His hokku are good but shallow. He is a writer who tried for what is shallow. Bashō cannot measure up to the strength in Kikaku's stanzas."[23]

In a sense Bashō does deal with the shallow. Not a little of his poetry is quite unimpressive when removed from its context in a haikai sequence or prose. But he possessed a rare ability to make something extraordinary out of what was ordinary, to create profundity from what seems casually discovered. He had seen into the genius of haikai, and he was willing to run risks. It is exceedingly difficult to avoid the showy or the drab in haikai, to get its two legs to move in good order. We can grant Kikaku that he was taking his art with a seriousness at least equal to

---

[22] See the commentary in *Renga Haikaishū*, p. 487. Kyorai is very unorthodox in suggesting that one ever sees enough of cherry blossoms, which are loved precisely because they fall before one can hardly enjoy them. As the old poem (*Shūishū*, 1-36) says:

Sakeba chiru	If in bloom they fall,
Sakaneba koishi	If not in bloom they make us yearn
Yamazakura . . .	Mountain cherry flowers . . .

[23] Kuriyama, *Haikaishi*, pp. 178, 179.

Bashō's. But he and the rest seem not to have taken life as seriously, probably lacking the talent to see beauty in the plain, and plainness in beauty. While the Bashō school broke down in squabbles of such kind (except for modest Kyorai, who retired to write down what he could remember from conversations), the Danrin school kept its popularity and its wealth, somewhat like the Ura-Senke tea school in the second half of this century.

About fifty years after the death of Bashō, and for another four decades, there was a resurgence of haikai. This Haikai Revival from about 1743 to 1783 was aided in part by a relaxation of the rigor of government rule and by an ensuing liveliness of temper among its subjects. The preference grew for what is unusual, what distinguishes individuals from each other. All social groups shared an alteration in manners.[24] No group of artists better represents the new sophistication than those called "bunjin." These *literati* got their name from the literary emphasis shown by their paintings. For our purposes one might call them studio poets. One of the outstanding painters was also the central figure in the Haikai revival, Taniguchi or Yosa Buson (1716-1783). He did not share Bashō's desire to live as a recluse. He did not feel the compulsion to set out in travel, not expecting to return. He did not have that tormented nature which Bashō sometimes shows, or that sense of death. In the enjoyment of good things Buson shows the fineness of a person born to art and the clarity of an acute mind. Everyone agrees that his haikai reveal a painter's visual sense at work, even when the imagery may also be oral.

Harusame ya	In the spring rain
monogatariyuku	a straw raincoat and fine umbrella
mino to kasa	go talking together

The scene is perfectly visualized, and there have been many people who prefer such perfectly realized observation to Bashō's involvement of himself in what he writes about. Buson's stanza uses the straw raincoat to represent a peasant, the umbrella a townsman or woman. Two different lives are brought together at this moment of gentle spring rain. A certain element of mystery remains, as in the style of painting favored for the

---

[24] *Ibid.*, pp. 187-88.

bunjinga. The question whether the umbrella holder is male or female prevents our imagining the conversation. The couple are half obscured in a haze-like soft rain, and they seem to be separated from the poet by some distance. No such masterly hand had been seen in haikai for a long time. Even if the art seems to run counter to Bashō's, it is altogether welcome. Buson leaves questions about the two figures unanswered, one might say, in the white of the painter's sheet. Those questions would have been just the ones Bashō would have sought out, getting his own life the more involved by his interest in theirs.

Buson achieves a wide range of effect and feeling. The world depicted seems to be wholly at his command to deliver the exact image he seeks.

Kanashisa ya	Sadness is there
tsuri no ito fuku	the line blowing on the fishing pole
aki no kaze	in the autumn wind

The thin line, the absence of any fish—and even of the holder of the pole—the rise of wind in the waning autumn light—all leave an unforgettable image. Here is my own favorite stanza.

Yanagi chiri	Willow leaves fall
shimizu kareishi	and in fresh waters weathered stones
tokorodokoro	scattered here and there

Various headnotes declare in effect that this describes a scene actually observed in travel. Certainly the scene is perfect in its combination of colors and wonderful peace. But, as the editors remark, Buson is also recalling an episode in Bashō's Narrow Road. On going to Ashino, the travelers had seen a willow known as that of Priest Saigyō (1118-1190).

Ta ichimai	I must depart
uete tachisaru	now that the single field is planted
yanagi kana	by Saigyō's willow

Bashō is recalling a poem by Saigyō (Shinkokinshū, 3: 262), one no less famous for having been celebrated in a nō.

Michi no be ni	Beside the path,
Shimizu nagaruru	Rippling in the fresh cool waters
Yanagikage	The willow image flows;
Shibashi tote koso	Intending but a moment here,
Tachidomaritsure.	How long I have enjoyed the shade!

Saigyō would like to stay on. Bashō feels himself there with the waka poet but required to move on. To Buson, the willow leaves are now withered, the stones of the stream are whitened with age, and the scene is empty of people. Saigyō and Bashō are gone from the earth, remaining however in the mind as a cherished idea shrouded in the mystery of memory.

Each literary tradition provides certain critical exercises. One in Japan is the comparison of Bashō and Buson. I shall give the reader the means to do so. What follows is a stanza that somewhat resembles Bashō's on the crow. Buson's is evocative of contrast and mutability.

Tsurigane ni	Upon the temple bell
tomarite nemuru	a little butterfly has come
kochō kana	to perch in sleep

A few more stanzas will give some idea of Buson's range.

Koiwataru	Loving in vain so long
Kamakura bushi no	the Kamakura samurai
ōgi kana	holds only a fan

★

Ikanobori	A single kite
kinō no sora no	flying in the same place of the sky
aridokoro	as yesterday

★

Utsutsu naki	No reality
tsumamigokoro no	is either in my desire to pluck it off
kochō kana	or the butterfly itself

One would like to linger over these famous stanzas from the approximately three thousand by Buson.[25] Whether the subject is the lovelorn samurai holding a fan instead of a sword, or a sense of shared Buddhist unreality in the phenomenal world, Buson is a masterly writer of stanzas. More will be said of his haikai ideals in the next chapter. For now, the examples given should at least make clear the so-to-speak unvarying excellence and especially the integrity of his stanzas. But we can also see that such fine qualities may pose serious difficulties for an art of sequential poetry.

Haikai continued to be practiced long after the energies of the Haikai Revival had dwindled. It had become institutionalized, as the success of the Danrin school shows so well. Such measures assured a general level of competence, but from the absence of any poet rivaling Bashō or Buson it seems safe to conclude that the institutionalizing did not promote originality. Buson posed another problem. His splendid hokku and the tendency toward integral separateness in his other stanzas must have enticed many a poet toward what would become haiku and away from haikai in its true sense. Perhaps there was also some danger that haikai might be insufficiently serious. In order to be properly serious, haikai had to be more than a frivolous game. It must also eschew solemnity and participate in the comic. Both aspects of the danger existed, the second particularly, because it was beginning to look as if poetic humor was being institutionalized in senryū.

Senryū is generally said to have emerged in the second half of the eighteenth century, probably in the Hōreki-Meiwa eras (1751-1772). It began as one species of haikai, and in particular of a linking of non-seasonal, that is miscellaneous (zō), stanzas. The name is derived from the style or pen-name of its early practitioner, Karai Senryū (1718-1790), and from a collection of ten thousand verses he published in 1757. At first this kind of writing evolved into a variety of maekuzuke that used the spoken language almost wholly, avoided the armory of cutting words, and tried to be pithily amusing. Later it reduced itself to that which we

[25] There are 953 selected for the "Haikuhen" of *Busonshū Issashū*, ed. by Teruoka Yasutaka and Kawashima Tsuyu (here Teruoka) Iwanami Shoten, 1959). In addition to hokku, other stanzas will of course be found in his renku.

know by the name today, in length a hokku or a haiku, and what has two unmistakably vulgar legs. Very much can be learned about Japanese life from senryū, although unfortunately one must know almost as much to begin with in order to get the point of most of them. But one fact is simple: even humor was becoming institutionalized in Tokugawa Japan.

The subsequent history of haikai and of its development into haiku does tend toward heavy seriousness. As Japan moved toward the nineteenth century, haikai seemed to have fallen into weaker days of competent mediocrity. One voice was heard in challenge. Buson and others of the Haikai Revival had used the slogan, "Return to Bashō!" The voice of Kobayashi Issa (1763-1827) cried instead, "I will be myself!" He spoke for animals and the weak, for those who, like himself, were in some sense orphans in a hostile world. Issa unquestionably opened the world of haikai to include more than it had comprehended before, but he had difficulty connecting his stanzas. His happiest solution came with an ages-old Japanese method combining the artistic poetic diary and the poetic collection.[26] One kind of writing shows him composing little sketches in prose that conclude with a poem.[27] These sometimes remind one of *Tales from Ise* and of jottings (zuihitsu) like those in Sei Shōnagon's *Pillow Book*. Or, if one more earlier example may be given, Issa's strongly plaintive autobiographical element is reminiscent of *Lady Daibu's Collection* (*Kenrei Mon'in Ukyō no Daibushū*), which mingles her sad accounts of life with waka poems. Issa's masterpiece is not such sketches. It is also not one of his three kasen, nor the full group of his hokku. It is rather the account he kept near the end of his life, one whole year, 1819: *Oraga Haru*.[28] In *Busonshū; Issashū* this occupies upwards of fifty pages (432-78). It mingles fact and fiction, as does Bashō's *Narrow Road Through the Provinces*, and is the better for doing so. The stanzas benefit by gaining a prose context, which supplies the connectedness that was being lost between one stanza and the next in haikai. The twenty-seventh stanza will serve as example.

[26] See *Poetic Diaries*, pp. 3-20.

[27] See Issa, *Bunshū* in the book cited in n. 25 (here edited by Kawashima), pp. 480-529.

[28] The title means "My Spring," but both the English title and translation given by Nobuyuki Yuasa should be recommended: *The Year of My Life* (Berkeley and Los Angeles: University of California Press, 1960).

Ima no yo mo   Even in our time
tori wa Hokekyō   the Lotus Sutra has been sounded
nakinikeri   in the cry of the birds

This might as easily be one bird, and there seems to be some of that sentimentality into which Issa drifts. The last two lines also have, at least on me, the effect of sounding like a rooster cry, since in Japan cocks cry "Kokekokkō." These problems vanish, once we set the stanza in its proper and necessary context.

> . . . after dusk had fallen on the 19th of the Third Month, a number of us gathered at my cottage, each of us waiting breathlessly, thinking that "Now"—or "Now"—we would hear, until bit by bit morning brightened the sky, and in the plum tree outside there did come one birdsong.

Ima no yo mo   Even in our time
tori wa Hokekyō   the Lotus Sutra has been sounded
nakinikeri.   in the cry of the warbler.

No heavenly music is mentioned, and neither is the warbler (uguisu) specified. But by long poetic tradition and valid enough associations it is the warbler that sings in the plum tree. We recall that Sei Shōnagon had written that dawn is the time of day for spring. Without so much as a mention, the fragrance of the plum blossoms rises to memory, and so also does the kalavinka, the bird that sings the Law in the Buddha's paradise. In such resonances, Issa's stanza seems beautiful, and a stanza added in true haikai fashion to develop what has been led up to by a previous unit (the prose) but not at all entailed by it. The next stanza mentions the warbler, the following a horse in spring rain, and its successor young sparrows. The method and spirit are those of haikai, even if we do not have 7-7-syllable stanzas alternating with the 5-7-5-syllable stanzas.

A freshening of poetic possibility came toward the end of the nineteenth century. It came partly in response to literary decadence at a time when much else was moving forward rapidly in a Japan newly opened to the world. It also came in good measure in the genius of

Masaoka Shiki (1867-1902), who was born just as Japan ended her long isolation as a "world within walls." Shiki wrote criticism, prose fiction, and tanka during his brief feverish life.[29] He would be remembered by very few today if it were not for what he did to the haikai tradition. Under his touch, the old and much rusted links were abandoned and haiku was freshly born. He and his followers managed to maintain certain elements of sequentiality in actual practice, as we shall see. If he saw very clearly the implications of Buson's practice in individual stanzas, his change in attitude is, after all, decisive. If before supposedly linked kinds were often breaking into separate units, the conception had always been one of linking: real, possible, or formal. And if with Shiki haiku were often combined, they were always considered as separate, integral units of 5-7-5 syllables. More yet than that, Shiki was so convinced of this that he (rather unfortunately) persuaded others that his predecessors were to be considered poets of single stanzas. He set poetic taste for the older poetry in ways that have remained influential to this day. No person can bring about a revolution singlehandedly. But if one person is responsible, it is this intense native of Matsuyama in Shikoku.

A revolution needs slogans and plans as well as leaders and timeliness. Shiki's slogan included a charge to return, not to Bashō, but Buson. The rather facile contrast between subjective Bashō and objective Buson is owed, with much else, to Shiki's movement. Yet once one decides that haikai is really not sequential at all but given to making sets of individual stanzas, a preference for Buson makes perfect sense. It is the premise that errs, not the inference from it. Shiki had another slogan, his most famous, "shasei," copying from life. He borrowed the term from the Western-style painter Nakamura Fusetsu (1866-1943)—and perhaps somewhat from the temper of the times. He also propounded "shajitsu," copying the actual. What he meant by these slogans has sometimes been termed opposition to lyricism and to overintellectuality. By lyricism he appears to have meant involvement of the poet's self in the world de-

---

[29] See the excellent essay by Robert H. Brower, "Masaoka Shiki and Tanka Reform," ch. 10 in *Tradition and Modernization in Japanese Culture*, ed. Donald H. Shively (Princeton: Princeton University Press, 1971), 379-418. The essay ranges beyond what its title suggests and gives useful quotations, as from Shiki's "Open Letter to Waka Poets," quoted in part below.

picted. By overintellectuality he seems to have meant wit, concern with technique, reflection, and much that a Wordsworth might have accused the eighteenth-century English poets of exemplifying. Shiki was not, however, simply negative. In addition to Buson, he espoused as a model the poetry of the great eighth-century collection, the *Man'yōshū*. To his mind that anthology was "sincere and compelling."[30] He also set a criterion of elegance, fūryū, one of those hardy Japanese terms whose meaning alters slightly from age to age. (Bashō had used it long before and it was old when he used it.) The following passage will show that Shiki was less radical than his rhetoric sometimes suggests. He is discussing the treatment of new subjects:

"When I say to treat new and unusual materials in your poems, some people will bring forth such 'machinery of civilization' as trains and railroads, but such notions are very mistaken. The machinery of civilization consists for the most part of inelegant, unpoetic things, which are difficult to put into poems. However, if one wishes to make the attempt, there is nothing for it but to arrange and harmonize these things with other materials that are tasteful. To treat them without such harmonizing material—to say, for example, 'The wind blows along the railroad tracks'—this is utterly flat and tasteless. It will give at least a somewhat better appearance if one combines these things with other materials, saying, for example, that violets are blooming beside the railroad tracks, or that the poppies scatter or the pampas grass waves in the wake of the passing train, and the like. Another good way of treating such unpoetic materials is from a distant point of view. One means of effacing their prosaic, tasteless qualities is to say, for example, that the train can be seen across the field of rape flowers, or that the train is passing in the distance beyond the broad fields of summer grass."[31]

Perhaps Shiki stated his central article of poetic faith most succinctly when he said, "*My fundamental principle is to express as clearly as I can the poetic quality that I myself feel to be beautiful.*"[32] The statement seems unexceptionable, but there are two things that deserve pointing out. There is some implication that as an individual poet he may find some things im-

[30] *Ibid.*, p. 415. The phrase is actually applied to an imitator of the *Man'yōshū* style but quite represents Shiki's feelings about that anthology.
[31] *Ibid.*, p. 393, from the "Open Letter."   [32] *Ibid.*, p. 395; the stress is Shiki's.

portant that others do not. A sense of relativism, and even of that dread
thing subjectivism, can be seen. Also what is important turns out to be
not true, good, or real so much as *beautiful*. Surely in that Shiki betrays a
devotion to "elegance" that unites him with many of the poets he
thought sophisticated.

Haiku are seasonal poems: the miscellaneous category is gone, and
such subtopics as love or travel or Buddhism must be got into seventeen
lines whose principal formal duty is to deal with a season. Because haiku
are short and seasons are long, poets often compose a large number of
haiku on the same or related subjects. Shiki took part in this practice,
which usually involves dropping weak poems, revising good ones to
make them better, and arranging them not so much in the order of composition as in one that has a certain aesthetic quality of its own. This is
still the practice in haiku magazines, and still the practice of many critics
discussing haiku.[33] In short, the old habits of integrating shorter units
into larger ones manifest themselves. One cannot call this true linked
poetry, since it is all too casual, too much *ad hoc*. But the *arrangement* of
short haiku is also not random.

We can recall from Issa that the integration of poems into prose had
been the means of achieving great beauty and meaningfulness early in the
nineteenth century—as it had been since *The Tosa Diary* (*Tosa Nikki*, ca.
935). Shiki used the same method, often in what might be translated
"diaries of sickness" (byōchūki). He suffered from a very painful kind of
tuberculosis, and since he pushed himself so hard, he frequently was near
collapse and had to stay put. One such moment came in 1899. It is quite
appropriate, given his admiration for Buson, that one of his friends
should have brought him some peonies during that illness. Here, then, is
Shiki's account of May 10th, which amounts to nearly half of *The Verse
Record of My Peonies* (*Botan Kuroku*).

May 10th.
After an enema in the morning I slept a little. I feel slightly improved.
It is always the case with this affliction of mine that when May
comes:

[33] See, for example, Konishi, *Haiku*, pp. 183–88.

Yakuzuki no	Month of bad omen
niwa ni saitaru	when they blossomed in the garden:
botan kana.	peony flowers

The unbearable pain makes me wonder what possesses me to wish to live on. I wonder, shall I die? Shall I die? I take a draught of medicine in resignation and, thinking I will die, know my life to be as precarious as dew. Come now: it might be worth some amusement to hold the most splendid celebration of a lifetime—on my Departing This Life. What I might try is to set a day, make my intent known to this person and that, and enjoin all the guests to come with flowers or fruit instead of the usual gifts for the dead. Soon after all were assembled, each one could compose an elegiac haiku. What a treat it would be to go through the fruit as it pleased me and, when the time came that my belly was full there among the mountains of flowers and fruit, take the compound with a good grace and quietly slip off into endless sleep.

Ringo kūte	Why not die then,
botan no mae ni	in front of the peony flowers,
shinan kana.	eating up apples?
Botan chiru	There is this silence
yamai no toko no	about the sickbed as the petals
shizukasa ya.	drop from the peonies!
Nihen chitte	Two petals fall
botan no katachi	and the shape of the peony
kawarikeri.	is wholly changed.

Hyōtei came by in the morning. Saemon came in the afternoon and the painter Fusetsu in the evening. The paper cover of these sheets has become a picture with the falling blossoms.[34]

Most of these haiku would have no interest whatever outside the *Record*. Also one cannot claim that the passage has the resonances of that by

---

[34] The text of the poems is taken from *Shiki Zenshū*, 15 vols. (Arusu [Ars], 1924–1926) 14, 340–42; the translation is from *Poetic Diaries*, pp. 202–203.

Issa, even though this is longer and has four times as many lines of verse. On the other hand, May 10th is very real. If we do not have the high art of Buson's bunjinga, we have something more creative than a photograph. And one haiku stands out, the last—the last of those in the passage given, not *necessarily* the last composed on that day. It alone of these has got into the anthologies. It has led many people to recall a hokku by Buson, as used in "Peony Petals Fell" (*Botan Chitte no Maki*, the last sequence given in Part Three).

Botan chitte	Peony petals fell
uchikasanarinu	piling one upon another
ni-sanpen	in twos and threes

The difference between what follows the three lines in each instance will clarify, if clarification be necessary, the distinction between haikai and haiku.

Given the Japanese inclination to preserve, however, the account just given of Shiki is overdrawn. His most important disciple, Takahama Kyoshi (1874-1959), wrote linked poetry. This fact is not well known. Kyoshi's son, Takahama Toshio, brought out a most interesting book just after the Second World War. This is *Haikai Tebiki* (Sōgensha, 1946), also known as *Shōwa Shikimoku*. As the titles and much in the book show, the conception of haikai (as opposed to the more usual modern word, renku) and of linked poetry itself had not died. In the tradition extending from critics like Nijō Yoshimoto, the author sets forth the canons to be followed and provides examples from earlier poets, notably of sequences by Bashō, Buson, and their colleagues. It also includes two kasen by the author, his father, and other poets.

To such a degree do the Japanese preserve their cultural inheritance, and to such a degree do Japanese poets seek to integrate their brief kinds into sequences drawing on other poetic units or prose. Given the revival of "renga" as a pastime late in this century, it seems just to say that the principle of linking and joining continues on, one way or another, in Japanese literary practice. No doubt it will outlive the few years remaining of the century. The sole question appears to be whether poets of sufficient genius will take up some version of linked poetry or, alternatively, whether it will remain perhaps an atavistic survival or merely an entertainment.

Each year thousands, perhaps millions, of haiku are written. But the real energy of Japanese poetry today works in free verse rather than in the old syllabic fives and sevens. Everyone admits that haiku and tanka are still alive. The challenging question is how much they matter. In a famous essay on "Second-Class Literature," Kuwabara Takeo attacked the feudalism of modern haiku teaching.[35] The attack was understood to be on haiku itself, and tanka as well, not merely on the schools. Are these kinds not intrinsically inferior today? His question can be answered only by Japanese, because only they can create a great literature in their language or debate on such grounds. My historical account ends with Shiki and his disciples. For those with hopes for linked poetry, the brightest opportunity must be sought in the past: from the outset the history of haikai at least has been one of sudden greatness emerging from pastime and mediocrity. "Time will shew." At this point the brightness of that haikai past beckons in the poetic ideals of Bashō and Buson.

[35] Kuwabara Takeo, "Daini Geijutsu" ("Second-Class Art"), *Sekai*, i, no. 11 (1946), 55-63.

5

The Haikai Aesthetic of
Bashō and Buson

"The basis of art is change in
the universe."—Bashō

WE HAVE BEEN seeing that haikai is a sequential art like renga, but that
sequentiality gradually diminished until haiku was born. The proportion
of hokku to sequence stanzas written rises from Bashō to Buson, and
Bashō is, in any event, much more likely to have integrated his hokku in
prose contexts or to have rescued them from some brief sequence. As
Homer nods, so on occasion even the greatest of haikai masters falters,
producing a connecting stanza that does not connect. Such is the
seventeenth in *Throughout the Town*, given in Part Three. We shall have
reason to see that what is exceptional in Bashō's practice is all too common even in Buson's. Konishi Jin'ichi puts this matter very well concerning Matsunaga Teitoku (1571-1653): "if one looks at him with haiku
eyes, he is an awfully useless character [hidoku tsumaranai yatsu], but
when we look at him with haikai eyes, he turns out to be a very impressive man [nakanaka erai otoko]."[1] Sequence distinguishes haikai from
haiku, and sequence joins haikai with renga.

If the sequential principle joins renga and haikai, they are distinguished
by another one of attitude shared by the poet and reader. Like early English novelists, haikai poets found a new world in exploring what seemed
"low" by comparison with what had gone before—renga and waka, in
the one instance, and the heroic narrative of Milton and Dryden, in the
other. This can be seen by reading a haikai after a renga, and it was set
forth very plainly by Shikō (1665-1731): "Haikai broadens art to that

[1] Konishi, *Haiku*, p. ii.

which is below the average, using a world lower in speech and conduct to guide the people of that lower road."[2] Bashō described the matter in more detail. He is reported to have said: "there are three elements in haikai. Its feeling can be called loneliness. That plays with refined dishes but contents itself with humble fare. Its total effect can be called elegance. That lives in figured silks and embroidered brocades but does not forget a person clad in woven straw. Its language can be called aesthetic madness. Language resides in untruth and ought to comport with truth. It is difficult to reside in truth and sport with untruth. These three elements do not elevate a humble person to heights. They put an exalted person in a low place."[3]

The thickly sown metaphors are part of the purpose of the passage, and from all Bashō said it would not be difficult to find some contradictions. But he has got at the role of haikai in a way that can scarcely be improved on. The problem he leaves to the poet is of finding ways of adjusting high to low, of achieving either some reconciliation of opposites or some margin between them. Bashō obviously thinks of a reconciliation that will impose humility on the exalted. Even his use of language suggests as much. His three central terms are variations of the central ones in waka criticism since the Preface to the *Kokinshū*. For "feeling" he uses "nasake" rather than "kokoro." For "language" he uses "gengo" rather than "kotoba." And he stays with "sugata" for "total effect." The cast of thought is traditional, but the decision worked out favors the low.

Bashō also sets limits to how low one should descend. "The profit of haikai lies in making vulgar speech right," he said; and Kuriyama Riichi does well to remind us that Bashō looked on himself as half-priest, half-layman, half-committed to religion, half-committed to the secular world. As he says further, there is in the poet's makeup a spirit opposed to the vulgar as well as a spirit attached to it.[4] As Bashō is reported to have said of himself on another occasion, he "resembles a priest but is soiled by the dirt of this world; and he resembles a layman but has a shaven head."[5] In these contrary inclinations we observe great tension. Bashō's art was born from such contrary energies in him, from his seek-

[2] Kuriyama, *Haikaishi*, p. 164. [3] *Ibid.*, p. 165.
[4] *Ibid.*, pp. 163, 164. [5] *Ibid.*, p. 163.

ing a lower world for higher things, and from knowing the religious world superior to that lay world in which alone the low could be found. His art was the other parent of those haikai that claim our respect. There may be some exaggeration in the idea that poetry "was for Bashō the way to salvation."[6] If we take "way" in the sense of that "michi" extolled by poets since the twelfth century, however, as a vocation in which Enlightenment can be obtained, the amount of exaggeration is minimal. It certainly is important that Bashō "does not deny the values of the present world." But he also concerned himself with those of the next. On his deathbed he told his grieving disciples, "Attain a high stage of enlightenment and return to the world of common men."[7] This Zen Buddhist commonplace had its counterpart for the poet in taking the world of the common as basis for Enlightenment. In terms borrowed from an older Japanese Buddhism, Bashō sought the Buddha nature in plants and trees, and in much that was even more humble.

This Old Man, this traveling hermit, has been so much studied that his career has been divided in many ways. According to Kyorai, his devoted student, Bashō's art developed in three stages. The first was a very lengthy one culminating in *The Narrow Road*, concerning a trip begun in 1689. That must be the year Kyorai meant, since Bashō was on the move almost constantly thereafter, except for a brief closing of the door of his hut in Edo. The second stage is represented by two collections, *The Gourd (Hisago)* and *The Monkey's Straw Raincoat (Sarumino)*. The third stage is represented by two late collections, *A Sack of Charcoal (Sumidawara)* and *The Monkey's Straw Raincoat, Continued (Zoku Sarumino)*. This scheme probably reflects Bashō's own views at the end of his life, with all the advantages that has. But it also has disadvantages. It divides the work into three periods, with the second and third occupying five years and the first all previous to them.

The creation of the shōfū, Bashō's mature style, is usually said to date from the stanza about the crow perching on a withered branch. That was 1680. Before then he had tended to write in wittier, showier styles. By 1680 he was living in Edo at the first Banana Plant Hut or Bashō An, from which he took his most famous *nom de plume*. The ensuing eleven

---

[6] Makoto Ueda, *Zeami, Bashō, Yeats, Pound* (The Hague: Mouton, 1965), p. 63.

[7] *Ibid.*, pp. 63 and 63–64.

years are usually taken to include five of searching and six of his greatest work. Those six may be termed, for simplicity's sake, as the period of sabi, an ideal we shall be considering. They are also the years in which he wrote his finest haibun or prose with verse, often concerning his journeys. In his last years (1692-1694) he was back in Edo, now not the Old Man but an old man and a great man. Much to the distress of some of his students and the embarrassment of not a few of his critics, Bashō gave up his ideal of sabi. These last three years can be typified by his new ideal, "karumi" or "lightness."

Even with these alterations in the scheme, Bashō's career shows a very long preparation and an achievement relatively brief: six to nine years. Some of the preparation may be worthy of notice. While living in Fukagawa in Edo, he became acquainted with the Zen Buddhist priest and haikai poet, Butchō (1643-1716), whom he mentions with great respect toward the beginning of *The Narrow Road*. It is believed that the priest was a major influence on Bashō's intellectual development, although actual evidence is not easily come by. There was also an incident that occurred when he was thirty-eight and of which he made much: "In the winter of 1682, my grass hut in Fukagawa became enveloped in a sudden fire. I somehow managed to live on by soaking myself in the tidal water, a stick on my shoulder, and surrounded by smoke. That was the beginning of my understanding of the mutability of human life. It was in that incident of a burning home that I understood how we are governed by change, and that my inclination [kokoro] for displaced life began."[8] Thereafter words like "life" and "death" appear more frequently in his writing. During a trip in 1684-1685—he was now living nowhere about as literally as a person can—he wrote *The Winter Sun* (*Fuyu no Hi*) while pausing in Nagoya. The trip was recounted in a travel diary whose title tells us something about his new mood: *The Moor-Exposed Skeleton* (*Nozarashi Kikō*).

Nozarashi o	The bones on the moor
kokoro ni kaze no	the wind blows on them through the heart
shimu mi kana	piercing my flesh

[8] Kuriyama, *Haikaishi*, p. 113. Bashō no doubt was led by the incident to recall the parable in The Lotus Sutra treating a burning house as a world emperilling enlightenment.

And on a visit to his native place in Iga Province, Bashō's brother showed him some of the hair left from their dead mother. It was snowy white.

Te ni toraba kien	White hair in my hands
namida zo atsuki	the tears pour out to vanishing
aki no shimo	like hot autumn frost

By 1686 he had composed the poem on the frog splashing into the old pond.

In the first year of the Genroku Era (1688), Bashō was once more on the road. This time he was off for Suma, where, among many other associations, he was led to weep over the end there of the young hero Atsumori. To Ensui (1640-1704) he wrote about that and his feelings: "The loss on that day and the pain of this—I shall never forget you among thoughts of life and death, the subservience of the weak to the powerful, mutability, and swift time."[9] Two years later, he stopped at the Unreal Hermitage (Genjūan) in Ōtsu, which he was to visit repeatedly, and where he flowered as a poet. Saintly as he was in many ways, Bashō basked among devoted followers and was in favor of a little comfort. Lacking one or the other, he would complain of illnesses that go unmentioned otherwise, and become grumpy, matters that he exposes forthrightly in *The Narrow Road*. His serious sense is expressed in one of his well-known stanzas.

Yagate shinu	The cicada's voice
keshiki wa miezu	gives no evidence it knows
semi no koe	that death is near

Everyone has favorite stanzas by Bashō, and it is probably memory of them more than anything else that has made him the most widely loved and known of Japanese poets. There are not many that I like as well as the following, which we shall see in its proper context in Part Three.

[9] *Ibid.*, p. 116. The intimacy of this letter derives from the fact that, like Bashō, Ensui was born in Iga Ueno. He was four years senior to our poet, under whom he studied haikai.

Hiru neburu   Sleeping at noon
aosagi no mi no   the body of the blue heron
tōtosa yo   poised in nobility

Standing in the water on one leg, its head under its wing, oblivious of the
world, the bird represents the achievement of complete enlightenment,
its dreams those of a higher reality. And yet our lesser world makes itself
known, as it always will. That "noon" is necessarily a moment followed
in the ceaseless flow of time, what can only take the bird away from its
majestic stillness. We should associate with such a stanza a comment reported from Bashō: "The basis of art [fūga] is change in the universe.
That which is still has changeless form. Moving things have change, and
because we cannot put a stop to time, it continues unarrested. To stop
something would be to halt a sight or sound in our heart. Cherry blossoms whirl, leaves fall, and both flit along the ground. We cannot arrest
with seeing or hearing what lies in such things. Were we to gain mastery
over things, we would find that the life of each thing itself had vanished
without a trace."[10] It is not so much that the heron will fly away when it
wakes as that the heron of our minds will not stay still. Out of that we
make art.

Bashō often spoke about his chief ideal, sabi. What he says about it,
however, may leave us recalling that if we do not understand such things
naturally we shall scarcely understand them at all. For example, he wrote
that "Sabishimi and okashimi are the bones of haikai style." "Sabishimi"
must be something other than "okashimi," which means that which is
peculiar, odd, and perhaps a bit humorous. Another passage says a bit
more. That which has sabi and that which is peculiar are the bases of
haikai style. "The peculiar is implied by the name, 'haikai'; sabi is the
fruit of art."[11] Haikai is peculiar in a double sense. It is peculiar because
waka and renga were considered norms. And it is peculiar because only
by opening art to that with less dignity could Bashō define his own poetic world, separate from the formerly normative ones. Sabi enabled him
to give to the peculiar not only humor but responsiveness to fellow humanity in that humor. Drawing on the resources of art, sabi also gave to
that which is peculiar a dignity and a meaning that it had not had.

[10] *Ibid.*, p. 118.   [11] *Ibid.*, p. 127.

Most explanations of sabi relate it not unnaturally to "sabishii," an adjective meaning "lonely." Two other glosses are much to be preferred. Kuriyama Riichi gives a linguistic explanation. By scrutiny of various words such as "sabi," "sabite," "sabu," "saburu," etc., he finds that the common element is alteration, particularly for the worse.[12] One agrees with him in the sense that if we took from the crow its withered branch to give it a flowering bough, the sabi would be gone. It is also not present in that version of the stanza on the frog's splash that begins with yellow roses rather than with an old pond. Konishi Jin'ichi has another explanation based on religious and literary grounds: "The better poems of Bashō composed during his forties all contain this element of 'quietness,' and this is what he terms sabi."[13] Again, if the crow stanza were full of cawing birds, there would be no sabi. And if the frog's splash did not intensify the stillness, there would be no sabi. This explanation requires that we consider quietness to be metaphorical or cognitive rather than purely sensory. The example always given is a stanza by Kyorai, since he reports in Kyorai's Notes (Kyoraishō) that Bashō said that "sabi-color is well shown" in it.

Hanamori ya	The flower wardens
shiroki kashira o	the white heads of two old men
tsukiawase	joined as companions

The stillness and attenuation are there, but I think that the blue heron provides a far better example.

If sabi and other qualities distinguish haikai, they distinguish it within the general category of poetry or art. A well-known passage touches on this: "[High art] is all one in nature, whether in Saigyō's waka, in Sōgi's renga, in Sesshū's painting, or in Rikyū's tea ceremonial. Moreover, in matters of art one follows the creative principle and accompanies the four seasons of the year. It is impossible to think of looking without looking for cherry blossoms, of longing without longing for the moon. Those who keep no image of flowers are like barbarians, and those whose hearts

---

[12] Ibid., pp. 127-28. Some of his examples, especially from early times, seem rather forced, but the idea is suggestive.

[13] Konishi "Image and Ambiguity," p. 63.

are not stirred by flowers are no better than beasts. One must expel such barbarity; one must leave the animals and join humankind, constantly pursuing or returning to the creative principle, he said."[14]

The flowers are the glory of spring, the moon the glory of autumn—Bashō is talking of all that is greatest, finest, in human experience of the natural world. It is of some interest that he has narrowed the ideas of Tsurayuki in the Preface to the *Kokinshū*. Tsurayuki had declared that animals, like people, are given to song, and among the poetic subjects there was love as well as nature. The restriction may be more apparent than real, however, since an abstractive or exemplary process is involved.

Bashō also presumed that years of practice and careful revision were required to be a poet. He knew that had been the case with himself. The assumption is an unspoken one throughout Japanese criticism.[15] Why else did one engage to work with a master? Here is an instance of one of those matters seldom if ever mentioned in Japanese criticism because it seems so obvious. So aware were writers of the kind of practice necessary that in their criticism they sought to stress a compensatory principle that would give a naturalness to expression: "In composing stanzas, there is becoming and making. A stanza can be said to become when a person who is used to devoting himself to what lies within responds to the world of things and the coloring of that thought becomes a poem. A stanza can be said to be made by a poet who does not devote himself to what lies within and must therefore compose by subjective will."[16] The idea is of course expressive: in composing a stanza. Yet more is involved than that: "When one enters fully into something, expressing its special qualities, and responding to its essence, then one makes stanzas."[17]

In addition to the expressive element, there is also the affective in responding. These elements make up the central tenets of classical Japanese criticism. But, as in earlier formulations of them, two other things are

[14] Kuriyama, *Haikaishi*, p. 134.

[15] In his *Art of Chinese Poetry* (Chicago: University of Chicago Press, 1962), James J. Y. Liu includes "The Technical View: Poetry as Literary Exercise" as the third of the four principal Chinese views of literature. For some relation of those views to Japan, see my essay "Towards a New Approach to Classical Japanese Poetics," cited in Ch. 1, n. 3 (p. 6),

[16] Kuriyama, *Haikaishi*, pp. 139-40 (Bashō).   [17] *Ibid.*, p. 141.

implied. If one can enter fully into something, then there is great assurance as to the poet's (and by implication the reader's) cognitive ability. In addition, if one can respond to the essence of something or to the world of things (as in the previous quotation), then there is a truly existent world that yet remains knowable.

Bashō's restatement of classical poetics has the very telling virtue of presenting the four entities necessary to any full literary theory: poet, reader, expression, and world. Japanese criticism, for all its oblique ways, is enduringly strong in such accounts, and in fact more so than most Western theories, for all their abstract sophistication. What distinguishes Bashō from earlier critics is, of course, sabi. Or rather, since sabi is a concern of earlier poets, it is not the sabi itself but the terms on which it exists in his poetry. On the assumption that sabi is required, it is that other term, okashimi, that matters. As Bashō said, that is implied by the very name, "haikai." The nonstandard, the low, the humorous (to a degree and of certain kinds) combine with the more refined, more severe, more affective sabi to define a new world of poetry. Bashō seems to have been quite clear in his mind that haikai offered a new kind of poetry. Was it not he who was the first to have written the new, genuine article? It is possible to think Bashō so original that he has no ties with earlier poets and critics. It is possible to show that his ideas have connections with those held for centuries. But it seems much more sensible to make two different assumptions. He is in the main stream of classical poetics; and yet he offers something new. "Newness is the flower of haikai," he said. "The old is not a flower but something that gives the aged sense of a clump of trees. . . . Something altogether without popularity has no newness."[18]

The novelty Bashō brought to linked poetry involves the adjustment of sabi to the okashimi of nonstandard renga, to haikai. It is like our Old Man, however, to abandon late in life that which had been new and that had made him respected. There are some authors who begin with the simpler and go to the more complex. Others turn to at least an apparently simpler style late in life. Shakespeare, Milton, Dryden, and Keats offer English examples. Tsurayuki and Teika offer Japanese precedents.

[18] *Ibid.*, p. 146.

In Bashō's case, the period of change was brief, running only a few years at the end of his life. The problem is what to make of the simpler style. In the case of Dryden's *Fables* or Keat's odes, we appreciate the change. Bashō's shift more resembles Shakespeare's to romances or Milton's to *Paradise Regained*, in being not only simpler but perhaps also less profound.

Bashō spoke not of simplicity but of "lightness": "karumi." Of course he had always worked painfully for natural, right expression. If he is the first genuine haikai poet, that is owed to his abandoning the mannered wit of earlier poets (and his own early work). Yet there is no question but that he changed his style. The new note is first sounded in a stanza written at home in Iga in 1690.

Ko no moto ni	Beneath the boughs
shiru mo namasu mo	eating soup, fish, and vegetables
sakura kana	flecked with cherry petals

This is none of your fancy outings but a simple meal to accompany what was deemed the acme of natural loveliness. It is rather like having a cheese sandwich and a beer at a performance of Bach's St. John Passion. The poet said of his stanza: "I tried to give it the atmosphere of a flower-viewing party and imparted a lightness to it."[19] By the time of Bashō's death, the new light style was known to be his poetic standard, to the distress of some of his followers. The loyal Kyorai appears to have been impelled to define and perhaps to defend Bashō's departure. He insisted that lightness must be distinguished from thinness, that the language was rich and the meaning no less than before. Lightness, he said, "derives from the depths of the body and is found naturally throughout the whole stanza."[20] Here is another stanza in the style, taken from the last year of Bashō's life.

Umegaka ni	The fragrance of plum trees
notto hi no deru	and the sun up all of a sudden
yamaji kana	on the mountain path

[19] *Ibid.*, p. 168. [20] *Ibid.*, p. 171.

It is worth mentioning that one thing has not changed. These famous stanzas are just that, stanzas, and in fact hokku for real sequences. They are not haiku. The "Fish, Soup, and Vegetables" sequence (*Shiru-namasu Kasen*) was composed by Bashō and two others in 1690. Since it was composed on the second day of the Third Month, cherry trees must have been in blossom. One even wonders if Bashō was not describing their lunch: and expecting a nice banquet later. "The Plum Fragrance" sequence (*Umegaka Kasen*) was a duo with Yaba (1663-1740).

The practice of composing sequences is the same. But the style differs. In what respects? The central alteration involves a reduction in the tension of pressing elements in a given stanza. (The matter of stanza relatedness in sequence is a quite separate subject and not involved in "lightness" *per se*.) In the light style we commonly find the lovely (cherry blossoms, the fragrance of plum trees) with what is common as to object ("soup, fish, and vegetables") or common as to language (and the sun up *all of a sudden: notto* hi no deru). There is still a considerable measure of the unexpected in such joinings, so that on such and other grounds the element of okashimi remains. There also seems to be less effort. Strong measures were not so necessary, as with the sabi style. The two examples of the new style also show a more conventional loveliness. The stillness and deterioration of sabi have less place. Yet even these differences do not seem the most important one. If sabi has to do with a lowered world apprehended in stillness, there are still strong elements of this. The major change lies in the diminished charge of what had been opposed to sabi and beauty together.

The change can best be shown by three examples to set against the two we have seen. Let us begin with the unfeeling although perfectly human comedy of a senryū.

Sano no uma	That old nag of Sano's
Tozuka no saka de	has tumbled over twice upon the slope
nido korobi.	leading to Tozuka.[21]

Poor Sano Gonzaemon, the author says, with a laugh showing that this.

[21] Kuriyama (*ibid.*, p. 133) compares this senryū to the hokku next quoted. I have added the prose context of the hokku (from *Poetic Diaries*, pp. 177-78) and the third example.

condition is not likely to touch Number One. As usual with comedy, our immunity allows us to smile. The second example comes from *The Narrow Road*. Bashō and his companion Sora have just left the grand ruins at Hiraizumi, where the romantic, chivalric figure Yoshitsune met his death. They are now making their way through what is unpleasant country: "Because there are so few travelers on this route, the barrier guards treated us with great suspicion, and we were let through only after much delay. We struggled up a steep mountain trail, and finding that the day had grown dark, stumbled into the house of a provincial border guard and asked to be let lodging for the night. A fierce rainstorm howled for three days, keeping us in those worthless lodgings in the mountains."

Nomi shirami　　　　Fleas and lice
uma no pari suru　　and the sound of horses pissing
makura moto　　　　next to my pillow

Here the poet and we are engaged directly with the experience. We do not laugh. There is an incongruity in the fact that the greatest poet of the time should be in such filthy quarters. Bashō saw it and was not amused. Neither are we, because this image of life has the possibility of including us, as that poor old horse does not.

The third example comes from 1690 and belongs to a thirty-six-stanza sequence that is given in full in Part Three: *Throughout the Town* (*Ichinaka wa no Maki* or *Ichinaka Kasen*). In the twenty-fifth stanza the poet writing before Bashō introduces the moon. Bashō adds a stanza presumably describing another member of the household or a close neighbor at a time a bit later on that long autumn night.

Kosokoso to　　　　Stealthily stealthily
waraji o tsukuru　　he plaits straw into sandals
tsukiyo sashi—　　　in bright moonlight—
—nomi o furui ni　　—and shaking fleas from the bedcovers
okishi hatsuaki　　　she wakes to early autumn

Is not the attitude of this less involved than the passage from *The Narrow Road* and more involved than in the senryū? If sabi means the still or the deteriorated, surely we have that in Bashō's stanza. But in the end it is less intense and so offers something of okashimi. The fleas do not matter so much. And yet, since the constituents are the same, the poetic world has not changed as much as is sometimes said. It is perhaps only natural that reaction should differ in response to one's own present experience from someone else's imagined experience. In short, I am suggesting what seems to be a somewhat unusual explanation: that the change in Bashō's late style is more a matter of hokku than of sequences. It may be that he sought to change his style in added stanzas (tsukeku), but that old habits and old ways of understanding lasted on in them far longer. In any event, the technique does not alter. It was easier to change in hokku when Bashō did not feel under the pressure of old habits of joining stanzas.

Any explanation, my own included, must hesitate from failure to consider all the evidence. The sequence from which the last example was taken is the 181st in what is supposed to be the canonical text of his poems,[22] and that counting does not include his haibun. The sequence *Throughout the Town* was written in 1690. On the 17th of the Ninth Month in 1694, shortly before Bashō died, he took part in his last sequence, which is especially interesting for having two or three women among the poets. How can one stress sufficiently that in his last four years Bashō took part in 108 haikai sequences? That is something like two sequences a month. From such practice, two just inferences may be drawn. One is that he wrote so much in so many circumstances, and especially late in life, that any rigid conception of changes in his style requires numerous exceptions. This puts in hazard my description as much as anyone's. The other fair inference is that Bashō does not become a more haiku-like poet as he grows older—quite the contrary. As he became famous, or at least as he came to know more people, he naturally joined more often with others in composition. If he had spent as much of his time on sequences in the last twenty years of his life as he did in the last four, he would have written, not about two hundred but almost 2200 sequences.

One might imagine that with such a legacy haikai could finance several generations. "The gods determined otherwise." There were of course

---

[22] *Teihon Bashō Taisei*, ed. Ogata Tsutomu *et al.* (Sanseidō, 1962).

able poets, but the situation degenerated. Bonchō did not like Bashō's late "light" style. Modest Kyorai retired and took few disciples. Kikaku criticized the Old Man caustically. On his death, Bashō's influence quickly waned. So did the quality of haikai. It was natural enough for former disciples like Kikaku and Shikō to set up their own schools. But in some sense it was a weakness in Bashō's kind of haikai that it did not lend itself to transmission. That weakness was also a version of its strength. Not just anyone could practice it. The peasant with a hoe in his hand could still get help from the Danrin school, which ticked right along.

This is a story of decline from true greatness until that Haikai Revival usually dated from 1743 to 1783. The fact that this period also is thought to close with the death of the second genius of haikai certainly lends some credence to the idea that individuals influence history or that history moves in periods of spirit. In any event, the second genius is a many-sided one. As is well known, Taniguchi or Yosa Buson (1716-1783) has claims for distinction as a painter and calligrapher as well as a poet. In recent years there has been fresh appreciation for his Chinese poetry. Such considerations lie out of bounds here, and it will not do to say simply that just as he is the greatest poet among Japanese painters, so is he the greatest painter among Japanese poets. Most people think Buson second to Bashō as a poet. So do I. But the greatness of Buson seems to me to involve a clarity that is difficult to find in his predecessor. Buson has less tension in his poetry, and there is no late change to worry over. One might say that his eyesight was clearer, even if he did not see so deeply.

Like Bashō, Buson had a good opinion of himself, and with good reason. This opinion can be seen in a note added in 1780 to his *Peaches and Plums* (*Momo Sumomo*). He talks there of his development and his early triumphs: "I entered the circles that honored Bakurin and Shikō, and consequently employed their rules for writing stanzas. Since there were things I liked about Kikaku and Ransetsu, I produced verse according to their taste. Practice with the masters in the capital led me to follow the styles of Tantan and Rajin. In short I was not without good reception anywhere I sought to go, and each place regarded my haikai as among the best in their circle. In fact I toyed with the world and felt nothing but contempt for the usual low styles of haikai." Less vainly and more strikingly, he said, "I do not follow Kikaku's style of howling at the moon."[23] No wonder he joined in the cry, "Return to Bashō!" It appears that Kikaku was sought after in some measure because he seemed complex.

Buson did not think his styles so difficult: "Kikaku is called the Po Chü-i of haikai. That is no less true because out of 100,000 stanzas not twenty give pleasure to hear. In his collection, the majority of stanzas are difficult to comprehend orally. But when they are read one can never have enough of them. That is where he excels. In any case, stanzas are best composed with a largeness of spirit that does not fuss over details."[24]

Does this imply that Buson thinks Bashō a Tu Fu? It does show that he wished Kikaku to be appreciated in the right way. And he referred to Kikaku more often than to anyone except Bashō. Clearly haikai now had its own tradition, and a poet of Buson's great powers could choose to set qualities of different poets as standards for emulation. Even Kyorai wrote that "No one touches Kikaku for being a grand show."[25]

In calling for a return to Bashō, Buson's preferences suggest a Bashō different from the figure usually conceived today. Again and again he praised poems that are now infrequently read. He liked those from the earlier period, from collections made about 1683 to 1685: *Chestnut Shells* (*Minashiguri*) and *The Winter Sun* (*Fuyu no Hi*). It is by no means clear that Buson's own writing resembles either the earlier or later Bashō that much, although perhaps the wit in some of the earlier writing had some appeal. Whatever else may be said, Bashō was a grand exemplar of what haikai might achieve, even if Buson's talents and the needs of his age were better met by other resources.

Something must be said of that age and of Buson's response to it. The Haikai Revival coincided with a relaxation by the government of its strict control over the lives of the people. We can predict the results. Entertainments, clothes, behavior, and ideas that were not permissible before became wanted and available. Along with a good deal of pleasure-seeking, there was also more open expression, and a more important place accorded the arts. At its best, and a best of which Buson is one

[23] Kuriyama, *Haikaishi*, pp. 237, 240.   [24] *Ibid*., p. 240.
[25] *Ibid*., p. 241.

prime representative, the age awoke to a new refinement and purification of tastes. Painters of bunjin-ga like him were particularly antipathetic to ostentatious vulgarity, preferring to explore the world with elegance of art and well-defined personal life. Each age has the faults of its virtues, and this age ran some danger of over-aestheticism and dilettantism. Certainly more things now seemed possible. Buson suggests as much in one of the most helpful of his many pronouncements: "There is no special entry to haikai. Our entry is solely by the gate of haikai itself. One proceeds by exhausting most kinds of possibility, saving one store from which the best may be chosen and got out to use. Still, there is no other rule at all but examination of the workings of one's own motives."[26] All people are self-aware, writers especially. Clearly Buson's awareness differs from that shown by Bashō. It would not be easy, however, to infer from this remark that Buson is more objective, less subjective, than the earlier poet.

Buson also proves somewhat elusive. In 1774 he wrote: "So that if I were to designate the school I follow at present, it would not be the open style of Sōa. I yearn solely for the sabi and shiori of Bashō and long to recapture the past."[27] It is not easy to separate a veneration of the past from poetic ideals. The same mixture characterizes another remark: "Old Master Bashō said, 'In haikai the language should approach the very low, and the spirit requires that we try for elevation.' Is this not a principle for the ages?"[28] Kitō (1741-1789), who was taught by Buson, added in 1787 that his master "would look for that dark shudder of the late Bashō, the refinement with which he produced stanzas, and he admired solely the greatness of *Chestnut Shells* and *The Winter Sun*."[29] Here is a problem. The collections Kitō names are early rather than late, and if a "dark shudder" is to be found it is in the second of Bashō's periods designated by Kyorai, not earlier or later. But one can believe that Buson liked whatever refinement he found in his predecessor.

Yet another remark, this time in 1782, seems to indicate a more revealing inclination. "Reducing my ambition," Buson begins modestly, "rather than devote myself entirely to sabi and shiori, I wish to link myself to one who writes stanzas possessing grandeur."[30] There is no reason

---

[26] *Ibid.*, p. 218. [27] *Ibid.*, p. 237. [28] *Ibid.*, p. 235.
[29] *Ibid.*, p. 237. [30] *Ibid.*, pp. 237-38.

why the desire for such an attachment should rule out Bashō, but it perhaps suggests a leaning toward Kikaku, who was, as Kyorai said, inimitable for a grand show. Even Bashō said that Kikaku was another Teika, probably thinking of himself as another Saigyō. Like Bashō, Teika ended with a simpler style that Kikaku is not likely to have esteemed very highly. But Kikaku could find much to respond to in Teika's early style of ethereal, refined charm (yōen, yōenbi).[31] A stanza by Kikaku will suggest his debt to Teika and some resemblance to Buson.

<table>
<tr><td>Kahashira ni</td><td>Mosquitoes swarm</td></tr>
<tr><td>yume no ukihashi</td><td>and on their cloudlike pillar hangs</td></tr>
<tr><td>kakaru nari</td><td>the floating bridge of dreams</td></tr>
</table>

This very impressive stanza obviously alludes to one of Teika's most famous poems (*Shinkokinshū*, 1: 38), one we have already seen.

<table>
<tr><td>Haru no yo no</td><td>The bridge of dreams</td></tr>
<tr><td>Yume no ukihashi</td><td>Floating on the brief spring night</td></tr>
<tr><td>Todae shite</td><td>Soon breaks apart,</td></tr>
<tr><td>Mine ni wakaruru</td><td>And from the mountaintop a cloud</td></tr>
<tr><td>Yokogumo no sora.</td><td>Takes leave into the open sky.</td></tr>
</table>

Kikaku concentrates some of Teika's central images, and his summer scene marvelously alters, to the haikai world, what before had belonged to the romance of spring. It is not evident that he achieves the religious and other complexities of Teika and Bashō. On the other hand, the scene seems closer to hand, palpably more real. In short, it seems to me that the Bashō whom Buson wished to return to was one adapted by that brilliant disciple, Kikaku. In both there is a clarity of focus and a range of evident effect that impress us deeply.

Buson is a master of writing stanzas at once particular and whole. He commands details, not they him. Even when they are low, an instinct to refinement purges the dross. This easily can be shown by spring stanzas, or by stanzas on his favorite flower, the peony. They can also be shown

---

[31] For discussion and examples of poems embodying these ideals, see *Court Poetry*, pp. 262-68.

by others that are somber, without flowers, as in these three involving trees, especially those late in the year.

Miidera ya	At Mii Temple
hi wa uma ni semaru	the sun's rays shrink at noontime
wakakaede	among young maples
★	★
Kusu no ne o	The icy drizzle
shizuka ni nurasu	quietly dampens the roots
shigure kana	of the camphor tree
★	★
Ono irete	Striking the axe
ka ni odoroku ya	I am surprised by the fragrance
fuyu kodachi	in the wintry grove

These stanzas show what Japanese mean in calling Buson objective. They do not lack emotional coloring, and in fact the emotion varies. In each instance the common ground of feeling derives from an aesthetic base. What is not needed is refined away, and what is needed turns out to be what might easily be missed by an eye and a mind less acute than his. Take the icy drizzle on a wintry day. It must be dampening the whole tree, since it falls from the sky. But it is darkest at the roots because there it is thickest and least dried by wind and because least shined on by whatever sunlight there may be. It has been said that such treatment amounts to the "minuteness of things."[32] Yet it is natural to think of roots of a tree like the camphor, which grows to the height of a hundred feet or so. Here is no bush. For that matter, although the axe of the third stanza bites into one tree, there is a sense of the whole grove, which is the more visible in winter. In the first stanza, a very carefully observed phenomenon of light seems to tell of the "minuteness of things," but we have a new stand of maples at a great temple. No wonder everyone thinks Buson the poet resembles Buson the painter. With great economy he selects telling details from a potentially large whole, not reducing the large to the small, but representing it by its chosen parts.

Buson resembles Shinkei in producing brilliant stanzas, and it could be

[32] Kuriyama, *Haikaishi*, p. 247, a by no means uncommon judgment.

argued that his frequently stand by themselves better than do Bashō's. This may provide more problems than virtues. One can link stanzas, but one cannot link paintings, and there seems to be a frame around many of Buson's best pieces. The frame tells us that it is a verbal picture, and it also sets off art from life. Buson was antipathetic in no small way to something said by Bashō: "The way of the world and the way of haikai are not distinct things."[33] The three stanzas given are all about the world, but a world rather more remote from love and death. Also, none has the hairiness or humor we expect from haikai. They are all but indistinguishable from renga stanzas in tone and diction. And in their framing we see something like proto–haiku.

Of course Buson is not always so. The collection *Peaches and Plums* (*Momo Sumomo*) contains two kasen, one opening with summer and the other with winter. Kitō starts the second with a bleakly cold hokku that gives the stanza its name, *The Wintry Woods* (*Fuyu Kodachi*). Buson's waki, or second stanza, is a joke:

kono ku Rōto ga   this stanza would give old Tu
samuki harawata   cold shudders in his belly

Tu Fu is meant, and here the haikai touch is very evident, both in the connection of stanzas and in the humor. Later in *The Wintry Woods* (stanza 15), Buson offers this:

Tsuki ochite   The moon has fallen
Kehi no yamamoto   and in the foothills of Mount Kehi
tsuyu kuraki   the dew grows dark

What a splendid stanza to develop Kitō's idea of a boat starting out in a heartless wind blowing autumn from behind! A little consideration of expectations in a kasen would show that this moon stanza really belongs seven stanzas earlier. (One so delayed is called a spilt moon.) There is nothing wrong with that, and it rather contributes to the first line. One other matter requires comment. This stanza exists earlier in a couple of variants on the second line, which in the others was situated in Izu or

[33] *Ibid.*, p. 197.

Tosa rather than in present Fukui, where Mount Kehi stands. Buson
seems to have had in his head an inventory of stanzas that he might begin
with or insert into sequences, revising when necessary. The technique
works very well here, but one must confess that it does not seem to be
fully true to the haikai spirit.

One of Buson's most often printed stanzas has great beauty.

Yūkaze ya	The evening breeze
mizu aosagi no	leads the waters to ripple on
hagi o utsu	the blue heron's legs

The order of images here is extremely important, and in that fact we understand that Buson is truly a poet in these stanzas, not a painter. The
pressure and coolness of an evening breeze lead to the waters on which it
blows, not too strongly. And there, at some distance, stands the blue
crane, feeding as dusk gathers. Let us recall Bashō's stanza with its predecessor in *At the Tub of Ashes* (given whole in Part Three).

Ame no yadori no	No more than cover from a shower
mujō jinsoku	is human life in ceaseless flux
hiru neburu	sleeping at noon
aosagi no mi no	the body of the blue heron
tōtosa yo	poised in nobility

As a simply beautiful stanza, Buson's might well be the one preferred.
But once we learn what Bashō's implies about ourselves, the world,
evanescence, and the Void (kū), how can we do anything other than prefer it?

Buson's life seems to have been happier than Bashō's. Things fell better into place: painting and poetry, friends and a wife (who was also a
poet), enough money and liberal times. With Bashō there is a tension,
even in those very last years. He tried most to hide away while in Edo,
for if that was not as large or as bustling as its successor, Tokyo, is today,
it was still the largest city in the world at the time. It seems to have made
him uneasy. While enduring the rigors of travel, he very much liked
meeting people. It is significant that he should have compared writing a

kasen to taking a journey in thirty-six steps, not expecting to return alive.[34] In this sense, haikai and the world were indeed not separate, and both were about life and death. After him, there was Buson, with his splendid aesthetic insight and penetrating intelligence. When Buson left the scene, the Haikai Revival quietly came to its end.

[34] This comparison is made much of, and to telling effect, by Andō Tsuguo in *Bashō* (Chikuwa Shobō, 1965), p. 227. Bashō wrote "A kasen consists of thirty-six footsteps." One implication is that haikai and travel participate in each other.

6

Some Canons of Haikai

"A kasen consists of thirty-six
footsteps."—Bashō
"Your stanza is self-indulgent."
—Bashō, laughing, to Kyorai

SOME BREVITY is possible on the topic, since most of what was said of the canons of renga also holds for haikai no renga—to give it its full name. There are some differences. The major technical one involves what was considered the normal sequence length. We have seen that for renga it was the hyakuin, one hundred stanzas, and that Bashō made the kasen predominate among those who practiced his style, his followers, and Buson. The kasen has been described earlier, and a look at Figure 5 will refresh the memory. But since the terms and indeed the ways of thought differ so from what we are used to, a little recapitulation may not be amiss.

A kasen uses two sheets of paper, each of which has a total of eighteen poems on its front and back sides. These sheets and sides have names:

First Sheet: Sho-ori
Second Sheet: Nagori no ori (also Ni no ori).

In each case the front is the omote and the back is the ura. This gives us sho omote and sho ura, and nagori no omote and nagori no ura.

A major feature of the kasen is its departure from the hundred-stanza requisites for flower and moon stanzas. A hundred-stanza sequence (hyakuin) should have one flower stanza on each of its four sheets and one moon stanza on each of its eight sides, although that on the back of the last sheet is sometimes omitted. In the kasen, there are two flower stanzas, as we might expect, since there are two sheets. But there are only three moon stanzas, although there are four sides. Each of the five special stanzas has a conventional place (za), although considerable freedom is allowed, especially with the moon stanzas. The stipulated places are as follows:

Stanza	Number in Part	Number in Whole
1st moon	5, front of first sheet	5
2nd moon	8, back of first sheet	14
1st flower	11, back of first sheet	17
3rd moon	11, front of second sheet	29
2nd flower	5, back of second sheet	35

All except the second moon stanza (eighth of twelve on the back of the first sheet) fall in the penultimate spot on its side of paper. Such insistence on avoiding the first or last or middle position is very Japanese, and so also is the lack of symmetry in this one exception. But more is involved. The second moon stanza does not come as the seventeenth, because the flower stanza has precedence. Moon stanzas are still not as important as flower stanzas, because there are more of them, even if only three to two. As a kind of corollary, the moon stanzas get shifted about a good deal. One of the haikai kasen given in Part Three is *Throughout the Town*, in which the first stanza itself is a moon stanza. That is not unparalleled. In *The Wintry Woods (Fuyu Kodachi)*, for example, Kitō does the same. The next stanza by Buson protests, but not about having an opening stanza a moon stanza. It will be recalled that he protests only about the cold, which would give Tu Fu a bellyache. Of all supposed fixed places, the most commonly honored is the second flower stanza, which conventionally falls in the thirty-fifth stanza, the last but one. Even sequences that move the first flower stanza and the moon stanzas about with freedom usually honor this one location. Yet in *The Wintry Woods* the first flower stanza is the one in place (number seventeen, or the eleventh on the back of the first sheet) whereas the second appears as the thirty-fourth instead of the thirty-fifth stanza.

These conventions may well induce headaches such as many of us felt on first dealing with Latin verbs or remembering rime royal, Spenserian stanzas, sonnet forms, and the like. Yet it is with such matters as with fugues, dances, and pictures of Virgin and child. Unless one knows what is to be expected one can form no notion of what is unexpected. With that pedantic pronouncement, let us return to more of the same.

As in renga, so in haikai Spring and Autumn are the prized seasons, and they usually run from as few as three to as many as five stanzas in succession. Summer and Winter stanzas may go in runs of three, but after the third stanza (daisan), they usually go in shorter runs. A shift from one season to another usually involves one or more intervening miscellaneous stanzas. But exceptions are frequent. As in renga, about half the stanzas in a haikai sequence are Miscellaneous. Also as in renga, such subtopics as Love or Travel or Shinto may accompany either a Seasonal or Miscellaneous topic. The flower stanzas of haikai require the word "hana," not a named flower, just as in renga, although we recall that in one instance Kyorai named weeping cherries (itozakura). In haikai the word "hana" has now come to mean solely cherry blossoms. It does not mean plum blossoms unless so specified (ume no hana). These matters can be exemplified from *The Wintry Woods*. The flower stanzas are the seventeenth (Buson) and the thirty-fourth (Kitō). In addition there are stanzas with two named flowers and therefore not flower stanzas: "sumire" or violets in the fifth (Kitō), and "yamabuki" or yellow roses in the twenty-fourth (Buson).

Bashō realized that for a kasen the development section is very brief (stanzas seven through thirty) as opposed to a hundred-stanza sequence (stanzas nine through ninety-two). That being the case, the subtopic of love, which was considered the most agitated, required special care. Usually it was used twice in the Development section, and two stanzas were considered a sufficient run. Because of the lower decorum of haikai (and the misogyny that had grown so strong in Japanese society), the love stanzas often have comic elements in which women are depreciated or other treatments that would be out of place in renga and waka. At one point in *Peony Blossoms Fall* Buson gives a love stanza on male homosexual love. Two more things must be said of this stanza. It is not *so* male homosexual but that Kitō can easily add a stanza making his and Buson's heterosexual. The second is that the essence or hon'i of love is maintained in the homosexual stanza: it is unrequited love, or yearning love, as the older man wishes for the young boy to appear. The same poets have another pair of unusual love stanzas in *The Wintry Woods* Kitō has a stanza about a bowsman at Noto Bay. The prey imagined by Buson (stanza eleven) turns out to be a female fox with strong resentment against her lover. Foxes are enchanters—more often enchantresses—so often in Japanese stories that they were hunted, feared, and treated as demonic lovers. It is a very clever transition. Kitō then (stanza twelve) makes an equally radical alteration—of the fox into a lady of high class, probably of the court, whose hair is dishevelled as she rises in the morning after a night of love. This stanza illustrates another feature of love stanzas. They must be capable of adapting to non-love meaning with another stanza: women can awake with messy hair from causes other than love-making.

As such matters indicate, in general haikai canons are taken from renga but modified. A chief factor in modification involves diction. Like waka, renga uses solely Japanese diction, and that of an especially pure or poetic kind. Haikai admits sinified words and compounds. Its style is therefore much less mellifluous, harsher, and also more capable of certain kinds of abstraction. In a single stanza a poet will often have one or two lines that are indistinguishable from renga in the waka-like purity of their language and then use a line that sounds highly sinified and therefore contrastingly haikai-like. The result need not be a lowering in tone at all. For example, in *At the Tub of Ashes* (the third sequence given in Part Three), Yasui (1658-1743) gives us just such a stanza as the thirty-second of the sequence:

| ame no yadori no | no more than cover from a shower |
| MUJŌ JINSOKU | is human life in ceaseless flux. |

Perhaps one could use mighty terms like EVANESCENCE ACCELERATION to convey the non-native origins of "mujō jinsoku," but after a certain amount of experimentation in such matters one translator has decided that his license does not extend to large and unwieldy carriages. More importantly, even the ordinary Japanese diction employed brings into haikai a whole realm of quotidian experience that is new. Haikai abounds in things of daily use. It abounds in *things*. There are more products of handiwork, more items of daily use, more of natural life, from insects to animals. Children, architecture, apprentices, soldiers, crowds, food, pastimes, occupations—more indeed of customary reality. The translator of waka and renga may bite a pencil or thumb dictionaries in search of some passable equivalent for flora and fauna. The translator of haikai has pretty well bit off the one and torn up the other. Even when there are Western equivalents, they have mostly disappeared from common usage in the last forty or fifty years. Few readers today have any clearer notion of a smith's forge than of a case knife, of a crupper than of a whiffle-tree. Of course people who have never seen or felt such things as leeches, fleas, and lice will have sufficient idea of what they may be. Some things can be explained easily enough, as for example a piece of bamboo bowed so that its springing will ward off badgers. But those last thirteen words make no easy translation of "shinohari no yumi." Everyone reading haikai must be struck by scenes crowded with things or with people, even as some stanzas may give the larger, clearer, freer vistas of renga and waka.

The concept of essential nature, hon'i, is maintained from renga. The moon is still the autumn moon unless otherwise qualified. But the multiplicity of things, abstractions, and human activities introduce much for which no hon'i had been set and for which only a computer could keep track. This balance is of crucial importance for haikai. It maintains, on the one hand, a status as haikai *renga*, while insisting, on the other hand, that it is *haikai* renga. In general, the thinginess of haikai presses away from renga, just as seasonal matters press toward renga. But the exceptions are very numerous. A sinified word such as a Buddhist term has an inherent dignity unless guyed in some fashion, whereas seasonal details can be set a bit askew and be made to seem very appropriate to haikai. For example, Kyorai (1651-1704) concludes *Throughout the Town* (the second sequence in Part Three) with language wholly Japanese and yet comic in its serious way.

kasumi ugokanu   The spring haze hangs motionless
hiru no nemutasa.   at the drowsy midday hours.

Kyorai has deflated the happy but very peaceful and essential spring image of haze into sleepy stasis. The vitality of haikai can be found in that alteration of the high tradition into a lower, in one genuine sense more real, context without sacrificing poetic validity.

Such greater informality testifies to the degree of freedom haikai poets enjoyed within the general traditions of renga. Other symptoms are not hard to find. Sōgi still used those directives, fushimono, although they served as little more than a title. Haikai poets do not bother with them. The titles of most haikai sequences offer some version of the first line rather than something like *Minase Sangin Hyakuin*, which designates Minase as place of composition, the number of poets as three (sangin), and the number of stanzas as one hundred (hyakuin). There also grows a tendency to treat haikai as parts of a book, either with or without a number of hokku lacking successive stanzas. Bashō's disciples helped make such collections for him, and later Buson saw to the publication of the two sequences included in *Peaches and Plums*. He prefixed to it a preface in which he jokes with facts and the reader. Other prefaces are more solemn.

These matters suggest another shift. The actual moment of composition is coming to matter less. There seems to be little desire to end matters with a fine banquet or with a presentation to a shrine, temple, or some commissioning potentate. In this respect, haikai sequences are poetry more as we know it, composition that may be published in a book. If this is true, readers matter more than details of composition. *Peaches and Plums* shows as much. Its two sequences were talked about and started in the late spring of 1780 and were not finished until winter (from the Third Month to the early part of the Eleventh). There is a note dating from the twenty-fifth of the Seventh Month telling that a new hokku has been introduced to begin the summer sequence. That new one is the present one, which had in fact been composed earlier. For that matter, so had been the one that it replaces. For such reason, the opening stanza of *The Wintry Woods*, which would have had such dire effects on Tu Fu, need not have been composed in winter at all, as some critics think. It would be just like the Kitō or Buson of *Peaches and Plums* to have written it in the heat of summer, so to suggest that it would give the Chinese poet the chills even on a blistering day.

Such developments appear to signify a growing tendency to fictionalize. In waka, spring poems could be written in summer, travel poems in the winter, poems "by" women actually by men, and so on. Such developments are often thought to signify artifice, especially by the Japanese, and especially by Japanese today influenced by the kind of thinking encouraged by Masaoka Shiki. In truth, Japanese literature is often less fictional—or at least more autobiographical—than Western. But the deities in the ancient records were given for their speeches verse composed earlier, and in the *Man'yōshū* poems by sophisticated poets mask as compositions by the humble or even by animals. For that matter, any change from the first stanza introduced into linked poetry by the second stanza involves variance from the circumstances of composition. It is a matter of fine balance. The sabi style of Bashō's great period is itself a specially fine balance—as it were—between the fictionalizing aestheticism of Buson and the more autobiographical character of Bashō's own late and "light" style.[1]

The age of haikai brought a new kind of poetry, because conditions differed from those which had been best understood by renga. As we have seen, most of the great renga masters emerged from obscurity, became nominal priests, and then found patronage with the powerful. Haikai masters tend to come from better families, often the military aristocracy. They tend to resign their military status in favor of study and teaching, especially of haikai. They reach out, not to the high and mighty, but to people like themselves and to those of humbler status. *The Narrow Road* shows Bashō meeting person after person interested in haikai, including even merchants, supposedly the lowest social group. Haikai poets do not come, on the whole, from obscure origins, but such poetry enabled many writers of lower rank to make a mark on the world. As part of this change, women once more gradually come to be known as poets. One of the best known—if only for a few stanzas—is Kaga no Chiyo, or Nun Chiyo (1703-1775). She studied with Shikō, among others, and was also an accomplished painter. Like Buson's wife, herself a poet, she took orders after her husband's death—apparently that granted women the freedom that nominal priesthood had given the renga poets.

One of Chiyo's stanzas has what might be termed valid or earned sentiment. She recalls the loss of her only son, imagining, as parents so often do in such a situation, what he would be doing if still alive, or even that he still lives.

[1] This point is made by Konishi Jin'ichi in "Image and Ambiguity," pp. 76-80.

Tombotsuri	How far away
kyō wa doko made	has he gone off today in chase
itta yara	of dragonflies

One need not say that Japanese children like to catch insects. If one doubts the poetry of such a stanza, one need only wait until one is a parent, and if one disbelieves it, one need only wait until someone deeply loved dies. A yet more famous stanza suffers from a degree of preciosity.

Asagao ni	The well-ladle is claimed
tsurube torarete	by the morning glories that twine it
moraimizu	so I beg water elsewhere

We can use the same standard: if one thinks that matters such as this constitute universal poetry, one need only wait until someone deeply loved dies.

Yet in a tradition uniquely distinguished for its female writers, it is good to hear such a voice again. We may be reminded by this one that haikai coincided with the treatment of women by serious male writers. Ihara Saikaku (1642-1693) treated women as seriously as he did men in his brilliant prose fiction, and if Chikamatsu Monzaemon (1653-1724) did not always do so, he treated both women and men more seriously in his plays than did Saikaku or other Edo writers. It is also worth recalling the prostitutes of Niigata whom Bashō added out of fictional inspiration and humanity to *The Narrow Road*. The virtues of haikai include chiefly the intrinsic interest of individual sequences. But they also include a widening of vision in Japanese literature of the Edo period. That widening involves much more than the presence of women, although that one matter is certainly symptomatic. The new reach of experience makes its way differ from the way of renga, although they differ in the same way from the kinds of literature practiced elsewhere in the world. This double difference will be our last concern before examples of major sequences of linked poetry.

7

Distinctive Features of
Linked Poetry

> "Immersed in the transshifting of dream and reality."—Sōgi
> "High art is all one in nature."—Bashō

LIKE ALL other literature, linked poetry matters for providing a special understanding of the world, knowledge that freshens and deepens the understanding of those of us living centuries later and in another culture. Like all other literature, linked poetry derives from contingencies of a nation, a language, a time, and individual poets. It is now time to draw some of these elements together in order that we may have a definite conception of why we should prize this quite unusual kind of literary art. The full provision will come only with the sequences themselves in Parts Two and Three.

We can trace renga from antiquity to Yamada Yoshio and haikai from about the twelfth century to the nineteenth. The period of greatest achievement, from Sōgi to Buson, is of no such length. Some three centuries or so elapse between the outbreak of the Ōnin War (1467-1477) and the end of the Haikai Revival (1743-1783). We can extend the period of flourishing to earlier and later times, but in terms of truly high art, we have just over three centuries to consider.

Renga came to its glory under social conditions of furious civil strife, the breakdown of old institutions, and the dispersion of power to numerous local centers. Rapacity, treachery, and mindless destruction scoured the countryside like the horsemen of the apocalypse. After barely catching its breath, the exhausted nation was aroused to even longer exertions during the period of "sengoku," as the Japanese term it, meaning both a nation at war and war among provinces. Local military lords swung their swords and set the land ablaze in the effort to enlarge their power. From this period in the middle of the sixteenth century until the beginning of the eighteenth, a succession of strongmen and their adherents sought to unify and pacify the country under their own power. At last the Tokugawa family emerged as a ruling and indeed totalitarian regime, setting social patterns that Japanese historians, at least, term feudal (hōkenteki). Whatever the term, rule was legitimized by the powerless emperor in Kyoto, whose supposed wishes were carried by the military regime in Edo. In theory the people were divided into four classes, exclusive of the court nobility, whose increasing powerlessness is suggested by their seldom being mentioned. The military aristocracy constituted about seven percent of the population and was incomparably better off in its higher echelons than anyone else. Next came the farmers, about eighty percent of the population of thirty million. Every effort was made to extract the last possible koku of rice from the peasants, most of whom struggled to evade and to keep it. In *Throughout the Town* (Part Three), Kyorai's eighteenth stanza gives a glimpse into the lot of a small peasant.

nen ni itto no	each year it is but a peck of rice
jishi hakaru nari	but the land-tax is paid in full

This honest peasant must have a minisculur holding if so little rice satisfies the government: it is a grinding, poor life. In theory, merchants and artisans ranked below peasants, but, apart from the urban poor, many of these townspeople acquired increasing wealth and status. In the same sequence Bonchō describes another poor person—whether of the city, a town, or a village is not certain. But his twenty-fifth stanza tells a great deal. National industriousness—and poverty—manifest themselves in the light of the most precious symbol of autumn.

kosokoso to	stealthily stealthily
waraji o tsukuru	he plaits straw into sandals
tsukiyo sashi	in bright moonlight

This society had sumptuary laws, regulations against selling land or changing occupations, and against intercourse with foreigners. The family was told to defer to the male head of the house: it was "danson-johi," favor for the male, disfavor for the female. The philosophical underpinning of this system was derived from neo-Confucianism, especially the kind termed "shushigaku," Chu Hsi studies. Given the treacheries of the early part of this era, the Japanese differed from the Chinese in stressing loyalty more than filial piety.

This description has been given in terms of laws and with disclaimers such as "in theory." The Japanese have always had a streak of anarchy in them as well as a yearning for order, and a sense of the need to compromise born out of the conflict between anarchy and regulation. The more closely—at least the longer—one looks at anything Japanese, the more one realizes that things are not as they seem, but then also not as they do not seem, either. By Buson's time, Edo had over a million inhabitants. The society seemed to be getting on better than most do. Tokugawa rule was never monolithic and was in constant adjustment. The shogunate was forced to innovate when the eighteenth century brought a series of problems involving famines and uprisings. The eighth shogun, Yoshimune (1684-1751), reinstituted personal rule and managed to weather some crises flexibly. Under his son Ieshige (1711-1761) the councillors of the shogunate again held power. One of the most interesting of them, Tanuma Okitsugu (1719-1788) introduced bribery, currency debasement, liberalized concepts about what individuals might do, and new opportunities for people. His brilliant, corrupt improvisation seemed to work until 1783-1787, years of famine and other disasters that culminated in a three-day rebellion in Edo itself. By 1790 Tanuma had been dismissed and died, a more rigid and prudent leadership was in, and the Haikai Revival was done.

This brief sketch shows how linked poetry managed to thrive. Renga reached its peak in anarchy and violence. Bashō lived under repression. Buson basked under a liberalized policy. It cannot be wondered that Sōgi should describe himself "immersed in the transshifting of dream and reality"; that Bashō should be overcome by "thoughts of life and death, the subservience of the weak to the powerful, mutability, and swift time"; or that aesthetic exploration and intelligent observation should matter so much more to Buson. Neo-Confucianism had remarkably little effect on the practice of linked poetry, although it did tend to rule out women and establish poets in houses with disciples loyal to masters. It enters much more into the plays of Chikamatsu Monzaemon (1653-1724). His characters are caught in a conflict between giri or duty (to superiors) and ninjō, human feeling. Even Chikamatsu resolves the dilemma in Buddhist terms. Perhaps nothing testifies better to the prosaic nature of Confucianism than the steadfast indifference to it shown by Japanese poets. Or perhaps one should say the testimony bears on the debt of linked poetry to its waka origins. The ages-old Shinto delight in a pure world continued to be enriched by Buddhism. Of these two elements, Shinto changes relatively little. Buddhism does change, and for any given believer the question arises of the congeries of emphasis and selection making up the belief.

A central tenet of all schools of Mahayana Buddhism, the dominant kind in Japan and China, is that the things of the phenomenal world hold no existence in themselves. This is the doctrine of the Void: "śūnyatā"; Japanese "kū," the character for sky and emptiness.[1] Late in the twelfth century, waka poets begin to draw on this doctrine to express new aspects of human experience and to deepen those already familiar. A descriptive symbolism emerged with ideals of loneliness (sabi), of mystery and depth (yūgen), and ethereal beauty (yōen). The result gave attraction to the humble and an overwhelming sense of the Void and of dream.[2] The long attested Buddhist sense of the evanescence and insubstantiality of things (mujōkan) took on intensified meaning during Sōgi's lifetime, when violence and upheaval were daily realities. Apparently despair is a luxury available only to those who live in somewhat less terrible times or is the lot of those who suffer the dire fate of totally impossible times. Instead of despair, the renga poets give us a sense of suffering and even an aesthetic of sorrow.

The idea of mujō insists that nothing remains as it is. The idea of the Void holds that all existence is the same and lacks substance. Konishi Jin'ichi gives an example: "Without birds there are no desks, and without water there is neither brightness or heat." These are not causal propositions, since cause involves karma. Rather, they tell us that nothing has substance, and existence derives from relation (kankei). "Moreover, be-

---

[1] This part of the discussion of Buddhism and poetry draws on Konishi, Sōgi, pp. 120-22. See Abbreviated References, pp. xvii-xviii for such curtailed citations.

[2] See Court Poetry, pp. 236-71.

cause such constituents and their causes [birds, desks, and what causes each] do not exist as any fixed entities, all existence lacks substantial character, and all existence is only 'relation.' That all existence possesses only relation is expressed in Buddhist terminology as 'dependence and interdependence' [soe-sōkan]."[3] Most of us would think such Buddhist ideas to have an epistemological basis requiring the premise of subject and object. But, as renga shows, the Void and mujō are taken as conditions of the world itself:

Shimo oku nohara	Wide fields settling with the frost
aki wa kurekeri	autumn has reached toward its end
naku mushi no	the insects cry out
kokoro to mo naku	but without regard for such desires
kusa karete	the grasses wither

Autumn is known by its relation to frost, which is explained by the insects' sounds. All passes: autumn, frost, the grasses, insects.

Relation—dependence and interdependence—is of special relevance to linked poetry. "When we think that all exists in dependence and interdependence, we understand that without the whole there can be no part, and that the part is not distinct from the whole."[4] As Yoshimoto said, "In renga connection [kakari] comes first. Connection is its poetry. Its poetry is connection." Do not all wholes have parts and are not all parts aspects of a whole? Yes, but let us consider for a moment. Yeats's "Sailing to Byzantium" is made of several stanzas, like *The Faerie Queene*. But the stanzas lead in a *continuous* semantic order, joining the first with the fifth and with others yet more remote. The first and the fifth stanzas of a renga have no continuous semantic relation: their conditions will differ, their speakers will differ, their characters will differ, their times and places will differ. To presume, with such things in mind, that the first and the fifth exist only by relation means something far more radical.

The relation, the interdependence and dependence, are founded on sequential presence (two stanzas in the same sequence). The relation also depends on such things as rules of continuance and discontinuance, sheets of paper and sides, moon and flower stanzas, timely appearance of love stanzas, and much else. The sequence itself is one in which two stan-

---

[3] Konishi, *Sōgi*, p. 121.   [4] *Ibid*.

zas join to predicate at any given time, with the identity of those two changing, and the predication of a given stanza differing as it is joined to its predecessor or joined by its successor. The idea of essential character or hon'i governs and relates also, since everything important must be essential in this sense. The haze at the beginning of *Three Poets* tells us essentially of spring, and each stanza thereafter tells us essentially of something that is added. But what is essential at each stage is not substantial and acquires existence solely from complex relation.

Such thought is human thought and is therefore inconsistently held. A medieval French monk faithfully chronicling his order and the saints it had produced has, in one sense, jeopardized his salvation by removing his mind from love of God. The rest of us who are nominally Christians spend much of our time as if the Sermon on the Mount did not exist. We know the renga masters also intermitted. In acquainting us with the Void, they use essentially chosen words that give us a sense of something very like substantial worlds. It should not be assumed that every reference to the sky in Japanese poetry is a figuralist term for the Void, any more than every tree in Western literature represents the cross of Jesus or is a "Freudian symbol." It must be said as well that haikai often seems to lead us farther from the Void by its crowding of the world with people and objects. But there is also Bashō's blue heron dreaming at noon. The sense of the Void, without being a didactic postulation at every point, is crucial to the art of linked poetry.

Linked poetry rose to greatness at a time when Zen Buddhism flourished. In general, renga probably emphasized the ideas associated with the doctrine of the Void more than did haikai, whereas haikai of Bashō's and some other kinds drew more on Zen Buddhism. For example, Bashō was connected with Butchō, as we have seen, and when he read Chinese poetry he read it in editions prepared by Zen monks. (The situation alters after Bashō.) The monks took great pains to avoid introducing Buddhism into poetry that was written with other emphases, but "despite their cares, the spiritual condition resulting from training in Zen was bound to be manifested in some form, however indirectly."[5] The manifestations involve two quite different aspects of haikai. One con-

[5] Konishi, "Image and Ambiguity," pp. 57-58. It is striking that Chinese poets were far less affected by Buddhism than were Japanese, and that the reverse is true with Confucianism.

cerns imagery. In the handling of imagery Bashō sometimes seems to make little logical sense.

Shizukasa ya	The quiet is entire
iwa ni shimiiru	into the boulders penetrates
semi no koe	the cries of cicadas

This familiar hokku derives from that long-standing Japanese aesthetic precept: that a given state is most like itself and most appealing when modified by something else. The rim of a round tea bowl satisfies as roundness only by a dent at one point or by coloring differing from that predominating. It would be difficult to argue logically that silence comes only when cicadas make their long sustained, rasping sounds. Yet we see that to be the case when we put the hokku in its proper context. In *The Narrow Road*, Bashō and Sora go out of their way at one point to see Ryushaku Temple.

> It was still afternoon when we arrived. Arranging with the priests for temple lodgings at the foot of the mountain, we ascended the slope to the temple proper. The mountain seemed to be built up of rocks upon boulders. The pines and oaks were manifestly old, and the very stones and earth, lying under their smooth shroud of moss, gave off an atmosphere of great age. The doors of the temple pavilion up there on the rocks were all barred. There was not so much as a sound. Coasting around the brink of the grounds, as if we were creeping over the stones, we worshipped after a fashion at the temple, but it was the scenery that struck stillness in our hearts, purifying them from worldly defilement.

> In seclusion silence
> shrilling into the mountain boulders
> the cicadas' cries.

"There was not so much as a sound."[6] This is false. The insects rasp so loudly that their cries bore into boulders. That is also false, impossible. It *is* true that Ryushakuji means Temple of Standing Stones.

The quiet that assists in purifying their hearts is conditional upon

[6] The text is from *Poetic Diaries*, pp. 179-80.

sound. The hokku is predicated on the existence of the prose before it, as if it were a joined stanza, tsukeku, in a haikai. "Only connect," said Yoshimoto and (centuries later) E. M. Forster. "Existence is defined by relation," said the Buddhists. Certainly the meaning is impoverished by separation. The appropriateness of a silence heightened by sound joins two seemingly conflicting things, and, although the joining depends on no particular Zen doctrine or precept, Bashō's familiarity with Zen Buddhism makes such relations feasible. In Freudian terms, the connection is subconscious, made at some "deeper level" of our minds. In terms of current knowledge of the brain, this conjunction is typical of the right cerebral hemisphere, which functions by appositions rather than by those true-false propositions of the left hemisphere. The left is also the language hemisphere, and the right the hemisphere dealing with forms and place (as with Bashō and Sora, perched with some danger on the margin of the temple). To connect apposition with proposition and gestalt with words, as we do all the time, involves the cooperation of the two hemispheres. A similar process occurs in the metaphor-making of Western poetry. The difference is one only of degree, of slight stress. Western poets typically choose to make a somewhat more definite propositional, left-hemispheric matter of metaphor. Japanese poets typically choose to make more of a right-hemispheric matter of it, allowing for more possibility and worrying less over ambiguity. As a result, as Konishi Jin'ichi points out, it is often impossible to identify the exact tenor of Japanese figurative language, what an image "really stands for."[7] The mute right hemisphere insists that the linguistic translation by the left does not adequately convey what it knows, and we are left quite literally to know in that episode things that cannot be known by words, as in fact we do all the time.

What is true of metaphor is particularly true of Japanese metaphor, and what is true of Japanese metaphor is particularly true of Bashō's metaphor. We know for a fact, however, that the right-hemispheric gestalt was very slow in coming for him. He was, after all, working out of the logic of empirical reality. What he actually wrote on the day he visited Ryushaku Temple was:

[7] Konishi, "Image and Ambiguity," p. 15 and Ch. 8. But the whole essay bears on such matters.

Yamadera ya   The mountain temple
ishi ni shimitsuku   its stones are struck and pierced
semi no koe   by cicadas' cries

The whole appositional, non-propositional point of silence earned from sound has not yet been grasped by Bashō himself, as he works within the grounds of propositional knowledge. He tried two other versions. They also did not begin with silence, but with sadness and rocks: "Sabishisa no / iwa ni . . ." and "Sabishisa ya / iwa ni. . . ." It should not be thought that the process toward silence involves Bashō reaching enlightenment, satori. But the result does seem very much in one Zen mode of thought. And it certainly relates to his injunctions about composition: "One must first of all concentrate one's thought on the object. Once one's mind achieves a state of concentration and the space between oneself and one's object has disappeared, the essential nature of the object can be perceived. The moment one achieves this perception, it must be expressed in words. If one ponders it, the essential nature will vanish from the mind."[8]

Bashō is not saying that one can be a poet without arduous preparation and constant practice. He does not say that the profound insight rules out revision that may make the mediocre great. In fact, he does not pronounce on a division of emphasis between the two major kinds of Zen Buddhism in Japan. The Rinzai tends to confront the world and the self and thereby resolve all doubts in one grand feat of mind. The Sōtō tends to arrive at profundity gradually as one cultivates oneself in all the humble actions of daily life. The difference is that between rapid enlightenment (tongo) and gradual enlightenment (zengo). Since both are but versions of a single process, both emphasize the need to carry on normal human activity, including the daily tasks involved in keeping a monastery working.

If Bashō was assisted by Butchō of the Rinzai sect, he would have sought sudden enlightenment, perhaps as at that moment when "the scenery . . . struck a stillness in our hearts" at Ryushaku Temple. On the other hand, the working out of the hokku was clearly a matter of "gradual enlightenment." "Half priest, half lay," he worked back and

---

[8] *Ibid.*, pp. 64–65, slightly modified. See pp. 3–13 for a discussion of Buddhist matters related to this.

forth in both worlds, often with tension. His late style seems to have arisen from a number of personal crises and from doubt about the sabi ideal he had been propounding. If he had once had sudden enlightenment, more light was needed. He did say that the new style that he called light in another sense was not as plain as it looks. He asked his friends to read stanzas in that style carefully until they grasped what they were about.[9] Much as he had worked over his own stanza composed at Ryushaku Temple?

The second major feature of haikai that responds to Zen Buddhism is its emphasis on the secular world. This is very unlike the Tendai Buddhism we see in *The Tale of Genji* and many other earlier writings. Earlier kinds had tended to emphasize reclusion, austerities, rites, magic, and such pious acts as writing out sutras, or even repeating some address to the Buddha. Both major kinds of Japanese Zen Buddhism emphasized that after enlightenment, whether sudden or gradual, one was to take a religious self into the dust of this world to aid others. Bashō felt strong attachment to the old idea of reclusion, and he liked to think of himself—especially in swarming Edo—as a person who had thrown away the world (yosutebito). But we have seen that he was a driven hermit, almost always on the go.

Sōan ni	For a little while
shibaraku ite wa	he remains at his hermitage
uchiyaburi	then breaks off again

So his twenty-ninth stanza in *Throughout the Town*. Or we can also recall his deathbed advice to his disciples: "Attain a high stage of enlightenment and return to the world of common men."[10] The imperative derives from Zen Buddhism, which is very practical. When Konishi Jin'ichi was living for a time at a Zen temple in Tokyo, just after the ravages of the Second World War, he asked the head priest about the central tenet of the faith. The answer was no kōan as to one hand clapping. It was: "Live a better life today than yesterday." By returning to the world to lead a good life, one assists one's fellows to find their enlightenment.

Bashō was not a priest, and his religious ideas seem to have involved

[9] *Ibid.*, pp. 69-70.

[10] Makoto Ueda, *Zeami, Bashō, Yeats, Pound* (The Hague: Mouton, 1965), pp. 63-64.

some hesitations. But there is a sense in which his haikai seek to accommodate enlightenment and the world. It would be wrong to say that the two are always there, or that the presence of one either implies or denies the presence of the other. But haikai more than renga represents the ordinary world more fully. An abundance of things and people distinguishes haikai from renga, where, besides the speaker, there is seldom more than one other person, such as a lover. Yet Bashō's world was one under great political repression, and his resignation of his samurai status could not have given him any merit in the minds of the authorities. So he took a walking trip. Then another, and yet others, expecting he would not return.

> The months and days are the wayfarers of the centuries, and as yet another year comes around, it also turns traveler. Sailors whose lives float away as they labor on boats, horsemen who encounter old age as they draw the horse around once more by the bit, they also spend their days in travel and make their home in wayfaring. Over the centuries many famous men have met death on the way; and I, too, though I do not know what year it began, have long yielded to the wind like a loosened cloud and, unable to give up my wandering desires, have taken my way along the coast.

So *The Narrow Road* begins.[11] So Bashō went on foot, or so he went in mind, taking his steps in the stanzas of kasen.

Buson does not seem to have suffered from the sense of the Void or from the tension Bashō engendered in himself during an age of repression. In his liberalized era, hopes could run higher, and along with occasional jollity one discovers a clear freshness in his haikai. Most people seem to recall his poetry as something more static than in fact it is. His verbs are commonly active ones. What is called his stasis is really a full realization, the result of his composure. In choosing some hokku that I personally like, I begin with one showing his peculiar humor and end with one of his most famous.

Yuku haru ya	Spring reaches its end
senja o uramu	the poet resents the anthologist
uta no nushi	who would not select him
★	★

11 *Poetic Diaries*, p. 157.

Kusa kasumi	Plants fill with haze
mizu ni koe naki	and in the waters only quiet
higure kana	twilight everywhere
★	★
Yuku fune ya	The boat goes off
aki no hi tōku	those days of autumn grow
narimasaru	ever more distant
★	★
Haru no mizu	The waters of spring
yama naki kuni o	through a landscape without hills
nagarekeri	they flow slowly on
★	★
Haru no umi	The sea in spring
hinemosu notari	rising the livelong day
notari kana	falling and rising

One can see where these stanzas might come in a sequence. The second and the last are true opening stanzas. The fourth would make a first-class third stanza (daisan). The humorous first stanza belongs in the development section (9-30), especially toward the beginning of the front of the second sheet (19-30). The third would be ideal either as the last stanza of an autumn sequence with a moon stanza or at the beginning of the fast close (about stanza 31). If such remarks seem obscure or perverse, let me invite the reader to return to them after studying the sequences in the next two parts.

In such brief fashion have we considered renga in terms of an aesthetic of the Void, Bashō's kind of haikai in terms of religion and tension, and Buson's style in terms of examples and their places in a sequence. The point is surely that only a dead art is unchanging. Yet the sense of the Void hovers in Bashō's world as well as Sōgi's. Buson often creates a tension of aesthetic elements. And the renga masters frequently write beautiful poetry, with Sōgi a master over effects of haze. Apart from such sharings or exceptions, there are distinctive qualities about linked poetry set against the rest of world literature. Inevitably it proves hard to disentangle what is Japanese about Japanese linked poetry from what is linked about Japanese linked poetry. But we can try, and since the close relation of linked poetry to waka has been stressed, we can try to consider the two linked kinds as far as possible on their own terms.

We must recall features of the canons of linked poetry, those things it takes twenty years to master. They include: the three-part rhythm of preparation-development-fast finale (jo-ha-kyū), topics and subtopics, the number of stanzas one may or must use to continue a topic, the number of stanzas that must intervene before repeated use, the number of moon and flower stanzas per sheet or side, and various categories of connection between stanzas.[12] Such elements have a number of functions, but the most important is unmistakably the defining of the integrity of a sequence. Simple sequence alone has no meaning, as if we were to scramble all the words of *The Tale of Genji*. The words would still come to us in a sequence, since sustained verbal expression can be known only in time, but the sequence known would be gibberish except for random conjunctions and purely accidental reproduction of the original. The integrity ensured by the conventions of linked poetry includes certain cognitive elements that are essential to all literature: beginning and ending, parts in that stipulated whole, and knowledge that our proceeding from a given beginning to a given ending entails a purposive order.

Presuming, therefore, from various evidence of conventions that linked poetry provides directed, non-random sequence, we may concern ourselves with sequentiality. All literature is sequential, because it cannot be known by its maker or its readers at one time, although it may be remembered, as memory serves, at a number of particular times. We expect narrative and dramatic creations to continue sequence for a length greater than those of lyrics. Narrative also has the possibility denied to drama and lyric of making plots yield *naturally* to sequence. Nothing is more natural than for narrative to interrupt plot, unless it be to tell events that are happening at the same time. There are, for example, portions of *The Tale of Genji* that are temporally coexistent with other portions in the plot. That is perfectly reasonable, since different events may happen at the same time, providing only that they happen to different people in

---

[12] I have felt the categories of connection to be omissible, because they relate somewhat more to composition than understanding in reading. Also, to include all would be to clutter what is already complicated. For discussion, however, see Konishi, *Sōgi*, pp. 89-95 and much in pp. 124-35. Some of the things I have omitted will be found in the very useful translation from *Sōgi* by Brazell and Cook: see Ch. 3, n. 2 (p. 59).

different places. Yet the author of that long prose narrative had to decide which of a given two simultaneous episodes she would place first in the sequence of telling. Because narration is as it were a single present event, it has only one event going on at any given moment of the reader's continuum. It can narrate two simultaneous plot events, but it cannot narrate them simultaneously. Sequence has a claim prior to plot and therefore must be thought more radical to literature than plot.

The question whether linked poetry is narrative necessarily intrudes at this point. Of course that depends on what one means by narrative. It is reasonably easy to distinguish narrative and lyric from drama, because, although both may be recited, neither is represented. The distinction leaves the puppet theatre (bunraku) a drama because of representation by manipulated puppets and either narrative or lyric because of separate recitation. Anyone who has heard such a reciter will know that narrative mingles with part-taking. The differences between lyric and narrative have proved excessively difficult to ascertain. The native Japanese word for "poem" is "uta," or "song," and the word for "prose narrative" or "story" is "monogatari," which means "relating things." That distinction helps some. But surely a more adequate distinction involves the centrality of the lyric speaker versus characters in narrative beyond the speaker / narrator and perhaps a lover addressed. To the extent that another character or characters become independent of the close dominance by the speaker, a poem or narrative takes on narrative qualities. (We have ruled out drama on other grounds of representation.)

It is a frequently observed literary fact that one of our sets is present as a dominant element and another as a subordinate: we may speak of genre and sub-genre or even at times of co-genre and counter-genre. The fact that we say that such-and-such a song is "dramatic" means (if it means anything other than our liking it), that although a lyric it has features akin to representation. Numerous Japanese lyrics, especially those in the early literary period, have strong narrative sub-genres: Hitomaro's great poem on seeing the body of a man among the stones on the shore of Samine is a splendid example. Japanese lyrics less often have a dramatic sub-genre, and when they do it is usually in poetic exchange or dialogue: Okura's affecting dialogue by a poor and a destitute man is the greatest example.[13]

[13] Hitomaro (fl. ca. 680-700) and Okura (?660-?733) are two of the major poets repre-

It is an Anglo-American prejudice to think that "dramatic" is intrinsic praise rather than mere description. If there is a comparable Japanese prejudice, it favors narrative after lyric. The readiest examples derive from *Tales from Ise*, very short episodes made up of poems by, or attributed to, Ariwara Narihira (825–880) and poetic responders, using a kind of brief prose continuo. Here is one such brief episode (the 123rd).

Formerly there was a man who, by degrees, grew tired of a woman who was living in Fukakusa [literally, Deep Grasses]. He sent her the following poem.

Toshi o hete	The years have passed
Sumikoshi sato o	And I must leave Fukakusa
Idete inaba	Where I have spent this time—
Itodo Fukakusa	To what extent will its deep grasses
No to narinan.	Turn into a rampant moor?

The woman replied,

No to naraba	If it becomes a moor,
Uzura to narite	I shall live on just like the quails
Nakioran	Crying plaintively,
Kari ni dani ni ya	But will you not come here again
Kimi wa kozaran.	If only for brief falcoming?

Taking great pleasure in seeing what she had written, he abandoned his inclination to leave her.

Surely the small number of people involved in the poem and its reply suggests to an Anglophone reader a "dramatic" cast to lyrics. On the other hand, the prose would seem to present a mini-narrative. The Japanese title for these lyric episodes is *Ise Monogatari*, *"Tales from Ise."* Narrative. In Japanese literature, lyric and narrative have an extraordinary affinity. This little episode begins, "Formerly there was a man" ("Mukashi otoko arikeri"). The very long *Tale of Genji*, *Genji Monogatari*, has a similar beginning, stressing time and person: "In what

sented in the *Man'yōshū*. Hitomaro's Samine poem and envoys are, in that collection, 2: 220-22; and Okura's *Dialogue* and envoy in 5: 892-93. For translations, see *Court Poetry*, pp. 97-98, 121-23; or *Introduction*, pp. 48-49, 59-61.

emperor's reign was it?" ("Izure no ōntoki ni ka?") This long, long narrative also has almost eight hundred poems complete and numerous bits of others with songs and allusions to, or quotations from, Chinese poetry. These are lyrics. The point is that in Japan—in China also, for that matter—prose narrative developed out of lyric poetry. Moreover, lyric poetry defined the basic aesthetic that narrative had to prove equal to—and modify.

The task is to relate these matters to linked poetry. Both renga and haikai came well after the emergence of prose narrative. Sōgi was born four centuries after the death of Murasaki Shikibu (c.978-c.1014), whom we believe to be author of *The Tale of Genji*. She died some three centuries after that great lyric poet, Hitomaro. Yet such early emergence of esteemed (prose) narrative after another genre—the lyric—had defined the basic poetics unique to Japan. In China as well, however, (prose) narrative develops out of lyric poetry, or alongside it, as is the case of historical prose narration. In neither country is there any evidence for an early narrative poetry resembling the Homeric or Germanic epics.

So much for the historical and generic matters. Linked poetry is a kind of narrative, both by Japanese affiliations and by the criteria we have been using. The only other alternative is to say that it is lyricism given a narrative sub- or co-genre. The problem is a very large one in Japanese literature, since it applies as well to integrated sequences of waka, whether in the lengthy imperial collections or in such waka sequences as of a hundred poems (hyakushuuta). Only two obstacles lie before one who would argue that linked poetry is narrative with a lyric sub-genre. One is the lyric character of the stanzas. The other is the common understanding that narrative requires a plot. Whatever else may be meant by plot, it is usually assumed that it involves logical continuance and development of characters, time, and place. "Logical" implies some kind of causality, contingency, or even chance. Inspection would show that many or most of the poetic diaries of travel written in Japan have minimal plot. The traveler encounters a succession of places and people, with none of whom a lasting connection can be established. *The Narrow Road* belongs to a category of what Bashō himself termed "diaries of the road."[14] Only

---

[14] In his *Essay from a Traveler's Book-Satchel* (*Oi no Kobumi*) in *Bashō Bunshū*, ed. Sugiura Shōichirō *et al.* (Iwanami Shoten, 1959), p. 53.

Bashō and Sora remain constant, and even the intermittently mentioned Sora leaves toward the end. We encounter a sequence of episodes ordered by the actual succession of places visited by Bashō, with varying license for artistic effect. And the prose has, interspersed in it, lyric poems that interrupt the prose sequence to heighten its affective qualities. It may be added that many important works of the court period come down to us with three highly different designations: diaries (nikki) tales (monogatari), and poetic collections (kashū, -shū). Can there be another tradition in world literature so likely to stymy the Western critical computer?

Of course the possession of minimal plot is not the same as having no plot, although it also differs from being highly plotted. Perhaps we can find greater clarification by inquiring into the lyric genesis of narrative in Japan, both in plot kinds and in solely sequence kinds. It is generally agreed that what the Japanese term "tsukurimonogatari," that is, prose fiction, develops in parallel with "utamonogatari," "tales of poems," such as the episode given above in *Tales from Ise*. Also, the generative process of narrative growing from lyric with prose interludes can be found in *The Records of Ancient Matters* (*Kojiki*) and *The Records of Japan* (*Nihongi*) as well as in *The Narrow Road*. Because lyric poetry defines normatively and even descriptively what literature is over so many centuries, any kind of esteemed narrative would have to develop from the lyric. Now that the great classics of Chinese prose fiction are being re-translated with their abundance of poems, it has become possible to see that much the same thing happens in China. In classical Japanese prose fiction (tsukurimonogatari) and Chinese the prose has come to dominate, and with it so does plot.

Renga and haikai link lyric stanzas, without prose continuo, into sequential narrative. *One Hundred Stanzas by Three Poets at Minase* could almost be called *Tales from Minase* (*Minase Monogatari*). The total absence of prose ligatures makes a crucial difference, and the true model for the renga lay in the one-hundred-poem sequence of waka. But in renga the art of connecting is more highly developed than it had been in the waka sequences. There still is no plot. Some people have assumed that the integration of waka, whether in imperial collections or in shorter sequences, implies that a plot had been made. Plot is, however, wholly infeasible. The speaker and any other character change with each poem or stanza. Times change. and places. Yet the continuance can be wholly satisfying, and what satisfies is precisely "lyric" and plotless—that is, sequential—narration.

The achievement of sequential narrative seems to have been founded on a factor making the possibility of greatness even more precarious than usual. Linked poetry appears to be an unstable art. The factor making it genuinely feasible is multiple authorship at a sitting. There are exceptions, even among the sequences included here, to such composition. But such was the rule. It required not only that all the poets participating be capable of creating great poetry but also that they know each other's ways well enough to do so together. It seems significant that after his frequent composition of weak stanzas in *Three Poets* Sōchō should have revived for the far superior renga composed later at Yunoyama. Yet how often could such poets who knew each other well and who were so gifted be assembled? Even knowing each other well could pose problems, since there was a constant temptation (we know this because it was yielded to) for poets to compose impressive stanzas rather than seek to create impressive sequences. We see this with some of the best poets—Shinkei and Buson, for example. They heightened the *lyric* quality of individual stanzas while threatening the *narrative* properties of the sequence. A few great poets managed this most difficult art, and usually they had at their center a Sōgi or a Bashō as a kind of conductor able to work out a musical narrative. Otherwise we can say that as linked versifying is easy, so greatness is proportionally difficult of attainment.

The idea that linked poetry gives us sequential narrative finds confirmation in the parallel between its development and that of plot narrative in several literary traditions. It is possible to differentiate between renga and haikai by labeling the one romance and the other realism. Neither term really fits, but together they make the crucial distinction in attitude. In renga the poets and we consider the world of the lyric narrative to be at times like ours but is usually superior. As I have been at pains to emphasize, haikai is particularly difficult, and at times can rise very high or sink very low. But its genius is to keep "below" renga without yet "falling" into the disgusting or the merely humorous. If we allow for the spatial metaphor of a horizon shared by the poets and the reader, the world of renga typically lies above and that of haikai below.

Haikai obviously represents the innovation in all this. Before it, that which was inferior to the poet and ourselves had no more importance in narrative poetry than it did in England before the eighteenth century. That to which we deem ourselves superior can of course be accepted by traditional societies: on the condition that it be comic or satiric. One may recall the would-be bard at Ominato in *The Tosa Diary* and the marvelous Lady from Omi in *The Tale of Genji*. But Japan has less comedy and satire and parody in its older literature than do most Western national traditions. If there is a problem in treating the "low" seriously, Buson saves himself by selecting and refining aesthetically. To admit, as does Bashō, the humor and real lowness of an inferior world and yet to regard that world as truly serious probably requires either a very complex or a very sane mind. It also constitutes a revolution.

Bashō represents an achievement of Edo literature that is remarkable, one he shares with his two contemporaries, Ihara Saikaku and Chikamatsu Monzaemon. All three were involved in creating a literature of full seriousness out of what was inferior in attitude. This has many complexities and some exceptions, but simple comparison will show how centrally true it is. Bashō's stanzas need only be compared with Sōgi's, Saikaku's prose fiction with *The Tale of Genji* or *The Tale of the Heike*, and Chikamatsu's plays with the nō by Zeami. It is remarkable that one generation should have produced masters of the "lower" in all three kinds. It is also remarkable that this change should anticipate by fifty to one hundred years the birth of the novel in England. The novel was born only when the higher attitude of prose romance and heroic verse narrative by Milton and Dryden yielded to the inferior attitude of Defoe, Richardson, and Fielding. It is significant that not only their contemporaries but those of Austen, Dickens, and Joyce should have considered their work "low" or "comic."

That the alteration from renga to haikai parallels that from the romance to the novel testifies better than anything else to the fact that linked poetry offers narrative. Chikamatsu represented plots on the stage and Saikaku related plots in books. Sōgi, Bashō, and their fellows offered narrated but plotless sequences of lyrics on their sheets. Their narratives are not only sequential but made from lyric constituents, from brief stanzas. It is a very special achievement and therefore holds special interest for comparative and theoretical study as well as for intrinsic appeal.

Haikai steers the more difficult course. It dare not forsake the low any more than may senryū or the usual Western epigram. But it also dare not commit itself to the senryū world. It is an *enfant terrible*, an extraordinary yet less-well-favored child of a brilliant, famous parent. Renga gave it birth and a rich endowment. But haikai must leave its parent without deserting it. In that respect at least, renga is the easier art to practice. Haikai runs prodigious risks, gaining success only by realizing as had never been done—in lyric narrative—the "realistic" and "novelistic" possibilities of sequentiality. Its freedom from plot helped break the shackles of romance. In freeing the enchanted lady with its tin trumpet, it may show her to be a wench—or a lovely girl. But the lyric element constituting this narrative, and which is inherited from renga as well as waka, enables the authors and ourselves to *care* for that wench (or girl) just as we had for the highborn lady. Is there another literature in the world in which lyric poetry should be the medium for narrating what prose does in the novel?

As Bashō trudged up and down the paths of Japan, he knew that he was walking in Sōgi's footprints. Where Sōgi spoke of his violent age in terms of another walker-by being taken off by mist and rain and twilight, Bashō wrote of the monkey-master and his charge. The haze of Sōgi will be seen more than once in the renga sequences that follow. In the haikai sequences, Bashō's forlorn master and monkey will be found swept up in time. They are also given a beauty that Sōgi would have recognized, as they make their humble way in the light of the autumn moon. It only remains for us to recognize this very unusual and wonderful achievement.

FIGURES

Figure 1. Details of a Hundred-Stanza Sequence

See also Chapter 3 and the Commentary in Part Two

For renga, there is one flower stanza per sheet and one moon stanza per side of a sheet, although the last may be omitted. The specifications below therefore apply more to haikai than to renga.

1-22	First Sheet (sho-ori)	
	1-8	Front (sho-omote): moon 7
	9-22	Back (sho-ura): moon 18; flower 21
23-50	Second Sheet (ni no ori)	
	23-36	Front (ni no omote): moon 35
	37-50	Back (ni no ura): moon 46; flower 49
51-78	Third Sheet (san no ori)	
	51-64	Front (san no omote): moon 63
	64-78	Back (san no ura): moon 74; flower 77
79-100	Fourth Sheet (nagori no ori)	
	79-92	Front (nagori no omote): moon 91
	93-100	Back (nagori no ura): moon omitted; flower 99

The stipulated places for moon and flower stanzas in haikai are often not used, but this nominal positioning shows that the last stanza but one on a side and a sheet are thought especially important. In renga the positioning of flower stanzas on a sheet and moon stanzas on a side is very much freer. In Parts Two and Three will be found actual examples showing degrees of variance.

FIGURE 2. THE JO-HA-KYŪ RHYTHM

(In practice, the Jo and Kyū tend to encroach on the Ha in renga and haikai.)

A. *The one-hundred-stanza pattern (see Figure 1)*

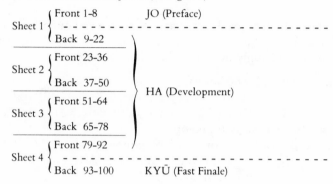

B. *Nō Plays*

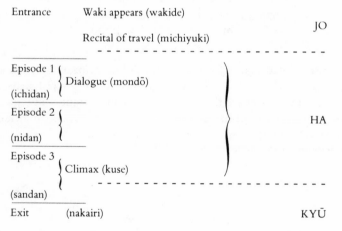

C. *The Thirty-Six Stanza Pattern (see Figure 5)*

FIGURE 3. A CLASSIFICATION TABLE FOR RENGA

See also Chapter 3 and the Commentary in Part Two

Title	Stanza Number									
		Poet								
Design/Ground										
Close/Distant										
Season/ Miscellaneous										
Travel, Grievance, Love, Evanescence, Buddhism, Shinto										
Persons, Birds, Insects										
Residences, Clothes										
Grasses, Trees, Cultivation										
Night, Radiance										
Falling Thing, Rising Thing										
Peaks, Waters										
Other										

FIGURE 4. A CLASSIFICATION TABLE FOR HAIKAI

See also Chapter 6 and the Commentary in Part Three

Title	Stanza Number	Poet							
Design/Ground									
Heavy/Light									
Season/ Miscellaneous									
Love, Grievance, Travel, Evanescence, Buddhism, Shinto									
Persons, Animals, Birds, Insects									
Residences, Clothes, Human Products									
Plants, Trees, Cultivation									
Night, Daytime, Radiance									
Nobility, Warriors, Peasants, Townspeople									
Peaks, Waters									
Other									

FIGURE 5. DETAILS OF A THIRTY-SIX STANZA SEQUENCE PARTICULARLY FOR HAIKAI

1-18   First Sheet (sho-ori)
    1-6   Front (sho-omote)

- -

    7-18   Back (sho-ura)

19-36 Second Sheet (nagori no ori)
    19-30 Front (nagori no omote)

- -

    31-36 Back (nagori no ura)

★   ★   ★

Names for Stanzas in Renga and Haikai

1st	——	hokku
2nd	——	waki
3rd	——	daisan
All others	——	hiraku
last	——	ageku (also a hiraku)

★   ★   ★

In a kasen certain stanzas are also given special names.
(See the parts specified above.)

    6 —— orihashi

- -

    7 —— shoku

    19 —— oritate
    30 —— ni no omote orihashi

- -

    31 —— shoku

Figure 6. Joined Poems, Stanzas, Verses

In Japan and China as well as in other countries poets of course may join poems in a series. The practice resembles renga and haikai composition only if it involves more than a single poet, only if it also involves disjunctive linking.

In Japan there were two kinds of joined stanzas or verses that went under the name of "rengu" ("ren" is Ueda 9325, Nelson 3713; "ku" as in "renku"). The basic kind of rengu involved two or more poets joining successive stanzas in Chinese verse. There was also a variation, wakan rengu (or kanwa rengu), in which Chinese verses and Japanese stanzas were joined in succession. Such practice goes back to Heian times, but it did not develop into a full-fledged art with the elaborate canons of true linked poetry. In fact, it has something of the air of great refinement or pedantry about it, and it clearly had no possibility of becoming a popular—or very widely understandable—poetic genre. (Today these kinds are also pronounced "renku.")

In China there was a more important practice of joined poems, "lien-chü." These also did not develop the canons of renga and haikai, but they sometimes engaged the talents of poets of importance. For a historical account and examples, see Stephen Owen, *The Poetry of Meng Chiao and Han Yü* (New Haven: Yale University Press, 1975), ch. 7.

PART TWO
TWO RENGA SEQUENCES

One Hundred Stanzas by Three
Poets at Minase

SŌGI, SHŌHAKU, AND   *(Minase Sangin Hyakuin)*
SŌCHŌ

JAPANESE who have read but one renga sequence have read the *Hundred Stanzas by Three Poets at Minase (Minase Sangin Hyakuin)*. And Japanese who remember no other lines from a renga still know those of the hokku:

Yuki nagara	Despite some snow
yamamoto kasumu	the base of bills spreads with haze
yūbe kana	the twilight scene

In fact, those who have studied renga prefer *A Hundred Stanzas by Three Poets at Yunoyama (Yunoyama Sangin Hyakuin)* and *A Hundred Stanzas on Person by Sōgi Alone (Sōgi Dokugin Nanibito Hyakuin)*. *Sōgi Alone* is given as the second sequence in this part, and something will be said in this introduction to *Three Poets* about *Yunoyama* as well. (The inconsistency in abbreviation is deliberate to help those without knowledge of Japanese keep the sequences in mind as distinct literary creations.)

Numerous people have read *Romeo and Juliet* or *Oliver Twist* who have not advanced much further into works by Shakespeare or Dickens, and so have never learned how much greater are *King Lear* or *Bleak House*. If that seems a pity, there is also an obligation for critics, especially those seeking to explain what is not well known, to include the more familiar along with the less. Konishi Jin'ichi makes very clear in his *Sōgi* how much he prefers *Sōgi Alone* and *Yunoyama* to *Three Poets*. And yet it is the last that he carefully sets forth. There is another advantage to beginning with it. It is somewhat less complex, and the lack of artistic maturity of

Sōchō—a stripling of forty at the time—produces certain weaknesses that enable us more easily to see what the strengths of renga may be.

Four years before Columbus arrived in the New World, in the very early spring of 1488, our three poets gathered to write this sequence. Sōgi's first stanza as usual faithfully refers to the time and scene before them. It is dusk. It is the 22nd day of the First Month (of a lagging lunar calendar), and some snow still lingers as the haze that represents spring makes its appearance. Sōgi is sixty-seven years old. To his hokku, the waki is added by Shōhaku, who is next in seniority at forty-five. The daisan is added by Sōchō, who is much liked by Sōgi but who has not yet acquired the skill he shows three years later in *Yunoyama*. The composition takes them about five or six hours, which means a stanza is written every three or three and a half minutes. Later they will make a fair copy and present it to the shrine of Emperor Gotoba, who had a palace in that area and who had come to be thought of as a patron divinity for poets. Sōgi appropriately weaves into his hokku an allusion to the Emperor's most famous poem, an allusion so apposite as almost to make one think their visit was deliberately timed so that they could see that dusk at spring which Gotoba had discovered, against most Japanese preferences, to equal that of autumn.

Miwataseba	As I look about,
Yamamoto kasumu	Where spring haze drifts below the hills
Minasegawa	Along Minase River,
Yūbe wa aki to	I wonder what could have made me think
Nani omoiken.	That autumn is the only time for dusk?

Sōgi builds half his stanza with words italicized in this poem (the 36th in the *Shinkokinshū*), written somewhat over two and a half centuries earlier.

In all likelihood, Sōgi later chose the fushimono—which is *hito*, "person" or "persons"—for a kind of title. As he sat with his two colleagues, they had to consider four pieces of paper. Each was folded, and they would be writing poems for the front and back of the outside portions of each sheet. Long before them, the method had been established for getting one hundred stanzas on the eight sides of four sheets. On the front of the first and the back of the last, they wrote eight stanzas, and on the six other sides fourteen each, giving eighty-four to add to the sixteen.

With each sheet the poets shift their order for composing stanzas. In *Three Poets*, the alternation used is the same for the first and third sheets, but the second and the fourth differ from each other as well as from the first and third.

1-22	Sōgi, Shōhaku, Sōchō	(ABC)
23-50	Shōhaku, Sōgi, Sōchō	(BAC)
51-78	Sōgi, Shōhaku, Sōchō	(ABC)
79-100	Sōchō, Shōhaku, Sōgi	(CBA)

The comparable *Yunoyama* sequence does not follow that pattern. In it, the order of composition is the same in the first and fourth sheets, with the second and third differing.

1-22	Shōhaku, Sōchō, Sōgi	(ABC)
23-50	Sōchō, Sōgi, Shōhaku	(BCA)
51-78	Sōgi, Shōhaku, Sōchō	(CAB)
79-100	Shōhaku, Sōchō, Sōgi	(ABC)

Both schemes of composition allow for order to a degree and alteration to a degree, so representing the larger genius of renga. Both schemes ensure that the composer of the hokku will write thirty-four stanzas and his two fellow poets thirty-three, so yielding the hundred stanzas sought. As all this shows, varied possibilities exist within which the poets may work out both the expected and the novel.

The sheets-side arrangement has a further importance in giving a sequence wholeness and making possible the jo-ha-kyū rhythm. In *Three Poets*, a simple explanation of the kyū can be given in terms that will also illuminate features of the earlier two divisions. One of the chief means of contrasting runs of stanzas is the use of seasonal or miscellaneous (non-seasonal) topics in runs of length that vary from the possible minimum of one to five or six or more. To the Japanese, the seasonal seem more "objective" and *in general* more appealing; the miscellaneous stanzas seem more "subjective" and in general to deal more directly with human affairs such as Love, Grievances, Buddhism, etc. After we have had a number of Seasonal stanzas, we therefore expect to come to a run of Miscellaneous, wondering if it will concern Love or be simply Miscellaneous, with no subtopic. Conversely, a run of Miscellaneous stanzas arouses the expectation of Seasonal stanzas.

The front of the fourth sheet begins with three Seasonal stanzas (spring, 79-81) that are quite attractive and that use up (81) the fourth flower. Five Miscellaneous stanzas follow on Love and then Grievances (82-86). The front concludes with six stanzas (87-92) with natural imagery but with strong coloring of human affairs. Certain other elements are also deployed.

87 Miscellaneous in mountains or hills; pines; human misery
88 Miscellaneous at an ocean bay; greater misery
89 Autumn at seashore, miseries of Travel
90 Autumn in the mountains
91 Autumn in the plains
92 Miscellaneous in the plains

Certain other details must be mentioned

87 —
88 Named Place, Bay of Uruwa
89 —
90 Moon stanza
91 —
92 Named Place, Great Moor of Ada

The postponement of the moon stanza to a point so near its last possible position, stanza 92, begins to arouse expectations, and with the shift to autumn in 89 we know that we can expect it in one of the next two stanzas. The situation of 91 and 92 in moors or plains stresses these places and makes the named place of 92 perhaps less important evocatively in some respects but also useful in making us look ahead to the back sheet, with questions whether we shall have seasonal or miscellaneous poems, so giving us some "speed."

Sōgi begins the back of the last sheet with a Miscellaneous stanza (93) and the word "dream" (yume), which therefore cannot be expected again, so giving a further sense of moving to an end. In 94 Sōchō echoes Sōgi's concern with the past, but adds the present, so moving along. In

95 Shōhaku introduces the future when the Buddha will return. In 96 Sōgi translates that hope into splendid spring imagery. In 97 Sōchō "hurries on" with a question about how many frosty nights, and in 98 Shōhaku gives at once a slowing (with an image of smoke rising peacefully) and a quickening (it happens at a temporary dwelling). The requisite minimum of three spring stanzas has been given, and, when 99 is miscellaneous, we know that we have reached the end of alternations and the sequence.

By such means are renga sequences fitted into integral creative patterns. The experience of the reader, and particularly of the reader to whom renga is a novelty, will not be so much one of stanzas as of striking integers. That is beginner's luck. Because, to the best readers of renga, and to the composing poets themselves, the immediate concern involves tsukeku, stanza connection. Such connections are conceptual as well as verbal (if such a distinction may be drawn). For example, in the jo or preface of *Three Poets*, in its first eight stanzas, which everyone agrees are above any reach of fault-finding, the first three are on the topic of spring, the next is a Miscellaneous stanza enabling us smoothly to skip summer, and in 5-7 smoothly to progress to autumn. The eighth is Miscellaneous. Within the three autumn stanzas there must be ways of accounting for stanzaic connection that retain what is essential but that also vary and therefore advance the sequence. One possible means is the introduction of such subtopics as Love or Travel, but in fact they do not enter in 5 to 7. Another means involves the use of motifs. The three stanzas "move" in such a fashion as follows.

5. Autumn. Night. Radiance. Rising Thing (mist).
6. Autumn. Falling Thing (frost).
7. Autumn. Insects. Plants.

The Night category of 5 would probably be day by Western standards, since dawn or daybreak is meant. In 6 we have a daylight scene as autumn "grows dark" or heads toward its end. We do not classify it as day, however, partly because the category is not used, and partly for the classification to be employed we would need some word or essential conception designating day, e.g., "asa," "morning." Still, we have knowledge that it is day—and later than 5—because the imagery of frost on fields is visual. Because frost was closely associated with plants and plants with insects, the 7th stanza introduces imagery of plants withering (with the frost of 6) and insects crying in the plants as frost promises their end as much as autumn's in 6.

Such relations particularly involve the techniques of progression and association used in waka sequences—that is, those alterations in degrees of impressiveness and closeness of relation which have been explained in Chapter 3. The matter of relatedness is perhaps the most important and most difficult. Because each stanza after the first and before the last functions twice, its meaning may vary considerably. Even in the usual Close-Distant or Distant-Close relation, a stanza has its meaning determined by connection with its predecessor and then acts to help determine the meaning of its successor. The degree of determination varies with closeness or remoteness of connection, but it varies by other means as well, and some help is needed to understand the relatedness itself. In fact there are numerous named kinds of connection that I have decided to omit on the grounds that they are likely to confuse more than to clarify this discussion. Of the thirteen kinds set forth by Konishi (*Sōgi*, pp. 124-135), I have referred to two, connection by diction (kotobazuke) and connection by conception (kokorozuke). In the commentary I shall be glancing at three other kinds. These may involve allusion to a foundation poem (honka), which may join two stanzas but never run through three. The poems alluded to are waka, not renga. The use of a foundation story (honzetsu) functions as with the allusion to an earlier poem, except that no words will be borrowed from the original. This is therefore somewhat more conceptual, atmospheric. The third is the use of place-names (nadokoro). If one stanza concerns cherry-blossoms, the next may be joined by mentioning Yoshino, which was famous as a place to see those flowers.

Any study of this kind is certain to number among its readers a few who are intimately acquainted with renga. For them, the pleasure of recognition will sometimes be tempered with the displeasure of disagreement. I have yet to encounter a book on renga that excited universal agreement or that did not have demonstrable mistakes, and this will be no exception. For readers of all kinds, then, the commentary on *Three Poets* provides what is essentially an education in linked poetry. Thereafter we assay to use our education. To follow the commentary on the left-hand pages, it may be useful to look at Figure 3 to refresh the memory concerning the various categories and alternatives. But there follows a sample that shows how the table can be used, including the usual Japanese abbreviations of the poets' names:

Gi = Sōgi
Haku = Shōhaku
Chō = Sōchō

Under two ruled lines, there are the following categories: impressiveness, closeness of relation; main topic (Season, Miscellaneous), any subtopic (Travel, etc.); Motifs (Persons, Birds, Insects; Residence, Clothes; Plants, Trees, Cultivation; Night, Radiance; Falling/Rising Things; Peaks, Waters); and an open category, Other (such as indication that it is the fourth moon stanza, or dream, or Named Place, etc.). Here are the results for the three autumn stanzas, 5-7, on the front of the first sheet of *Three Poets*.

The method of presentation used for *Three Poets* will be followed for *Sōgi Alone* and for the haikai sequences. Something should therefore be said of it. On the right-hand page, the reader will find romanized Japanese, with a number for the stanza appearing next to the first line of the *added* stanza, along with a translation and the poet's name. Here, for example, is stanza four with five introduced as we first have it in the sequence,

	Fune sasu oto mo	Daybreak comes on distinctly
	shiruki akegata	with sounds of a punted boat
5	tsuki ya nao	does not the moon
	kiriwataru yo ni	of a fog-enveloped night
	nokoru ran	stay yet in the sky
	Shōhaku	

On the left-hand page will be given various categories such as have been discussed and some brief comment. Here, for example, is the commentary on Sōchō's 6th stanza as it appears to the left of the text and translation given above.

6. Ground. Close-Distant. Autumn. Falling Thing.
The stanza has commonplace imagery and is syntactically fragmented,

Number	5	6	7
Poet	Haku	Chō	Gi
Design–Ground	Ground-Design	Ground	Design
Close–Distant	Close-Distant	Close-Distant	Close-Distant
Season Misc.	Autumn	Autumn	Autumn
Subtopic			
Persons Birds Insects			Insects
Residence Clothes			
Plants Trees Cultiv.			Plants
Night Radiance	Night, Radiance		
Falling Rising	Rising	Falling	
Peaks Waters			
Other	1st Moon stanza		Unnamed insects, once in 100 stanzas

but it fits well in the sequence, opposing a falling to a rising object and suggesting that the end of autumn made the moon more appreciated in 5.

My hope is that this method will enable a reader so inclined to ignore the commentary, and with all earnestness I invite anyone who has read the left-hand pages also to indulge himself or herself thereafter in the treat of going through the right-hand pages alone.

This introduction to *Three Poets* is necessarily longer than the rest, because it is here that we get our bearings. Let us conclude, then, by returning to questions of the larger integrity of this particular sequence. Most renga and haikai consist of about half Seasonal and half Miscellaneous stanzas. The proportion of Seasonal stanzas tends to be highest in the jo or prefatory unit, 1-8, as is certainly the case in *Three Poets*. Strongly human concerns such as Love, Grievances, and Buddhism are out of place in this first part, and it will be observed that the two Miscellaneous stanzas (4 and 8) are almost Seasonal season-less stanzas, since they contain imagery fitting well with Seasonal stanzas.

The long ha-development section from the back of the first sheet through the front of the fourth (9-92) introduces those human concerns which the preface avoided. But just as the last kyū-finale section begins a stanza (92) before the last side, so the first in the development section (9) continues the miscellaneous, quasi-seasonal emphasis of the preface. (Actually, the preface may be thought to continue through 10, but let us stay closer to the orthodox pattern.) There follow three more Miscellaneous, all three of them ground stanzas (10-12), like 9. After this plateau following the splendid things of the preface, we suddenly get three spring stanzas, 13 and 14 rising to Design status, and 15 falling to Ground. Such fluctuations assist in the sense of development.

We observe larger matters. All stanzas of the first sheet—including 1-8 as preface and 9-22 as first stage of development—use relatively Close relations between stanzas. There is none that is Distant, and Close-Distant predominates. This alters markedly in the second sheet, where both sides use much more distant relation, including eight Distant stanzas, a very high proportion, and a number of Distant-Close. Toward the end of the back side of the second sheet, however, the tendency is once again to Close and Close-Distant. The third sheet differs front and back. The front (51-64) is entirely intermediate (that is Distant-Close or

Close-Distant), except for its last stanza (64) which is Close and which prepares the way for the back (65-78) with its four Close and no Distant. The front of the fourth sheet (79-92) concludes the development section with a repetition of kinds on the front of the third sheet. That is, it is dominantly intermediate in relation of stanzas until towards the end; then there came three (88, 89, 92) of Close relation. The kyū-finale (again, in orthodox fashion, meaning 93-100) is also intermediate with a proportion of three Ground in eight (94, 95, 100). Only one stanza of Distant relation is used in the second half of the sequence, and that comes just halfway on (75). On the other hand, the distribution of full Design and full Ground stanzas is more even in the two halves: of twelve Design, seven are in the first half and five in the second; and of thirty-four Ground, twenty are in the first half and fourteen in the second. One can go on in this fashion, making numerous distinctions, but enough has been suggested to enable anyone who chooses to follow through in greater detail. A few other considerations may therefore claim attention.

Some remarks of critical assessment by Konishi Jin'ichi are worth attending to. At the end of the front of the second sheet he pauses to consider its emphases (Sōgi, p. 200). He remarks that in the former half Seasonal poems predominate, and as to Design or Ground emphasis, Design predominates. In the latter half, however, Miscellaneous stanzas predominate, with a Ground emphasis. He remarks on the imageless stanzas that conclude the side (33-36). At the close of the back of the second sheet, he remarks (p. 208) that on the front and the back there have been sixteen stanzas devoted to the subtopics of Grievances, Love, and Buddhism— and that eleven of those appear on the back—so intensifying there one of the major features of the lengthy development section. At the close of the front side of the third sheet he remarks (p. 215) that the side twice goes through scenery of the ocean and mountains, and that there is a strong emphasis on the experience of reclusive life, with the chief emphasis falling on a renga-like handling of the three seasons treated in *Three Poets*— spring, autumn, and winter. Konishi's appreciation (p. 222) is strongest at the end of the third sheet. Looking back to the front of that sheet, he remarks that it begins (in 51) with a kind of India ink painting and ends (in that very beautiful 78th stanza) with a loveliness that cannot be shown by a picture. Those stanzas which, on the whole, make the strongest appeal come on this sheet.

Throughout the sequence one is often lost in admiration at being able to move along so unexpectedly, and yet so naturally, that suspense can build as a flower stanza is awaited, or surprise can be caused by the early appearance of a moon stanza. The one thing that prevents *Three Poets* from becoming more than a masterpiece of renga, and in short a masterpiece of its literature and the world's, is Sōchō's performance. At times he measures up beautifully, but often he lapses into what Konishi terms his subjective tic. That involves stanzas without imagery and with directly expressed emotion that verges on the platitudinous or sentimental. On the other hand, it is fair to say that anyone who has heard *Three Poets* recited aloud (in Japanese, of course) knows that Sōchō's diction is especially pleasing to the ear. It may be that for renga purposes, it is too lovely, too much like that of waka. One symptom of Sōchō's "subjectivity" is his use of presumptive verb endings without much point. (They are the "-n" or "-mu" final inflections as in "ran," "sen," etc.) These do become a bore. His deflections enable us to appreciate the more his successes, and of course the incomparable art of Sōgi in stanza-relation, than whom renga never knew a greater master. Those who are familiar with his reputation will find it justified here and transcended in *Sōgi Alone*. In many ways, however, the happiest surprise is the performance by Shōhaku, who is not so often spoken of. Again and again he does the right thing, even if we had not known what that was. That means that when he follows Sōgi the results are wonderful. Following Sōchō is sometimes like trying to pick up potatoes from a burst bag and look charming for the photographer at the same time.

Konishi's final assessment (pp. 234-35) must excite general interest; it runs somewhat as follows. The front and the back sides of the first sheet are properly realized, with ability and appeal always appropriate. It is natural that the first eight stanzas should have been praised over the centuries as a model. This promise continues into the second sheet, but just before we get to the back, Sōchō's inadequacies become more noticeable. There is some failure in smoothness of development from the back of the second to the back of the third, which is a pity since this should demonstrate greatest interest in the sequence. With the last sheet, the succession is well managed, and with Sōchō's recovery we are left with the conviction that *Three Poets* is a masterpiece.

To conclude with my own responses, I think that others like myself with Western tastes are likely to find the ending decorous enough as to its topics but somewhat flat. If so, we must reflect that our standards are not universal. We can also return to the unquestioned delights of the front of the first sheet and the back of the third as well as to the steady variation, even when stanzas are less striking.

The text used is that of Konishi Jin'ichi, *Sōgi*.

1 Design. No relation. Spring. Rising Things. Peaks.
In this most famous of renga hokku, haze designates spring, a season long
thought best for dawn, as autumn was for evening. Emperor Gotoba had a
palace at Minase, where he wrote a tanka Sōgi echoes (see p. 172, above). The
"kana" termination is usual in a hokku.

2 Design. Close. Spring. Waters. Trees. Residences.
The movement suggests temporal progress with the melting of snow in 1.
"Yuku mizu" seems to recall a poem in the *Kokinshū* (15: 793) on Minase
River. This waki (or wakiku, second stanza) is not a flower stanza, because it
uses a named flower (na no hana), the plum ("ume").

3 Design-Ground. Close. Spring. Waters. Trees.
This daisan (third stanza) advances spring a bit more, suggesting that willows
are in full leaf but still fresh. When stirred by wind they were thought loveliest.
The "-te" conclusion is a usual one in this stanza. Konishi sets the relation as
close-distant.

4 Ground-Design. Distant-Close. Miscellaneous. Waters. Night.
Daybreak is considered nightbreak: hence, Night. So also does Sōgi emphasize
what is heard. The connection is that between the boat and the river of 3.
"Shiruki" (distinct) relates to both "oto" (sounds) and "akegata" (daybreak),
as in 1 "kasumu" (to haze), yokes "yamamoto" (base of hills), and "yūbe"
(evening). This yoking is common in linked poetry.

A Hundred Stanzas by Three Poets at Minase

(Minase Sangin Hyakuin)

Nanibito o fusuru renga.

A renga related to "person."

1

Yuki nagara
yamamoto kasumu
yūbe kana
Sōgi

Despite some snow
the base of hills spreads with haze
the twilight scene

Yuki nagara
yamamoto kasumu
yūbe kana
2 yuku mizu tōku
ume niou sato
Shōhaku

Despite some snow
the base of hills spreads with haze
the twilight scene
where the waters flow afar
the village glows with sweet plum flowers

Yuku mizu tōku
ume niou sato
3 kawakaze ni
hitomura yanagi
haru miete
Sōchō

Where the waters flow afar
the village glows with sweet plum flowers
in the river wind
a single stand of willow trees
shows spring color

Kawakaze ni
hitomura yanagi
haru miete
4 fune sasu oto mo
shiruki akegata
Sōgi

In the river wind
a single stand of willow trees
shows spring color
daybreak comes on distinctly
with sounds of a punted boat

5 Ground-Design. Close-Distant. Autumn. Radiance. Night. Rising Things.
The language is somewhat prosaic (although it would be poetic in haikai), but
the image of the moon ensures that this is not a ground stanza. Shōhaku emphasizes the stillness implied by 5 with night fog. In it a faint glow suggests
that the moon has not yet set. The first moon stanza.

6 Ground. Close-Distant. Autumn. Falling Things.
The stanza has commonplace imagery and is syntactically fragmented, but it
fits well in the sequence, opposing a falling to a rising thing and suggesting that
the end of autumn made the moon more appreciated in 5.

7 Design. Close-Distant. Autumn. Insects. Plants.
This is fresh in conception and yet central to Japanese thinking about autumn
and insects. Given the essential character (hon'i) of renga imagery, unnamed
insects were thought more comprehensive and moving. This is, therefore, the
sole use allowed in a hundred stanzas.

8 Design-Ground. Close-Distant. Miscellaneous. Residences.
"Arawanaru michi" (the once-covered path) is new in renga diction, and it
suggests that the person visited is as much gone as the path is changed. This
concludes the front of the first sheet: three poems on spring and three on autumn, the two most esteemed seasons.

♦   ♦   ♦   ♦

9 Ground. Close-Distant. Miscellaneous. Peaks. Residences.
The high winds associated with mountains have been still enough not to blow
down leaves and cover the road here. The idea resembles *Kokinshū*, 5: 288.
"Fukaki" (deep) yokes, "yama" (mountains), and "sato" (village). Sōchō
much affects presumptive verbs (as here, "ran").

Fune sasu oto mo
shiruki akegata
5   tsuki ya nao
kiriwataru yo ni
nokoru ran
Shōhaku

Daybreak comes on distinctly
with sounds of a punted boat
    does not the moon
of a fog-enveloped night
    stay yet in the sky

    Tsuki ya nao
kiriwataru yo ni
nokoru ran
6   shimo oku nohara
aki wa kurekeri
Sōchō

    Does not the moon
of a fog-enveloped night
    stay yet in the sky
as wide fields settle with the frost
autumn has approached its end

Shimo oku nohara
aki wa kurekeri
7   naku mushi no
kokoro to mo naku
kusa karete
Sōgi

As wide fields settle with the frost
autumn has approached its end
    the insects cry out
but without regard for such desires
    the grasses wither

    Naku mushi no
kokoro to mo naku
kusa karete
8   kakine o toeba
arawanaru michi
Shōhaku

    The insects cry out
but without regard for such desires
    the grasses wither
as I come to the fence in visit
the once covered path is clear

    ♦   ♦   ♦   ♦

Kakine o toeba
arawanaru michi
9   yama fukaki
sato ya arashi ni
okuru ran
Sōchō

As I come to the fence in visit
the once-covered path is clear
    has not the storm raged
till it grows late in the village
    deep in the mountains

10 Ground. Close-Distant. Miscellaneous.
"Sumai" (place) is unspecified as to dwelling and grounds. If it does not allow for the sweetness of melancholy, it must be a miserable place. The image-free style suggests a coming switch to Love or Grievances. Konishi considers that the preface (jo) actually ends only with this stanza (*Sōgi*, p. 114).

11 Ground. Close-Distant. Miscellaneous. Persons. Grievances.
We seem to move from an isolated place to a town or the capital, where a person lives a reclusive life for some unexplained reason. The time is ripe for a change in subject, in impressiveness, and in relation of stanzas.

12 Ground. Close. Miscellaneous. Grievances.
The voice seems to be that of a priest admonishing the speaker of 11 for expecting more from this world of dust. Konishi remarks on Sōchō's failure to shift the sequence enough, saying that the poet's strength seems not yet up to the task. Sōchō likes this moralizing, subjective style.

13 Design. Close-Distant. Spring. Evanescence. Falling Things. Cultivation.
Sōgi delivers the sequence from its problems with a splendid design stanza after four ground stanzas. The evanescence, for which dew is an emblem, relates this stanza more closely than it seems to the particular grievances of 12. "Falling things" such as dew were thought to change the color of leaves and blossoms. This is the first flower stanza; "hana" need not mean cherry flowers until the sixteenth century.

14 Design. Close-Distant. Spring. Radiance. Rising Things.
The sun has been setting and coloring the dew of 13, and now it is about to be lost to haze and then to darkness. Shōhaku very skillfully widens the scene from 13 while shortening the moment depicted. The sun remains but is setting; the haze just begins but is increasing. The words imply almost their opposites.

Yama fukaki
sato ya arashi ni
   okuru ran
10   narenu sumai zo
sabishisa mo uki
Sōgi

   Has not the storm raged
till it grows late in the village
   deep in the mountains
a place one cannot get used to
turns even loneliness to grief

Narenu sumai zo
sabishisa mo uki
11   ima sara ni
hitori aru mi o
   omou na yo
Shōhaku

A place one cannot get used to
turns even loneliness to grief
   more than ever now
for one who lives in solitude
   such thoughts are vain

   Ima sara ni
hitori aru mi o
   omou na yo
12   utsurowan to wa
kanete shirazu ya
Sōchō

   More than ever now
for one who lives in solitude
   your thoughts are vain
that all life is vicissitude
surely you knew that long ago

Utsurowan to wa
kanete shirazu ya
13   okiwaburu
tsuyu koso hana ni
aware nare
Sōgi

That all life is vicissitude
surely one knew that long ago
   disliking its own fall
the dew on the flowers it withers
   suffers for their loss

   Okiwaburu
tsuyu koso hana ni
   aware nare
14   mada nokoru hi no
uchikasumu kage
Shōhaku

   Disliking its own fall
the dew on the flowers it withers
   suffers for their loss
the yet remaining rays of light
in a scene just taken on by haze

15 Ground. Close-Distant. Spring. Birds.
This is rather interesting in that the birds are personified: that they speak tells us that they are heard, not seen, because of haze and night following 14. The birds go home (kaeru) to their northern grounds. Another "ran."

16 Ground. Close-Distant. Miscellaneous. Travel. Peaks.
This is a skillful connection. The birds go home; the person here travels on to a yet more remote area dark even in daytime. The darkness and the movement interplay in the connection. Perhaps the birds have made it home, while the traveler struggles on.

17 Ground-Design. Close-Distant. Winter. Travel. Falling Things. Clothes.
The character and the freshness of Shōhaku's language is hard to convey, since in English sleeves–clothes may seem redundant, and since "sode wa shigure" (rather than "sode no shigure") cannot be represented in a language without topics. The drizzle is real, cold rain, but it also represents the tears of a suffering traveler.

18 Ground-Design. Distant-Close. Autumn. Travel. Night. Radiance.
"Kusamakura" (grass pillow) always implies travel, by definition not toward the capital. One cut grass or fine bamboo to rest one's head. The moon glimmers in the drizzle-tears on the pillow. Here is a "san" presumptive. The second moon stanza.

19 Design-Ground. Distant-Close. Autumn. Love. Night.
The speaker is thinking of his wife or lover. "Itazura ni fushi" means to sleep alone without a loved person. Konishi quotes appositely from "Hahakigi" ("The Dwindle Bush"), the second chapter of *The Tale of Genji*. Sōgi introduces love for the first time here near the end of the first sheet.

Mada nokoru hi no
uchikasumu kage
15   kurenu to ya
nakitsutsu tori no
   kaeru ran
Sōchō

The yet remaining rays of light
in a scene just taken on by haze
   "has not dusk come"
the birds crying out in flight
   seem homeward bound

   Kurenu to ya
nakitsutsu tori no
   kaeru ran
16   miyama o yukeba
waku sora mo nashi
Sōgi

   "Has not dusk come"
the birds crying out in flight
   seem homeward bound
entered in the mountain fastness
no light distinguishes the sky

Miyama o yukeba
waku sora mo nashi
17   haruru ma mo
sode wa shigure no
   tabigoromo
Shōhaku

Entered in the mountain fastness
no light distinguishes the sky
   even in clearing moments
the sleeves wet with the cold drizzle
   on the traveler's clothes

   Haruru ma mo
sode wa shigure no
   tabigoromo
18   waga kusamakura
tsuki ya yatsu san
Sōchō

   Even in clearing moments
the sleeves wet with the cold drizzle
   on the traveler's clothes
my wet grass pillow of the journey
gives a weakened image of the moon

Waga kusamakura
tsuki ya yatsu san
19   itazura ni
akasu yo ōku
   aki fukete
Sōgi

My wet grass pillow of the journey
gives a weakened image of the moon
   sleeping by myself
dawn breaks on many yearnings
   and autumn nearly done

20 Design-Ground. Distant-Close. Autumn. Love. Night. Plants.
Shōhaku intensifies the shift to love by introducing dream (yume). It may not be used again for seven stanzas (and actually appears but four times in the sequence). The specificity of wind on the reeds stresses the dream's beauty and insubstantiality.

21 Ground. Close-Distant. Miscellaneous. Persons.
Sōchō populates the dream of 20 with specific people. His "mishi" (seen) is an associated word (engo) with dream (yume) in 20. Without that association, the relation would be Distant-Close.

22 Ground. Distant-Near. Miscellaneous. Grievances.
The rememberer of the people in the capital now becomes an aged man. Sōgi ends the first sheet (sho-ori) with a very plain stanza.

◆ ◆ ◆ ◆
◆ ◆ ◆ ◆

23 Ground-Design. Distant-Close. Miscellaneous. Grievances.
The Grievances continue into the second sheet, but fresh imagery emerges. "Koto no ha" (leaves of words) relates as "leaves" to the preceding line and also means "words." "Shire" ("know") is exclamatory rather than imperative. The order of composing changes with this stanza.

24 Ground. Distant-Close. Miscellaneous.
"That too" (sore mo) refers within the stanza to the sky. In connection with 23 it probably implies that the "leaves of words" are poems. Poetry and the evening sky, or poetry on the evening sky, are the speaker's companions.

Itazura ni
akasu yo ōku
  aki fukete
20   yume ni uramuru
  ogi no uwakaze
    Shōhaku

        Sleeping by myself
        dawn breaks on many yearnings
          and autumn nearly done
        the wind rustles upon the reeds
        begrudging the brief dream of love

Yume ni uramuru
ogi no uwakaze
  mishi wa mina
21   furusatobito no
  ato mo nashi
    Sōchō

        The wind rustles upon the reeds
        begrudging the brief dream of love
          all those people
        once seen often in the capital
          are gone without trace

  Mishi wa mina
furusatobito no
  ato mo nashi
22   oi no yukue yo
  nani ni kakaran
    Sōgi

          All those people
        once seen often in the capital
          are gone without trace
        what do the years of human life concern
        and what can I rely upon

♦ ♦ ♦ ♦
♦ ♦ ♦ ♦

Oi no yukue yo
nani ni kakaran
  iro mo naki
23   koto no ha o dani
  aware shire
    Shōhaku

        What do the years of human life concern
        and what can I rely upon
          colorless themselves
        the leaves of words alone are left
          for those who know the sorrow

  Iro mo naki
koto no ha o dani
  aware shire
24   sore mo tomo naru
  yūgure no sora
    Sōgi

          Colorless themselves
        the leaves of words alone are left
          for those who know the sorrow
        and that too becomes a companion
        the tint of the sky at twilight

25 Ground-Design. Close-Distant. Spring. Rising Things. Trees. Peaks.
What seemed flowers turn out to have been clouds after the flowers had all fallen. Sōchō recollects a poem by Shunzei, *Shinchokusenshū*, 1:57 (*Court Poetry*, p. 295). "Kumo ni kyō" is unusual syntax. Yamada, *Renga Gaisetsu*, p. 235, and Konishi, *Sōgi*, p. 194, give neither Trees nor Cultivation for "hana" here.

26 Ground-Design. Close-Distant. Spring. Birds.
Shōhaku advances the season slightly from flowers to birds on return (see 15). "Kikeba" (listening) implies necessary effort. *Shinkokinshū*, 1: 62 provides background and another use of "ima wa" to mean "farewell."

27 Design-Ground. Distant-Close. Spring. Persons. Night. Radiance.
The stanza echoes a poem in the *Sagoromo Monogatari* asking someone to linger (Mate shibashi), since the moon is just rising and little else can be done to slow the troubles of life. The third moon stanza.

28 Design. Distant-Close. Autumn. Falling Things. Night.
Time moves from night to dawn, spring to autumn, taking 27 as an autumn moon and not possibly a person. With recall of *Shingoshūishū*, 10: 908, Sōchō gives a scene of melancholy and beauty in one of his finest moments in *Three Poets*.

29 Ground-Design. Close-Distant. Autumn. Residences. Rising Things.
"Sueno" sounds like a place name but means the same as "nozue," at the end of the moor or fields. It may be that the speaker is on a hill and sees the fields at the end of his vision, with the village at the fields' end. "Haruka ni" (in distance) yokes "sato" (village) and "kiri tachite" (mist thickening).

Sore mo tomo naru
yūgure no sora
25   kumo ni kyō
hana chirihatsuru
     mine koete
Sōchō

And that too becomes a companion
the cast of sky at twilight
     entering the clouds
today I crossed the peak where flowers
     had completely fallen

     Kumo ni kyō
hana chirihatsuru
     mine koete
26   kikeba imawa no
haru no karigane
Shōhaku

     Entering the clouds
today I crossed the peak where flowers
     had completely fallen
listening I hear farewells
in cries of spring geese overhead

Kikeba imawa no
haru no karigane
27   oboroke no
tsuki ka wa hito mo
     mate shibashi
Sōgi

Listening I hear farewells
in cries of spring geese overhead
     oh stay on a while
can you also think so common
     this cloud-dimmed moon

     Oboroke no
tsuki ka wa hito mo
     mate shibashi
28   karine no tsuyu no
aki no akebono
Sōchō

     Oh stay on a while
can you also think so common
     this cloud-dimmed moon
in the dew on a traveler's bedding
glistens the light of autumn dawn

Karine no tsuyu no
aki no akebono
29   sueno naru
sato wa haruka ni
     kiri tachite
Shōhaku

In the dew of a traveler's bedding
glistens the light of autumn dawn
     at the wide fields' end ·
a village in the thickening mist
     is lost in distance

30 Ground. Distant. Autumn. Clothes.
Apparently the mist of 29 has closed in, so that vision yields to hearing. The first stanza of distant relation, this does not connect with imagery or diction but with a sense that the pathetic life of the female beating clothes has some connection with the village of 29.

31 Ground. Close-Distant. Autumn. Persons. Clothes.
"Sayuru" implies clear as well as cold. The clothes of 30 seem to have been lost to the speaker here. "Sode" means sleeves and implies tears, hence being used instead of clothes, for which it is metonomy. The season may possibly be winter instead of autumn.

32 Ground. Distant-Close. Miscellaneous. Grievances. Peaks.
The shivering person of 31 is now a hermit lacking proper fuel to keep warm. The concept of hidden dwelling (kakurega) implies Grievances in renga.

33 Ground. Distant-Close. Miscellaneous. Grievances.
In conception this is Distant; the nearness derives from "tsuki-" (consumed), being an associated word with "tsumagi" (firewood) in 32. There is an air of Narihira from the memory of Gosenshū, 15: 1084, although that poet is not the speaker here.

34 Ground. Close. Miscellaneous.
Here begins a number of unsatisfactory stanzas by Sōchō: over-subjective, moralistically simple or sentimental. This is the fourth ground stanza in succession. Relation has been changing, but Sōchō should have changed degree as well.

	Sueno naru	At the wide fields' end
	sato wa haruka ni	a village in the thickening mist
	kiri tachite	is lost in distance
30	fukikuru kaze wa	it is the wind on which there comes
	koromo utsu koe	the sound of someone beating clothes
	Sōgi	

	Fukikuru kaze wa	It is the wind on which there comes
	koromo utsu koe	the sound of someone beating clothes
31	sayuru hi mo	even the days are cold
	mi wa sode usuki	and I shiver in my thin sleeves
	kure goto ni	as each night falls
	Sōchō	

	Sayuru hi mo	Even the days are cold
	mi wa sode usuki	and I shiver in my thin sleeves
	kure goto ni	as each night falls
32	tanomu mo hakana	the firewood gathered in these hills
	tsumagi toru yama	all too soon betrays my trust
	Shōhaku	

	Tanomu mo hakana	The firewood gathered in the hills
	tsumagi toru yama	all too soon betrays the trust
33	saritomo no	even if it be so
	kono yo no michi wa	the road leading through this world
	tsukihatete	is utterly consumed
	Sōgi	

	Saritomo no	For all that can be said
	kono yo no michi wa	the road leading through this world
	tsukihatete	is utterly consumed
34	kokorobososhi ya	it has grown too much to bear
	izuchi yukamashi	and one is left without escape
	Sōchō	

35 Design-Ground. Close-Distant. Miscellaneous. Love. Night.
Shōhaku well introduces a stanza as love. The freshness of treatment as well as
the topic enlivens things. Usually lovers part in the early morning (kinuginu
ni) with hopes to meet. The woman now waits instead for death, having no
better expectation. This may recall *Kokinshū*, 18: 965.

36 Ground-Design. Close-Distant. Miscellaneous. Love. Persons.
The metamorphosis of the woman's feeling is remarkable. Near death from
her lover's neglect, she suddenly finds she still loves him. As Konishi well says,
this resembles Late Classical poetry (see *Court Poetry*, ch. 7; the poem on p.
378). This is fresh in renga. So concludes the front of the second sheet.

♦　♦　♦　♦

37　Ground-Design. Close. Miscellaneous. Love. Persons.
This stanza reads best as if a message from the lover of the woman in 36. But it
does not sufficiently advance the sequence. The first line has an extra syllable,
as does no other in the sequence.

38 Ground. Close-Distant. Miscellaneous. Love.
Shōhaku finds himself unable to do very much after Sōchō's weak stanza.

39 Ground-Design. Distant. Miscellaneous. Grievances. Cultivation.
Sōgi moves things to a fresher subject. At this stage, the sequence holds most
interest in the characteristic renga play of variety in impressiveness and, especially, in relation.

Kokorobososhi ya
izuchi yukamashi
35 inochi nomi
matsu koto ni suru
  kinuginu ni
 Shōhaku

It has grown too much to bear
and I am left without escape
  only the end of life
is now worthy of my waiting
  at this love-parting

  Inochi nomi
matsu koto ni suru
  kinuginu ni
36 nao nani nare ya
hito no koishiki
 Sōgi

  Only the end of life
had been worthy of my waiting
  at that love parting
for what reason can it be
that even he should seem so dear

   ◆ ◆ ◆ ◆

Nao nani nare ya
hito no koishiki
37 kimi o okite
akazu mo tare o
  omou ran
 Sōchō

For what reason can it be
that you should seem so dear
  apart from you
who else appeals forever
  and holds my love

  Kimi o okite
akazu mo tare o
  omou ran
38 sono omokage wa
nitaru dani nashi
 Shōhaku

  Apart from you
who else appeals forever
  and holds my love
compared with that remembered form
no other person bears resemblance

Sono omokage wa
nitaru dani nashi
39 kusaki sae
furuki miyako no
  urami nite
 Sōgi

Compared with that remembered form
nothing else bears resemblance
  to the very shrubs
the legacy of the ancient capital
  is lost in regret

40 Ground. Close-Distant. Miscellaneous. Grievances. Persons. Residences.
Sōchō's powers revive somewhat. It is not that impressive stanzas must be written one after the other, but that the variation in continuity should satisfy.

41 Ground. Close-Distant. Miscellaneous. Grievances. Persons.
"Tarachine no" (she who suckled you) is an old pillow word for "haha" (mother), etc. Shōhaku's use of the epithet for what it designates has novelty and interest.

42 Ground-Design. Distant. Miscellaneous.
Sōgi uses distant relation for the second turn in a row, and "dream" (yume) for the first time in this sheet. This is not a moon stanza, because "tsuki-" here means month. Konishi rates this simply Ground.

43 Ground-Design. Distant-Close. Miscellaneous. Travel. Waters.
Since dream (in 42) usually designates Love or Travel, Sōchō appropriates the preceding stanza to Travel—as it were from a remote, dreamlike land. "Morokoshi" is written with the characters for "T'ang boat."

44 Ground. Distant. Miscellaneous. Buddhism.
See Konishi, *Sōgi*, for details on Shōhaku's rather complex but very appropriate use of T'ang echoes. There is no other connection with 43. For more Buddhist stanzas, see the close of *Three Poets*.

	Kusaki sae	To the very shrubs
	furuki miyako no	the legacy of the ancient capital
	urami nite	is lost in regret
40	mi no uki yado mo	even the house where once I suffered
	nagori koso are	seems dear in memory of the past
	Sōchō	

	Mi no uki yado mo	Even the house where once you suffered
	nagori koso are	seems dear in memory of the past
41	tarachine no	take your comfort
	tōkaranu ato ni	in the traces not yet disappeared
	nagusame yo	of her who suckled you
	Shōhaku	

	Tarachine no	Take your comfort
	tōkaranu ato ni	in the traces not yet disappeared
	nagusame yo	of her who suckled you
42	tsukihi no sue ya	at the end of many months and days
	yume ni meguran	all of that would whirl in dreams
	Sōgi	

	Tsukihi no sue ya	At the end of many months and days
	yume ni meguran	everything seems whirled in dreams
43	kono kishi o	with this shoreline
	morokoshibune no	the boats plying from far Cathay
	kagiri nite	end their outward tour
	Sōchō	

	Kono kishi o	With this shoreline
	morokoshibune no	the boats plying from far Cathay
	kagiri nite	end their outward tour
44	mata umarekonu	how I should like to be taught the Law
	nori o kikaba ya	that I might end the chain of births
	Shōhaku	

45 Design. Distant. Autumn. Love. Falling Things.
Sōgi introduces Love for the second time on this sheet, though the first on the back. This sounds like a man's poem sent after returning from a night of love. The light connection with 44 involves the dew-impermanence emblem as a shift from Buddhism to Love. That emblem leaves scope for a change in tone and speaker. Sōgi's third Distant relation in three turns.

46 Ground-Design. Close-Distant. Autumn. Love. Persons.
The speaker is now the woman, so soon abandoned, as the dew emblem had half-suggested, even in the speaker's denial in 45. "Aki-" means both Autumn and grown cold toward her.

47 Design-Ground. Close. Autumn. Love. Insects. Plants.
"Matsumushi" is the "pine cricket," also "waiting cricket" (for a lover). Pines associate with the wind of 46. It is a named insect (na no mushi)—see comment on stanza 7—and so should not go beyond one stanza. There is an allusion to a story (honzetsu), the "Yomogiu" chapter of *The Tale of Genji*.

48 Design-Ground. Close-Distant. Autumn. Peaks. Night. Radiance.
"Sumu" means both "live" and "be clear," joining the speaker and the moon. A poem by Shunzei (*Shinkokinshū*, 6: 1558) is recalled in a way relating also to 47: "Settled in retreat, / 'Will he come now?' I ask with longing / In these autumn hills / Where housed among the rampant weeds / I wait as the pining cricket cries."

49 Design-Ground. Close-Distant. Miscellaneous. Grievances. Night.
Temples were associated with hills (yama, 48). Hearing the bell from the temple on the hill in 48, the speaker awakes to thoughts of the future. Very well considered. In renga more often than in waka, lines end with parts of speech like the possessive "waga" here, giving a strong kind of enjambement.

45

Mata umarekonu
nori o kikaba ya
    au made to
omoi no tsuyu no
    kiekaeri
Sōgi

How I should like to be taught the Law
that I might end the chain of births
    until we met
I imagined that the dew of love
    only dried again, again

46

    Au made to
omoi no tsuyu no
    kiekaeri
mi o akikaze mo
hitodanome nari
Sōchō

    Until we met
I imagined that the dew of love
    only dried again, again
his chill and autumn's in the wind
yet I hope for him I cannot trust

47

Mi o akikaze mo
hitodanome nari
    matsumushi no
naku ne kai naki
    yomogiu ni
Shōhaku

His chill and autumn's in the wind
yet I hope for him I cannot trust
    pining like the cricket
voicing cries without avail
    in this abandoned field

48

    Matsumushi no
naku ne kai naki
    yomogiu ni
shimeyū yama wa
tsuki nomi zo sumu
Sōgi

    Pining like the cricket
voicing cries without avail
    in this abandoned field
the only clear companion is the moon
in mountains closed up to the world

49

Shimeyū yama wa
tsuki nomi zo sumu
    kane ni waga
tada aramashi no
    nesame shite
Sōchō

The only clear companion is the moon
in mountains closed up to the world
    mine the temple bell
mine alone the uncertain future
    sounding me awake

50 Ground. Close. Winter. Grievances. Night. Falling Things.
The speaker has been wakened many times by the bell of 49 and is now grown
old. "Shimo" (frost) suggests white hair and, according to a renga handbook
cited by Konishi (*Sōgi*, p. 208) connects with "kane" (bell) in 49. This concludes the back of the second sheet and half the sequence.

♦ ♦ ♦ ♦
♦ ♦ ♦ ♦

51 Design-Ground. Close-Distant. Winter. Birds. Waters.
This splendid stanza has a timelessness to it that fits with waka and haikai as
well. "Ashitazu" is a crane in the water along reeds, an expression from waka.
Konishi says that except for its bleakness, this would be a Design stanza. The
order of composition is now as on the first sheet.

52 Ground-Design. Close-Distant. Miscellaneous. Persons. Waters.
An excellent joining, enlarging the scope and changing attention from the bird
to a man suffering like it. It would be hard to disagree with someone rating this
Design-Ground. "Yūshiokaze" works both as "yūshio" (evening tide) and
"shiokaze" (tidal breeze).

53 Design-Ground. Close-Distant. Spring. Rising Things.
This fine stanza connects by developing the scenery and atmosphere of 52, and
also by relations of language: e.g., the destination of the boatman is unknown
(yukue naki).

54 Ground-Design. Close-Distant. Spring. Residences. Peaks.
We move from the sea to the mountains, where spring comes later. The haze
of 53 is taken as the messenger of spring (cf. *Goshūishū*, 1: 5), and ironically
since the haze is everywhere, the direction from which spring has approached
is unclear. The issue of the direction taken as posed in 53 and here is very Japanese.

Kane ni waga
tada aramashi no
nesame shite
50   itadakikeri na
yonayona no shimo
Shōhaku

Mine the temple bell
mine alone the uncertain future
   sounding me awake
night after night the many frosts
have brought their whiteness to my head

♦   ♦   ♦   ♦

♦   ♦   ♦   ♦

Itadakikeri na
yonayona no shimo
51   fuyugare no
ashitazu wabite
tateru e ni
Sōgi

Night after night the many frosts
have brought their whiteness to one's head
   withered by winter
the reeds where the crane has suffered
   the bay where it takes flight

Fuyugare no
ashitazu wabite
tateru e ni
52   yūshiokaze no
okitsu funabito
Shōhaku

Withered by winter
the reeds where the crane has suffered
   the bay where it takes flight
in the wind swelling with evening tide
the boatman labors out at sea

Yūshiokaze no
okitsu funabito
53   yukue naki
kasumi ya izuku
hate naran
Sōchō

In the wind swelling with evening tide
the boatman labors out at sea
   the haze drifts on
uncertain in its scope and place
   unknown in its end

Yukue naki
kasumi ya izuku
hate naran
54   kuru kata mienu
yamazato no haru
Sōgi

The haze drifts on
uncertain in its scope and place
   unknown in its end
in this mountain village spring
gives no sign of whence it comes

55 Design. Close-Distant. Spring. Cultivation.
A wonderful stanza. Depending on the flower meant, this has a Trees or Cultivation classification. Yamada, *Renga Gaisetsu*, p. 237, gives neither. Konishi, *Sōgi*, p. 210, gives Cultivation. In 56 Sōchō seems to take it as Trees.

56 Ground-Design. Close-Distant. Autumn. Trees.
As earlier in the sequence, we shift here immediately from spring to autumn. A nice touch here involves Sōchō's mentioning trees to connect with 55 but referring really to dew-laden plants under them. There are seven plants particularly associated with autumn. A review of the succession from 51 to 56 will clearly show the art of connecting seasonal stanzas in the Development section.

57 Ground-Design. Close-Distant. Autumn. Residences.
An allusion to *Kin'yōshū*, 9: 568 beautifully joins this with the former and makes clear (if clarification were necessary) that the cold autumn drizzle also implies the speaker's tears.

58 Ground-Design. Close-Distant. Autumn. Buddhism. Clothes. Night.
  Radiance.
Even this priest is moved to tears by the beauty of the moon. "Tamoto" refers to the baggy lower part of the sleeve, which one uses as a pocket. Of course the whole robe is meant as to color, the sleeves as to association with tears. The fifth moon stanza.

59 Ground. Close-Distant. Miscellaneous. Buddhism. Persons.
The conception involves a situation too much like 58. This would work well right after 57 but is redundant here.

Kuru kata mienu
yamazato no haru
   shigemi yori
taedae nokoru
   hana ochite
Shōhaku

In this mountain village spring
gave no sign of whence it came
   from luxuriant boughs
the shower of petals leaves behind
   greater riches still

55

Shigemi yori
taedae nokoru
   hana ochite
ko no moto wakuru
michi no tsuyukesa
Sōchō

From luxuriant boughs
the shower of petals leaves behind
   greater riches still
beneath the trees I pick my way
on a path bright with the dew

56

Ko no moto wakuru
michi no tsuyukesa
   aki wa nado
moranu iwaya mo
   shiguru ran
Sōgi

Beneath the trees I pick my way
on a path bright with the dew
   even my rock-bound place
somehow is entered by autumn
   drizzling with tears

57

Aki wa nado
moranu iwaya mo
   shiguru ran
koke no tamoto ni
tsuki wa narekeri
Shōhaku

Even my rock-bound place
somehow is entered by autumn
   drizzling with tears
on my mossy priestly sleeves
the moon has found familiar place

58

Koke no tamoto ni
tsuki wa narekeri
   kokoro aru
kagiri zo shiruki
   yosutebito
Sōchō

On his mossy priestly sleeves
the moon has found familiar place
   the elegant taste
of the renouncer of this world
   clearly is supreme

59

60 Ground-Design. Distant-Close. Miscellaneous. Travel. Waters.
I follow Konishi (*Sōgi*, p. 213) in treating this as an allusion to Fan Li. A loyal retainer at the time of the overthrow of the Wu, he decided to give up the search for glory and slipped away by ship. A great alteration of the renouncer of the world in 59. For another interpretation, see Ijichi, *Rengashū*, p. 357.

61 Design-Ground. Close-Distant. Miscellaneous. Rising Things.
The storm past, a clear still morning ensues. At this juncture, the happiness of human response is unalloyed.

62 Design. Close-Distant. Winter. Falling Things. Peaks.
Sōchō's loveliest stanza in the sequence, beautifully connected with Shōhaku's stanza, this gives a wide vista, as the clouds of 61 disappear utterly and full daylight shines.

63 Design-Ground. Close-Distant. Winter. Residences. Peaks. Trees.
We must recall a poem by Chōmei in his *Mumyōshō* ("Sabishisa wa"): "My solitude / Yet retains its saddened beauty, / For upon the leaves / That had totally obscured the road / Dawn reveals the snow's first fall." The allusion combines 63 with 62 very well—and poses a problem for Shōhaku, who needs to disentangle 63 from 62 and join 63 to his stanza.

64 Ground-Design. Close. Miscellaneous. Trees.
Shōhaku manages handily by recognizing Sōgi's allusion and taking from it those elements alone which are not in 62. He also shifts the topic and introduces another kind of tree, the pines, that hold their leaves. So concludes the front of the third sheet, with an excellent sequence well exemplifying the sequential art of renga.

♦　♦　♦　♦

Kokoro aru
kagiri zo shiruki
    yosutebito
60 osamaru nami ni
fune izuru miyu
Sōgi

The elegant taste
of the renouncer of this world
    clearly is supreme
it seems a boat launches forth
on a sea whose waves are stilled

Osamaru nami ni
fune izuru miyu
    asanagi no
61 sora ni ato naki
    yoru no kumo
Shōhaku

It seems a boat launches forth
on a sea whose waves are stilled
    in the morning calm
no trace remains across the sky
    of last night's clouds

    Asanagi no
sora ni ato naki
    yoru no kumo
62 yuki ni sayakeki
yomo no tōyama
Sōchō

    In the morning calm
no trace remains across the sky
    of last night's clouds
peaks ring the distance on all sides
pure with the snow that covers all

Yuki ni sayakeki
yomo no tōyama
    mine no io
63 ko no ha no nochi mo
    sumiakade
Sōgi

Peaks ring the distance on all sides
pure with the snow that covers all
    the leaves are fallen
but at the hut upon the peak
    there is more to live for

    Mine no io
ko no ha no nochi mo
    sumiakade
64 sabishisa narau
matsukaze no koe
Shōhaku

    The leaves are fallen
but at the hut upon the peak
    there is more to live for
the voice of the wind in pines
makes the solitude familiar

♦   ♦   ♦   ♦

65 Ground. Close-Distant. Miscellaneous. Buddhism. Persons. Night.
The waking involves both priestly rites in a temple and hearing the wind in the pines of 64. On the strong enjambement of "kono . . . ," see 49 and comment.

66 Ground-Design. Close-Distant. Autumn. Travel. Night. Radiance.
Because the dawn observances of 65 need not necessarily be Buddhist, Sōgi can shift to travel. Moonlight (that of the fading moon at dawn is meant) in travel is very evocative, but this is a poor stanza to come from Sōgi. The sixth moon stanza.

67 Design-Ground. Close-Distant. Autumn. Clothes. Falling Things.
It is natural and fitting to move from the rigors of travel in 66 to the tear-bedewed, frosty, moon-reflecting sleeve. Shōhaku extracts the good from Sōgi's weak stanza. The use of both dew (also of course tears) and frost—two Falling Things—is interesting.

68 Ground-Design. Close-Distant. Autumn. Plants.
The frost of 67 is imagined to have acted on the plumes to tint them slightly reddish. A nice development. There may be a recollection of *Kokinshū*, 4: 243 that relates wet sleeves (as in 67) to pampas grass.

69 Design-Ground. Distant-Close. Autumn. Birds. Peaks.
The cold of 68 is intensified in a stanza known for its description of the effect of the wind without mentioning it. From the conception of a poem (*Shinkokin-shū*, 5: 513) that may be alluded to, we would understand that the sun is setting. The cry of quails was thought especially piteous. A good candidate for Design status.

Sabishisa narau
matsukaze no koe
65   tare ka kono
akatsuki oki o
    kasanemashi
Sōchō

The voice of the wind in pines
makes the solitude familiar
    who will do such
waking for each dawn observance
    next after next

Tare ka kono
akatsuki oki o
    kasanemashi
66   tsuki wa shiru ya no
tabi zo kanashiki
Sōgi

Who will do such
waking for each dawn observance
    next after next
is not the lingering moon aware
how travel brings such sadness

Tsuki wa shiru ya no
tabi zo kanashiki
67   tsuyu fukami
shimo sae shioru
    aki no sode
Shōhaku

Is not the lingering moon aware
how travel brings such sadness
    so thick the dew
that its frost withers away
    the autumn sleeve

Tsuyu fukami
shimo sae shioru
    aki no sode
68   usuhanasusuki
chiramaku mo oshi
Sōchō

So thick the dew
that its frost withers away
    the autumn sleeve
regret comes even with the fall
of tinted plumes of pampas grass

Usuhanasusuki
chiramaku mo oshi
69   uzura naku
katayama kurete
    samuki hi ni
Sōgi

Regret comes even with the fall
of tinted plumes of pampass grass
    the quails cry out
the distant mountain falls in shadow
    and the sun grows cold

70 Ground. Close. Miscellaneous. Grievances. Residences.
The quails of 69 are used with other details here to recall *Kokinshū*, 18:973 (also episode 123 in *Tales from Ise*; see above, p. 154), in which a woman addresses a man about to leave her. Here the Love situation is changed to Grievances, and the response is personal, unlike 69 itself.

71 Ground-Design. Close-Distant. Miscellaneous. Love. Persons.
The allusion in 70 is recognized but not enough incorporated in the diction of 70 and 71 to make their relation close. Sōchō introduces an image-free style again, which runs through 74. "Hito" (person) as so often means "you."

72 Ground-Design. Close-Distant. Miscellaneous. Love. Persons.
This abandoned woman refers to her faithless lover in the first line, to herself in the second. The syntax and grammar are difficult, but her plea for affection is plain.

73 Ground-Design. Close. Miscellaneous. Love.
This is not much more impressive than Ground. We are on a relatively low level of impressiveness in preparation for rise at the end of the side and sheet.

74 Ground-Design. Close. Miscellaneous. Love.
This is disappointing in not changing in any classification. Having begun this imageless Love series, Sōchō did not need to continue in the same vein for a fourth stanza. Very lame.

Uzura naku
katayama kurete
   samuki hi ni
70 no to naru sato mo
wabitsutsu zo sumu
Shōhaku

      The quails cry out
the distant mountain falls in shadow
   and the sun grows cold
also in a village turned to fields
living here I suffer on

No to naru sato mo
wabitsutsu zo sumu
71   kaerikoba
machishiomoi o
   hito ya min
Sōchō

Also in a village turned to fields
living here I suffer on
   if you return
all my waiting, waiting, longing
   surely will be plain

   Kaerikoba
machishiomoi o
   hito ya min
72 utoki mo tare ga
kokoro naru beki
Sōgi

   If you return
all my waiting, waiting, longing
   surely will be plain
who is it who behaves so coldly
who can it be who has a heart

Utoki mo tare ga
kokoro naru beki
73   mukashi yori
tada ayaniku no
   koi no michi
Shōhaku

Who is it who behaves so coldly
who can it be who has a heart
   from olden times
only misfortunes have befallen
   those on the road of love

   Mukashi yori
tada ayaniku no
   koi no michi
74 wasuraregataki
yo sae urameshi
Sōchō

   From olden times
only misfortunes have befallen
   those on the road of love
how can one put from the mind
the world of love with all its pains

75 Ground. Distant. Miscellaneous. Persons.
Uncouth, miserable peasants could hardly be expected to distinguish the seasons *aesthetically*. The speaker seems to be an exile from the capital. Konishi sees a recollection by that speaker of the past that leads him to a Distant-Close classification. We are on our way up after four on the level.

76 Ground-Design. Close-Distant. Miscellaneous. Plants. Residences.
The overtones of summer lack diction justifying a Summer classification, although this is the closest to that season in the sequence. "Shiba no to" (the wattled door) probably means the door to a hut that is wattled in its entirety.

77 Ground. Close. Spring. Residences.
This excellent stanza lacks conventional evocative power but may be somewhat more impressive than indicated here. It is a fine stanza of close relation that yet gives development. "Kakiho" (hedgerow) refers to plants growing atop a fence or earthen wall or some other barrier enclosing the garden on the house. "Kaeshi" is a large hoe for digging in lieu of plowing.

78 Design. Distant-Close. Spring. Persons. Rising and Falling Things.
This magnificent stanza—to my mind the finest in *Three Poets*—is so because superbly led up to by 77 and indeed in contrast by the unimpressiveness of some earlier stanzas. There is some connection with 77, as if the person here is the long-gone farmer of 77. Haze rises, rain falls; the light fades as the person comes by. So the third sheet concludes, the best for variety, movement, and quality.

♦ ♦ ♦ ♦
♦ ♦ ♦ ♦

79 Ground Design. Close-Distant. Spring. Birds.
Whether the warbler has left or is there but does not sing cannot be told, but warblers often fail to sing when desired. Two presumptives ("sen," "ran") and a questioning particle ("ya") really are too much. The poem recalled (*Shinkokinshū*, 1: 82) is embarrassingly fine and makes comparison awkward.

Wasuraregataki
yo sae urameshi
75   yamagatsu ni
nado haruaki no
shiraru ran
Sōgi

How can one put from the mind
the world of love with all its pains
how can the peasants
distinguish spring from autumn
come to their mountains

Yamagatsu ni
nado haruaki no
shiraru ran
76   uenu kusaba no
shigeki shiba no to
Shōhaku

How can the peasants
distinguish spring from autumn
come to their mountains
shrubs never cultivated by the owner
stand thick by the wattled door

Uenu kusaba no
shigeki shiba no to
77   katawara ni
kakiho no arata
kaeshi sute
Sōchō

Shrubs never cultivated by the owner
stand thick by the wattled door
in that vicinity
the overgrown field by the hedgerow
covers the neglected hoe

Katawara ni
kakiho no arata
kaeshi sute
78   yuku hito kasumu
ame no kuregata
Sōgi

In that vicinity
the overgrown field by the hedgerow
covers the neglected hoe
the traveler returns drifting in haze
brought by twilight in light rain

♦ ♦ ♦ ♦
♦ ♦ ♦ ♦

Yuku hito kasumu
ame no kuregata
79   yadori sen
no o uguisu ya
itou ran
Sōchō

The passer-by drifts off in haze
brought by twilight in light rain
where can one lodge
unguided by the warbler on a moor
that it dislikes

80 Design–Ground. Distant–Close. Spring. Night. Trees.
"Sayo" (brief night) is a poetic diminuitive, here for a brief night in spring, when the flowers are seen more by imagination than by eyes. The stanza relates to 79 by virtue of the assumption that one would like to lodge for the night beneath flowering boughs. As Konishi says, this rivals Sōgi's skill in connecting stanzas.

81 Design. Close–Distant. Spring. Night. Cultivation.
Sōgi shifts the scene from a large to a smaller—and if a garden, these flowers are Cultivation. To see outside better, the speaker dims the lamps, as in a line by Po Chü-i (see Konishi, *Sōgi*, p. 224; *Court Poetry*, p. 388-89). Two stanzas designating cherry flowers should not be joined. By connection with 80, this may mean cherries, but not by itself or with 82. The fourth and last flower stanza.

82 Design. Close–Distant. Miscellaneous. Love. Persons.
The man recalls the beauty of that love and her pillowing his head on her arm, with the flowers of 81 part of the distant time that now is a dream. Konishi sees a recollection of the chapter "Hana no En" in *The Tale of Genji*.

83 Ground–Design. Distant–Close. Miscellaneous. Love.
Years pass. Now the woman of the dream of 82 recalls the man and his inconstancy. The lament is timeless in Japanese conceptions of the anguish of the abandoned woman.

84 Ground–Design. Close–Distant. Miscellaneous. Grievances. Peaks.
It is expected that an old person would seek to retreat from an unsatisfactory world and desire to enter a religious life. Here the person is already anxious to leave this world.

Yadori sen
no o uguisu ya
  itou ran
80   sayo mo shizuka ni
sakura saku kage
  Shōhaku

      Where shall I lodge
unguided by the warbler on a moor
  that it dislikes
even the brief night holds stillness
and cherries blossoming in dim forms

Sayo mo shizuka ni
sakura saku kage
81   toboshibi o
somukuru hana ni
  akesomete
  Sōgi

Even the brief night holds stillness
and cherries blossoming in dim forms
  with the lamp dimmed
the blossoms grown paler in the dark
  take on the tint of dawn

  Toboshibi o
somokuru hana ni
  akesomete
82   taga tamakura ni
yume wa mieken
  Sōchō

  With my lamp dimmed
the blossoms grown paler in the dark
  take on the tint of dawn
on whose arm was I pillowed
when that lovely dream appeared

Taga tamakura ni
yume wa mieken
83   chigiri haya
omoitaetsutsu
  toshi mo hen
  Shōhaku

On whose arm was I pillowed
when that lovely dream appeared
  he keeps on breaking
all the vows of love he promised
  and my long years pass

  Chigiri haya
omoitaetsutsu
  toshi mo hen
84   ima wa no yowai
yama mo tazuneji
  Sōgi

  He keeps on breaking
all the vows of love he promised
  and my long years pass
Though age brings me to bid farewell
I ask no mountain for retreat

85 Ground. Close-Distant. Miscellaneous. Grievances. Persons.
This person has retired to the mountain retreat—as if the speaker of 85 has changed the decision—and now reflects on the people of the world. Another "ran."

86 Ground. Close-Distant. Miscellaneous. Grievances.
Perhaps this speaker is a person thinking from the capital of the recluse in 85. "Kakaru" for "depend" as in 22. The soul (tamashi) was thought a jewel (tama) on a cord (o) which it might extend to leave the body. If the cord was broken, the person would die.

87 Ground-Design. Close-Distant. Miscellaneous. Trees. Rising Things.
Recluses often had to use pine needles as fuel or even, according to a passage from the *Utsuho Monogatari* (Konishi, *Sōgi*, p. 227), eat them. Since this is more realistic than that story, we may prefer the first alternative.

88 Ground. Close. Miscellaneous. Residences. Waters.
From the smoke of 87, Sōchō imagines fires for making salt of sea-water, an emblem of miserable life. Sōgi's imagery in 87 gets out of the Grievances sequence. But Sōchō ends with yet another subjective "ran."

89 Ground. Close. Autumn. Travel. Night. Waters.
The speaker becomes a traveler along the shoreline. The second line is fresh in its play on "araiso" (rough seacoast) and "isomakura" (the seacoast as pillow). But the last line (I lie in suffering) sounds like *Sōchō*'s emotionalism.

85
Ima wa no yowai
yama mo tazuneji
  kakusu mi o
hito wa naki ni mo
  nashitsu ran
Sōchō

Though age brings me to bid farewell
I ask no mountain for retreat
  people no doubt think
a hermit like myself long dead
  and care no more

86
  Kakusu mi o
hito wa naki ni mo
  nashitsu ran
sate mo uki yo ni
kakaru tama no o
Shōhaku

  People no doubt think
a hermit like myself long dead
  and care no more
well then it is this wretched world
on which one's fragile soul depends

87
Sate mo uki yo ni
kakaru tama no o
  matsu no ha o
tada asayū no
  keburi nite
Sōgi

Well then it is this wretched world
on which my fragile soul depends
  morning and evening
it is only needles from the pines
  that raise my smoke

88
  Matsu no ha o
tada asayū no
  keburi nite
Urawa no sato wa
ika ni sumu ran
Sōchō

  Morning and evening
it is only needles from the pines
  that raise my smoke
how do salt-makers bear to live
at Urawa the village on the bay

89
Urawa no sato wa
ika ni sumu ran
  akikaze no
araisomakura
  fushiwabinu
Shōhaku

How do salt-makers bear to live
at Urawa the village on the bay
  I lie in suffering
pillowed on the rough seacoast
  in the autumn wind

90 Design-Ground. Distant-Close. Autumn. Birds. Peaks. Night. Radiance.
As the traveler of 89 lies unable to sleep in the rough place, geese fly across the moon so large by the rim of the mountain. As Konishi says, this connects admirably with 89 and yet introduces new imagery to allow for quite different scenic development in a way special to Sōgi. The seventh and last moon stanza, there being none on the back of this last sheet.

91 Design-Ground. Distant-Close. Autumn. Plants. Falling Things.
Sōchō's stanza is the richer for an allusion to *Kokinshū*, 4: 221. But there is another presumptive ("min") and a subjectivism in the last line that is, Konishi says, Sōchō's tic.

92 Ground. Close. Miscellaneous. Persons.
One theory is that this is not Ada no ōno as a place-name, but a fickle, untrustworthy (ada na) moor. But we need a sense of speed at this stage, and the use of place-names (nadokoro) assists in that. The kyū or fast finale technically belongs only to the back of this sheet, but usually was thought best begun a bit earlier, with this or the preceding. So ends the front of the fourth and last sheet.

♦ ♦ ♦ ♦

93 Ground-Design. Distant-Close. Miscellaneous. Grievances.
This stanza does take Ada the place-name to mean untrustworthy, making a philosophical matter out of the difficulty of our distinguishing illusion and reality, wish and fact, etc.

94 Ground. Close. Miscellaneous. Grievances.
That is, past and present are as difficult to distinguish as dream and reality. Another presumptive, "sen."

	Akikaze no	I lie in suffering
	araisomakura	pillowed on the rough seacoast
	fushiwabinu	in the autumn wind
90	kari naku yama no	the geese cry out above the mountain
	tsuki fukuru sora	crossing the moon in the late night sky
	Sōgi	

	Kari naku yama no	The geese cry out above the mountain
	tsuki fukuru sora	crossing the moon in the late night sky
91	kohagihara	I shall see tomorrow
	utsurou tsuyu mo	the patch of bush clover with the dew
	asu ya min	that withers its color
	Sōchō	

	Kohagihara	I shall see tomorrow
	utsurou tsuyu mo	the patch of bush clover with the dew
	asu ya min	that withers its color
92	Ada no ōno o	the scene on the great moor of Ada
	kokoro naru hito	gives much to the respondent heart
	Shōhaku	

♦   ♦   ♦   ♦

	Ada no ōno o	The transient great moor
	kokoro naru hito	touches the respondent heart
93	wasuru na yo	oh do not forget
	kagiri ya kawaru	the bounds of life keep shifting
	yumeutsutsu	reality and dream
	Sōgi	

	Wasuru na yo	Oh do not forget
	kagiri ya kawaru	the bounds of life keep shifting
	yumeutsutsu	reality and dream
94	omoeba itsu o	by thinking so the present time
	inishie ni sen	merges with the bygone years
	Sōchō	

95 Ground. Close-Distant. Miscellaneous. Buddhism.
For all such problems, there is hope. Past and present may be a jumble, but the promise of a Buddha coming as formerly gives hope for the future.

96 Design-Ground. Close-Distant. Spring. Cultivation. Buddhism.
The metaphysical speculations are resolved by the chief allusion: at the death of Gautama, the paired sal trees where he preached withered. From the optimism of 95, the allusion is altered to the very hopeful renewal of the trees signifying the Buddha's presence and ultimate reality.

97 Design-Ground. Close-Distant. Spring. Peaks. Rising and Falling Things.
The seasonal aspects of 96 are redone quite appropriately, although Sōchō would give us another "ran." "Ikushimoyo" plays nicely on "ikushimo" (how many frosts) and "shimoyo" (nights of frost). Haze is the rising, and frost the falling thing.

98 Ground-Design. Close-Distant. Spring. Residences. Rising Things.
"Nodoka ni" (peacefully) takes the essence of 97, and renders the distant view near. Konishi remarks that *Three Poets* has often revealed the capacity for such lovely variation in the sequence: he gives as examples Shōhaku's connection of 2 to 1, 29 to 28, and 52 to 51; as well as Sōgi's relation of 24 to 23, 48 to 47, and 78 to 77.

99 Ground. Close-Distant. Miscellaneous. Persons.
This and the last stanza maintain a decorum of modest orthodoxy that may seem to others as well as myself to be much less interesting than what has gone before.

Omoeba itsu o
inishie ni sen
95   hotoketachi
kakurete wa mata
   izuru yo ni
Shōhaku

By thinking so the present time
may merge with distant years
   the many Buddhas
disappear from sight and yet again
   come into this world

Hotoketachi
kakurete wa mata
   izuru yo ni
96   kareshi hayashi mo
harukaze zo fuku
Sōgi

The many Buddhas
disappear from sight and yet again
   come into this world
the breeze of spring is stirring
even in the withered trees

Kareshi hayashi mo
harukaze zo fuku
97   yama wa kesa
ikushimoyo ni ka
   kasumu ran
Sōchō

The breeze of spring is stirring
even in the withered woods
   how many frosty nights
have these hills known before today
   whitens with warm haze

Yama wa kesa
ikushimoyo ni ka
   kasumu ran
98   keburi nodoka ni
miyuru kariio
Shōhaku

How many frosty nights
have these hills known before today
   whitens with warm haze
the smoke arises peacefully
for one in a makeshift hut

Keburi nodoka ni
miyuru kariio
99   iyashiki mo
mi o osamuru wa
   aritsu beshi
Sōgi

The smoke arises peacefully
for one in a makeshift hut
   however low one be
it is holding oneself in sway
   that is imperative

100 Ground. Close. Miscellaneous. Persons.

We come to rest with the same decorum. Konishi says this is successful in evoking the aura of the age of Emperor Gotoba (see comment on 1). But that success does not go very easily into another language, unless perhaps we recognize that this renga was to be copied out handsomely and presented to the local shrine devoted to Gotoba.

Iyashiki mo
mi o osamuru wa
  aritsu beshi
100   hito ni oshinabe
michi zo tadashiki.
  Sōchō

However low one be
it is holding oneself in sway
  that is imperative
all mankind without exception
should travel on the Way aright.

2

A Hundred Stanzas
Related to "Person" by
Sōgi Alone

(*Sōgi Dokugin Nanibito Hyakuin*)

AMONG MANY of the most impressive renga sequences, the one most esteemed is probably this one of the two sequences of hundred-stanza sequences composed by Sōgi alone. High claims may be made for others
on various grounds, and, as we shall see, this is by no means regular in
the conventional ways. But it does seem that, three years before his
death, the old renga master devoted four months to composing a sequence that would satisfy him. Such a long period is quite special, if not
unique, and we may well think that only an accomplished master could
make of it something particularly valuable. Sōgi described his process of
composition in the usual humble terms:

> . . . in 1499 I entered my seventy-ninth year, and about the 20th of
> the Third Month I found myself unable to let pass silently my emo-
> tions for the falling flowers and composed a brief sequence [iisute].
> As I later added one stanza and then another, I found myself enfee-
> bled in mind and at a loss for words, utterly lacking the ability to
> think. But while I looked on the moon in this mental stupor, I found
> myself unable to stop what I had begun. As I completed something
> more than half the sequence, I found myself wondering how it
> might turn out, and at last, by the end of the seventh month, I
> brought it to a close. (*Renga Haikaishū*)

If Yamada Yoshio was right in saying that one needed twenty years of
practice before one was able to show any talent in renga, Sōgi had passed

that point by about·four decades. In the 43rd stanza he alludes to his being within a year of the age at which Gautama died (eighty, in Japanese count, *aetatis suae*), and throughout the sequence we sense a practiced ease in raising those matters that interest him most. The danger probably lies equally in interpreting the sequence too biographically, too sentimentally—or too little as a product of Sōgi's real life and feeling. We can certainly admit that the Japanese have seldom made our rigid distinction between life and writing. In fact, there is a good deal of the old poet in this sequence, and it is all the more moving for that. Of course the poet is there as poet, not just as an old man. The best evidence for that can be given very simply. A quarter of the stanzas—a very unusually high proportion—have the subtopic of Love (25 of 100). At his age and as a priest of some earnestness of cloth, Sōgi meant so remarkably a stress on love in no simple autobiographical way. On the other hand, the longing and grief characteristic of Japanese love poetry must have seemed appropriate. We can connect his remarks to the sequence in other assured ways. He says that the flowers of the spring season and the moon made him write. That is no common gesture. The first stanza is a flower stanza, a rare thing, and, if not without parallel, still a clear realization of what he said got him started. And, instead of the usual eight moon stanzas (one for each side of the four sheets) there are in fact ten, although, as in *Three Poets*, here too is omitted that one expected on the last side, the fast finale section.

In many respects the sequence exemplifies Sōgi's practice. The Miscellaneous stanzas amount to almost half (43 of the 100; they might have exceeded the seasonal poems by that proportion ordinarily); and spring and autumn stanzas predominate among them, with 18 on spring and 25 on autumn. Both summer with 4 stanzas and winter with 6 are also represented. If there is any special emphasis in this, it surely involves the preponderance of autumn and winter stanzas, with their greater sense of sadness, of deprivation. Some of the subtopics are not easy to ascertain, as we shall see in a moment, but Love accounts for more (25) than the three others combined: Travel (4), Grievance (10), and Buddhism (5). Sōgi had a special fondness for Ground stanzas, and, if my assessments are correct, he has about twice as many (20) as Design stanzas (9). (Let me stress again that assessments of impressiveness and relation here are my responsibility. They should be taken as suggestions rather than as infallible decrees.) Of the stanzas using intermediate relation, the proportions are more nearly equal, with the Ground-Design (37) exceeding somewhat the Design-Ground (34).

The chief art involves relatedness and pacing of such relatedness. In this matter, the general statistics are not unusual:

Close	18	(55)
Close-Distant	37	
Distant-Close	32	(44)
Distant	12	

Statistics do not tell everything, however. The first instance of Distant relation comes with the twenty-fifth stanza, which suggests that such agitation grows when we get to the second sheet (stanzas 23ff.), and that is so on other grounds also. Here are some of our knowing editor's comments. At the end of the front of the second sheet (after 36), Kaneko Kinjirō remarks that it is heavy with Grievance and Love stanzas. At the end of the back of that sheet (after 50), he comments on the misery it treats. At the end of the front of the third sheet (after 64), he says that there is an acute sense of an age torn by strife. If minuteness of connection characterizes the next side (the back of the third sheet, ending with 78), the last side of the Development section (79-92) "is afloat with the gloom of old age." And the finale (93-100) closes amid the uneasiness of life.

In many important respects, this is an old man's poem. It concerns age, the past, a world present but soon to be lost, a sense of what religion requires, with perhaps a yet keener sense that one yearns for the world in spite of its insubstantiality. Because he is the sole author, Sōgi develops such concerns, sometimes to the point of being more self-revealing than elsewhere. If life in China is miserable, there is also no quiet in Japan (27-28). He wonders when a land under imperial sway will see peace, and he pities the common people whose lives were ruined by the ravages of those warring times (55-56). Surely his humble origins gave him a special sympathy. The sequence ends with imagery of a dream of clouds torn by winds, and of an old man awake through the night with a lamp—and a life—about to expire. No doubt Japanese critics often err in making too much of the autobiographical element in these matters, because traditional interpretations are apt to suppose too easy an identification between the poet and the speakers of poems. Yet in the West we sometimes err in the opposite fashion, assuming that the poet is as it were unacquainted with the speakers used. In this solo renga, we can allow ourselves somewhat greater license in connecting Sōgi with the voices we hear.

There are moments when technical problems arise for us, in particular two near the end of the sequence. Here are 85-86.

85	Yoshi saraba	If that is how it is
	sora mo shigure yo	the sky too may add its drizzle
	sode no ue	to that upon my sleeve
86	tagui dani aru	and let it join me as companion
	omoi naraba ya	to share the yearnings of my heart

The problem involves topics and subtopics. To one who follows a line of interpretation running from Satomura Jōha and *Ubuginu* to Yamada Yoshio and Konishi Jin'ichi, agreement is not always possible with so fine an editor and critic as Kaneko Kinjirō. He classifies 85 as a Winter stanza, because of "shigure" (drizzle). My interpreters allow for either Autumn or Winter, but I have accepted Kaneko's Winter, on the grounds that there have been three Autumn stanzas (82-84) leading up to this one, and three fulfills the usual minimum number for that season. Kaneko adds that "shigure" and "sode" (sleeve) indicate Love. That seems unlikely. *Ubuginu* does say (p. 301) that expressions such as "yoshi saraba" (If that is how it is) may be Love or not. But for "sode," it gives (p. 198) only the phrase "sode no ka" (scent of the sleeves) as a Love term. It adds, "With 'sode nururu' [sleeves are wetted], 'namida' [tears] may go for two stanzas. But it is not a Love stanza."

All this would be easy enough, except that in 86 "omoi" (yearnings of my heart) is a standard word to designate Love, and if this stanza deals with that topic it is the sole one to do so at this stage. A single stanza on Love simply violates renga canons. Usually three is thought the proper number, although in *Yunoyama* there are but two at one stage (74-75). Three possibilities exist. It may be that Sōgi is allowing himself a freedom in old age that he would not have felt permitted in youth and so has but one Love stanza (86). It may be, as Kaneko thinks, that both 85 and 86 are on Love. It seems more likely to me, however, that both are on Grievance—a topic otherwise represented relatively seldom in this most sober renga—and so I have judged them.

The last two stanzas pose similar problems, with Kaneko assigning Grievance subtopics that my authorities do not allow. Konishi Jin'ichi mentions (*Sōgi*, p. 235) that he has been using the criteria of Jōha style renga. If they do not apply to renga composed in Sōgi's time, then his discussion and analysis is faulty, he says; but "I know no other critical standards." We can use only those we know and make them as clear as we can by reference to our authorities. These include the later Renga Masters Sōboku (d. 1545) and Shūkei (d. 1544), whom Kaneko quotes on each stanza.

Fortunately, we have greater security in larger matters. Everyone thinks of *Three Poets* as the standard example of renga. On the other hand, *Yunoyama* is considered the finest of sequences composed by three poets (and those the same as in the renga written that spring evening at Minase). Yet the highest praise must go to *Sōgi Alone*. This estimation began with the poet, who has a remark somewhat loosely paraphrased by Konishi (*Sōgi*, p. 59) to the effect that "This is my renga of my world and my lifetime." Comparison holds particular difficulties in renga, where so much depends on ceaseless connection. But it will be recalled how beautiful a sequence there is in *Three Poets*, culminating at the end of the third sheet with Sōgi's stanza on the person going by in a haze of rain at evening (78). An even lovelier sequence in *Sōgi Alone* (65-68) culminates with a stanza on a little fishing boat anchored to the haze on the offing. For a comparable sequence in *Yunoyama*, we may take the following stanzas (36-39). The first (36) is by Sōgi.

36	Furuki miyako no	Long ago a capital stood here
	inishie no michi	and its road leads back into the past
37	saku hana mo	the flowers are in bloom
	omowazarame ya	and who would think that springtime
	haru no yume	should pass as in a dream
	Shōhaku	

	Saku hana mo	The flowers are in bloom
	omowazarame ya	and who would think that springtime
	haru no yume	should pass as in a dream
38	sakura to ieba	yet all I need say is "cherries"
	yamakaze zo fuku	and the wind storms from the mountains
	Sōchō	
	Sakura to ieba	One need only call them cherries
	yamakaze zo fuku	and the wind storms from the mountains
39	asatsuyu no	yet the morning dew
	nao nodoka nite	lingers with a special stillness
	kasumu no ni	upon haze-thickened moors
	Sōgi	

From all these examples, we learn that Sōgi followed the genius of the greatest poets before him: writing poetry because people must do so to convey what it is that moves them, involved deeply in a world prized, it seems, for Shinto attractions and deprived by Buddhist knowledge, and above all modulating misery with beauty. But Sōgi gave various versions of such motives. In one of his finest waka, the beauty predominates because the human self intrudes less (*Gunsho Ruijū*, 15: 489). The topic is "The Bell of an Old Temple."

Yume sasou	Inviting dreams,
Kane wa fumoto ni	The sound of the temple bell
Koe ochite	Tumbles on foothills,
Kumo ni yo fukaku	And with clouds the night grows deep
Mine no tomoshibi.	Where on a peak a lamp still glows.

A lovely poem. Yet it lacks the power and certainly the bleaker personality of the last two stanzas of *Sōgi Alone*. We find in them similar diction and images, but a wisdom earned by many years and many sufferings. Let it be emphasized as strongly as one can that they are the conclusion of a sequence informed by the wisdom of ripe age and modulated by a beauty of stanza connectedness with variation unsurpassed in renga. So understood, they are beyond my powers of critical description.

The text used is that of Kaneko Kinjirō in *Renga Haikaishū*.

Fushimono. Or "Nanihito." Another version gives "Nanikara," "Related to Cathay"

1 Design. No Relation. Spring. Trees.
  Sōgi begins with a flower stanza (hana, "flower"—rather than sakura, "cherry blossoms"—being the necessary word). All agreed that cherry blossoms were loved so much because their time of beauty is so very brief, briefer in Japan than North America. The first flower stanza.

2 Design-Ground. Close-Distant. Spring. Residences.
  "Shadows" is added to emphasize that the flower petals of 1 are falling in this scene. "Kururu" (to grow dusky) plays on "niwa" (garden) and both elements of "harukaze" (a spring breeze). Probably the wind is not responsible for making the blossoms fall but is a soft spring breeze fitting with the scene.

3 Design-Ground. Close. Spring. Residences. Night. Radiance. Rising Things. Peaks.
  The time of evening moves ahead a little. The speaker is now on the verandah of a house, but his attention is drawn farther outside. Kaneko quotes Shūkei on the tranquility of the relation to 2, so natural that "There is nothing special for the mind to note." It is a surprise to find a moon stanza so soon, especially after the flower stanza in 1. Also, the spring topic does not prepare us, since most moon stanzas are autumnal.

4 Ground-Design. Distant-Close. Miscellaneous. Travel.
  The connections lie between sky and the moon of 3 and "wakanu" (cannot be distinguished) and haze in 3. Travel is unusual in the first eight stanzas, and we expect a quick shift to a season, probably autumn—but we are wrong.

(*Sōgi Dokugin Nanibito Hyakuin*)

Nanibito   *Related to Person*

1   Kagiri sae   Now that they end
     nitaru hana naki   there is no flower that can compare
     sakura kana   with cherry blossoms

     Kagiri sae   Now that they end
     nitaru hana naki   there is no flower that can compare
     sakura kana   with cherry blossoms
2   shizuka ni kururu   the garden softly stirs with shadows
     harukaze no niwa   as a spring breeze brings the dusk

     Shizuka ni kururu   The garden softly stirs with shadows
     harukaze no niwa   as a spring breeze brings the dusk
3   hono kasumu   beyond the eaves
     nokiba no mine ni   faintly cast in haze the peak
        tsuki idete   brightens with the moon

     Hono kasumu   Beyond the eaves
     nokiba no mine ni   faintly cast in haze the peak
        tsuki idete   brightens with the moon
4   omoi mo wakanu   and the path I travel here below
     karifushi no sora   cannot be distinguished in my thoughts

5 Design-Ground. Close. Miscellaneous. Travel.
The connection exists between dream here and "karifushi" in 4, since the word can be read to mean lie down for a temporary sleep. The travel subtopic is also shared. The traveler is stationary in this stanza, while his dream (probably of someone loved) comes and returns (to her home?). "Yume" (dream) raises the stanza.

6 Ground-Design. Close-Distant. Miscellaneous. Travel. Persons.
This is perhaps Close in relation. The opening words are parallel with those in 5, and "mienu" (cannot be seen) is an associated word with "yume" (dream). The traveler has now been deserted by the dream of 5 and the friend here.

7 Design-Ground. Close. Winter. Falling Things.
This stanza emphasizes the loneliness of the speaker, who is now only implied. It is a surprise to have winter rather than autumn, the season paired with spring. Teika uses the phrase "shimo mayou" (doubtful in frost) for the sky (*Shinkokinshū*, 1: 63), and Kaneko quotes a stanza by Sōgi from *A Thousand Stanzas Related to Crossing* (*Nanikoshi Senku*) where the phrase is used for hills and no one is to be seen.

8 Ground-Design. Close-Distant. Winter. Plants.
The frost of 7 is the agent of the withering. It is very Japanese to assume that on seeing the withered patch the observer wonders what kind of grass it was. The front of the first sheet ends with a bleakness surprising after the loveliness of the first three stanzas. We shall see much of both, sometimes together, in what follows.

♦   ♦   ♦   ♦

9 Design. Close. Autumn. Insects.
This impressive stanza is like beginning with another hokku. The clump of grass left from the patch is, as Sōboku puts it, the insects crying-place (mushi no nakidokoro), closely relating the stanzas, although there is some jar in moving to autumn from winter, rather than the reverse. The topic of 8 is frequently carried over to 9, from front to back on the first sheet. Unnamed insects are restricted to a single use in one hundred stanzas.

Omoi mo wakanu
karifushi no sora
5   koshi kata o
izuku to yume no
kaeru ran

    Koshi kata o
izuku to yume no
kaeru ran
6   yuku hito mienu
nobe no harukesa

Yuku hito mienu
nobe no harukesa
7   shimo mayjou
michi wa kasuka ni
arawarete

    Shimo mayou
michi wa kasuka ni
arawarete
8   karuru mo shiruki
kusamura no kage

♦   ♦   ♦   ♦

Karuru mo shiruki
kusamura no kage
9   naku mushi no
shitau aki nado
isogu ran

The path I travel here below
cannot be distinguished in my thoughts
    from which quarter
was it that the dream appeared
    and to which returned

    From which quarter
was it that the dream appeared
    and to which returned
the friend who came cannot be seen
where the moors stretch on and on

The visitor cannot be seen
where the moors stretch on and on
    doubtful in frost
the course of the road beyond
    shows but faintly

    Doubtful in frost
the course of the path beyond
    shows but faintly
yet the withering is distinct
in the crumpled shapes of plants

Even the withering is distinct
in the crumpled shapes of plants
    why is it, Autumn,
that though insects cry they love you
    you hurry to your end

10 Ground-Design. Distant-Close. Autumn.
"Nowaki" designates typhoon winds. Kaneko regards the word as having special associations or derivation from *The Tale of Genji*, where it is the title for the brief twenty-eighth book and is mentioned elsewhere. There seems to be a degree of personification here, although not as strong as in 9. The preface or jo seems to end here.

11 Design-Ground. Close-Distant. Autumn. Night. Radiance.
The typhoon gales have passed, sweeping the sky clear of clouds. The second moon stanza again comes early in its part.

12 Design-Ground. Distant-Close. Miscellaneous. Night. Waters.
Kaneko gives a Travel subtopic because of Kiyomi Barrier, something not authorized by *Ubuginu* or Yamada in *Renga Hōshiki Kōyō*. In Japanese, dawn "opens" or "brightens" (ake-) which also applies to the door of the barrier gate (-sekido). We have here a "nadokoro," or named place that literally means "pure view," so giving some connection with 11.

13 Ground-Design. Close-Distant. Miscellaneous.
On the basis of the place name here, Kaneko again classifies the stanza as Travel. He may be right, but I am following another line of renga interpretation, as in 12. There are two Sumida Rivers mentioned in earlier literature, neither very far from Kiyomi Barrier. Since that barrier is on the coast, a river scene fits well here.

14 Ground. Close-Distant. Miscellaneous.
This stanza has a honzetsu the Ninth Episode of *The Tales of Ise*, on which Sōgi lectured. The fact gives credence to Shūkei's remark that the Sumida of 13 is the one in Musashi (present Saitama Prefecture and Tokyo), as mentioned in *The Tales of Ise*. This is a fine example of a Ground stanza, plain in language, no imagery. It also begins a run of stanzas greatly fluctuating in impressiveness.

Naku mushi no
shitau aki nado
  isogu ran
10   sono mama hageshi
nowakidatsu koe

    Why is it, Autumn,
that though insects cry they love you
    you hurry to your end
what sounds like the voice of gales
rises in its fearsome rage

Sono mama hageshi
nowakidatsu koe
  me ni kakaru
11   kumo mo naki made
  tsuki sumite

What sounds like the voice of gales
rose up in its fearsome rage
    with utter clarity
and not a cloud to arrest the eye
    the moon shines on

  Me ni kakaru
kumo no naki made
  tsuki sumite
12   Kiyomigasekido
nami zo akeyuku

    With utter clarity
and not a cloud to arrest the eye
    the moon shines on
and then the Kiyomi Barrier gate
opens as dawn moves on the waves

Kiyomigasekido
nami zo akeyuku
  itsu kite ka
13   Sumidagawara ni
  mata mo nen

The gate of Kiyomi Barrier
opens as dawn moves on the waves
    the River Sumida
when shall I come here again
    to wake upon its bank

  Itsu kite ka
Sumidagawara ni
  mata mo nen
14   hanareba tsurashi
tomo to suru hito

    the River Sumida
when shall I come here again
    to sleep upon its bank
it is painful not to share this
with the friend who left me here

15 Design-Ground. Distant-Close. Spring. Trees.
The conception fits well with 14, but there is little verbal or topical relation. This is the second flower stanza and is supernumerary, since the convention calls for but one per sheet, and this sheet began with one (1). Sōgi plays freely with the rules as an old man, wanting to satisfy himself.

16 Ground. Close-Distant. Spring.
"Whirling Flowers and Falling Leaves" tell of the transience (mujō) of life, something that someone in orders should know; he therefore should feel no attraction in the phenomenal world. But the Japanese love spring, and religious imperatives are easily set aside, making it all sadder and lovelier. The season was spring as Sōgi began.

17 Design-Ground. Close. Spring. Grievances. Residences. Rising Things.
In connection with 16, this stanza presents a person of religion who yet has an elegant taste for the seasons. By itself, the stanza is far less concerned with religion. The speaker is guided and hidden by the essence of spring: haze. Another fine example of Close relation.

18 Ground-Design. Close-Distant. Miscellaneous. Grievances. Rising Things.
The tone changes markedly. "Yukue" has a range of meanings from direction to being taken to death, most of which are well conveyed by the smoke image (a Rising Thing going toward the clouds), as death is suggested by its extinction. Haze in 17 and smoke associate well as Rising Things.

19 Design. Distant-Close. Autumn. Clothes. Night. Radiance.
The life of salt-makers was considered an emblem of human misery. Yet by virtue of the exile of Ariwara Yukihira (818-93) and of Prince Genji at Suma and Akashi, it also took on poetic richness. As in the nō, *Matsukaze* (the Yukihira story), the sisters carrying brine see the moon reflected in pails; here it is in tears on the sleeve. The third moon stanza.

15	Hanareba tsurashi
	tomo to suru hito
	  chigiriki ya
	aranu noyama no
	  hana no kage
		It is painful not to share this
		with the friend who left me here
		  did I pledge myself
		at this nameless hill upon the moor
		  meeting beneath the flowers

16	Chigiriki ya
	aranu noyama no
	  hana no kage
	yo o nogarete mo
	haru wa mutsumaji
		Did I pledge myself
		at this nameless hill upon the moor
		  to these lovely flowers
		though I have renounced the world
		spring appeals with transient things

17	Yo o nogarete mo
	haru wa mutsumaji
	  mi o kakusu
	io wa kasumi o
	  tayori nite
		Though I have renounced the world
		spring appeals with transient things
		  to put the world behind
		the growing haze acts as the guide
		  to my hermitage

18	Mi o kakusu
	io wa kasumi o
	  tayori nite
	kien keburi no
	yukue o zo matsu
		To put the world behind
		the growing haze acts as the guide
		  to my hermitage
		and I await the extinction
		of the smoke above my pyre

19	Kien keburi to
	yukue zo matsu
	  moshio kumu
	sode sae tsuki o
	  tanomu yo ni
		As they await the extinction
		of the smoke above their fire
		  and ladle brine at night
		even the saltmakers' sleeves
		  hope the moon will rise

20 Ground. Distant-Close. Autumn.
This is joined to 19 by the mention of autumn and concern with response to it. The u- of "uramin" suggests "u(shi)" miserable, so strengthening it from its usual meaning of "resent" to a stronger feeling.

21 Ground-Design. Distant-Close. Autumn. Love. Falling Things.
The connection with 20 involves "uramin" and the waka topic here of "uramu koi," resentful love. Perhaps (as my students have thought) this is really tenuous enough to be Distant. But both stanzas have an autumn topic. Sōgi introduces autumn love here so that he can go on to two further stanzas on love, effecting a transition to the second sheet.

22 Ground. Close. Miscellaneous. Love. Persons.
The woman assumes that if he has been faithless to her (21), he must be visiting another woman (who will discover the same thing in her turn). So the first sheet ends, and so also the initial stage of the development section (9-92). Autumn has been the dominant season. Human affairs also have mattered.

$$\begin{matrix} \blacklozenge & \blacklozenge & \blacklozenge & \blacklozenge \\ \blacklozenge & \blacklozenge & \blacklozenge & \blacklozenge \end{matrix}$$

23 Ground-Design. Close-Distant. Miscellaneous. Love. Plants.
The suffering, distraught woman now presumes that her estranged lover is promiscuous as well as faithless to her. The grassy fields are those he would cross to visit the other women at the trysting time of dusk. Any woman's field will do, she thinks.

24 Ground. Distant-Close. Miscellaneous. Travel.
This is a very skillful transformation from Love to Travel, with the promise now being to someone where he was born or possibly in the capital. (Travel is never toward the capital, but may be between two other points.) Both sides of the first sheet had Travel stanzas. This is a high proportion early on.

Moshio kumu
sode sae tsuki o
   tanomu yo ni
20   kokoro nakute ya
aki o uramin

Ladling brine at night
even the saltmakers' sleeves
   hope the moon will rise
yet they must lack refinement
hating autumn for its pain

Kokoro nakute ya
aki o uramin
   kakaru na yo
21   ada koto no ha no
tsuyu no kure

Is it to lack refinement
hating autumn for its pain
   I must never trust
his promises that turn to air
   like dew on leaves at dusk

Kakaru na yo
ada koto no ha no
   tsuyu no kure
22   tare o ka towan
aware to mo miji

   I must never trust
his promises that turn to air
   like dew on leaves at dusk
whom else does he visit now
indifferent to what I feel

♦ ♦ ♦ ♦
♦ ♦ ♦ ♦

Tare o ka towan
aware to mo miji
   chigirite mo
23   e ya wa nabete no
kusa no hara

Whom else does he visit now
indifferent to what I feel
   he may have promised
but the grassy fields he visits
   belong to everyone

Chigirite mo
e ya wa nabete no
kusa no hara
24   kaerikon o mo
shiranu furusato

   He may have promised
but the grassy fields he crosses
   cover everything
and though his native place waits on
it does not know if he'll return

25 Design-Ground. Distant. Miscellaneous. Travel. Rising Things. Waters.
The speaker is uncertain of the destination ("yukue": see comment on 18), especially in the perilous element of the sea. Attention goes to the distance, where clouds and waves mingle. The first line is decidedly Ground. Thereafter the tone rises.

26 Ground-Design. Close. Miscellaneous. Travel. Persons. Waters.
Now the sea is metaphorical ("nise no umi," pretended sea, in renga criticism); otherwise the sea image could not follow the boat image of 25. This interestingly restates 25, with the first word here, "nami(da)" or tears echoing the last there, "nami" or waves in sense and sound.

27 Ground-Design. Close-Distant. Miscellaneous. Grievances.
The traveler at sea has reached China, only to discover that the miseries of human life are everywhere. Because Morokoshi is thought of as a place to and from which boats ply in trade, this seems to me more Close than Distant (see the second line of 26). The impressiveness may be Design-Ground.

28 Ground-Design. Close. Miscellaneous.
Now back in Japan ("hi no moto," giving the native reading of the characters for Nihon, Nippon), life again turns out to be miserable. The human condition.

29 Design. Distant. Spring. Residences. Cultivation. Peaks.
The previous stanza is less agitated with this, "nodokeki" in 28 now meaning something like "calm." The absence of calm involves here the speaker's response to the end of the cherry blossoms and the lateness of the season.

30 Design-Ground. Close. Spring. Residence. Rising Things. Peaks.
Haze may come at any time in spring, including its very end, as here, where spring seems to disappear into the village far beyond. Sōgi next moves to autumn, a common enough shift. But by composing only two spring stanzas in succession, he violates one of the rules of renga, another sign that this sequence is composed for his own appreciation in old age.

Kaerikon o mo
shiranu furusato
25   ika ni seshi
funade zo ato mo
kumo no nami

Although my native place waits on
it does not know if I'll return
    why did I come aboard
a boat whose wake leaves far behind
    the clouds that join the waves

    Ika ni seshi
funade zo ato mo
    kumo no nami
26   namida no umi o
wataru tabibito

    Why did I come aboard
a boat whose wake leaves far behind
    the clouds that join the waves
crossing upon a sea of tears
bitter to the voyager

Namida no umi o
wataru tabibito
27   Morokoshi mo
ame no shita to ya
tsurakaran

Crossing upon a sea of tears
bitter to the traveller
    and does not China too
lie beneath this selfsame sky
    bound in misery

    Morokoshi mo
ame no shita to ya
tsurakaran
28   sumeba nodokeki
hi no moto mo nashi

    Does not China also
lie beneath this selfsame sky
    bound in misery
yet even in the sun's own land
anyone who lives will suffer

Sumeba nodokeki
hi no moto mo nashi
29   sakura saku
mine no shibaya ni
haru kurete

Even in the sun's own land
those years of life brought pain
    now the cherries bloom
as at the brushwood hut upon the peak
    spring nears its end

    Sakura saku
mine no shibaya ni
haru kurete
30   usuku kasumeru
yamagiwa no sato

    The cherries bloom
as at the brushwood hut upon the peak
    spring nears its end
and at the margin of the hills
the village merges with faint haze

31 Design. Distant-Close. Autumn. Birds. Night. Radiance.
The strong verb for the moon derives from its use for the wind in waka, whence it was taken up for renga by poets like Shinkei. We should imagine a pause as the moon falls behind the hills of 30 (the connection with that stanza), then as light appears in the haze, birds begin to sing. Lovely and natural. Fourth moon stanza.

32 Ground-Design. Distant-Close. Autumn. Love. Falling Things.
This connects with 31, because lovers parted in the morning. Dew is evanescent, soon gone. It may also suggest tears. Cf. John Donne, "Breake of day" (3): "Why should we rise, because 'tis light?" also spoken by a woman, rare as that is in Western poems by men.

33 Ground-Design. Close. Autumn. Love.
Lovers slept under their robes piled one on the other. Hence lovers' parting is called "kinuginu no wakare," parting of the robes, or as here by metonomy, sleeves (sode). He has left, and the wind that blew his sleeves as he parted chills her heart. The season is indicated by "mi ni shimeru."

34 Ground. Distant-Close. Miscellaneous. Love.
We move from morning to evening, from his departure to his subsequent neglect. 33 and this well show the typical version of love: the woman's unfulfilled yearning.

35 Ground. Close-Distant. Miscellaneous. Love.
The basic postulation of the stanza involves the opposition between "omou" (yearning) and "wasuren" (forget). Sōgi has descended from the heights to Ground generalization.

36 Ground. Close. Miscellaneous. Love.
It is not clear whether the woman addresses herself or is being addressed by another person. Five love stanzas in a row is sanctioned, but it is also unusual. It suggests the great misery of love, something heightened by three ground stanzas in succession (34-36) at the end of the front of the second sheet.

♦   ♦   ♦   ♦

	Usuku kasumeru	At the margin of the hills
	yamagiwa no sato	the village merges with faint haze
31	tsuki ochite	the moon sweeps down
	tori no koegoe	and then the songs of various birds
	akuru yo ni	break with morning light

	Tsuki ochite	The moon sweeps down
	tori no koegoe	and then the songs of various birds
	akuru yo ni	break with morning light
32	tsuyu nagori naku	do we then wake that we may part
	oki ya wakaren	like dew soon gone without regret

	Tsuyu nagori naku	Did we wake then just to part
	oki ya wakaren	like dew soon gone without regret
33	mi ni shimeru	all that I retain
	kaze nomi sode no	of his robe that covered us
	katami nite	is the wind's bleak cold

	Mi ni shimeru	All that I retain
	kaze nomi sode no	of his robe that covered us
	katami nite	is the wind's bleak cold
34	taekoshi kata no	and each long day yields to evening
	yūbe ni zo naru	with endurance of his neglect

	Taekoshi kata no	Each long day yields to evening
	yūbe ni zo naru	with endurance of his neglect
35	omou na yo	enough of yearning
	wasuren mo koso	such a suffering heart as mine
	kokoro nare	may well forget

	Omou na yo	Enough of yearning
	wasuren mo koso	such a suffering heart as yours
	kokoro nare	may well forget
36	tsuraki ni nomi ya	why should you grow accustomed
	narawasaru beki	only to the anguish of neglect

♦   ♦   ♦   ♦

37 Ground-Design. Distant-Close. Miscellaneous. Buddhism.
One part of a house remains, though in ruin. (A neglected house is always thought of as being overrun with growth of plants, weeds, and trees.) The "michi" here is the Way of the Buddha. Sōboku glosses the rampant growth as irreligious persons. The good live among the many bad.

38 Design-Ground. Distant. Spring. Cultivation.
An allusion to a poem by Ki no Tomonori (*Kokinshū*, 1: 38) is involved. His poem ends "Shiru hito zo shiru" (only those can judge who know the best), referring to plum blossoms. By connection with 37, this person with genuine taste is also a good person. Sōboku glosses: "A person who really knows flowers is a good person. The flowers also know that knowing person. . . ." Shūkei says much the same.

39 Design-Ground. Distant-Close. Spring. Clothes. Rising Things.
The connection is in conception; the words are not close. Once again Sōgi's favored succession is from flowers to haze: see 1 and 3, 29 and 30. This is the fourth appearance of haze (after 3, 17, 30) in the first two sheets. As a favorite of Sōgi's, it appears twice more (68, 79).

40 Ground-Design. Close-Distant. Spring.
Kaneko suggests that a line by Po Chü-i may lie behind this stanza, but numerous waka seem closer. A poem by Tsurayuki (*Kokinshū*, 1: 22) could be said to lie behind 39 and 40 in combination.

41 Ground-Design. Distant. Miscellaneous. Buddhism.
Kaneko splendidly recalls a poem (*Fūgashū*, 18: 2036) that relates 40 with this: "Be not surprised / That today should also close / In the world's Void; / Our miseries fill the sky / Sounding with the temple bell at dusk." Both Sōboku and Shūkei presume that the crematorium at Toribe is designated as the scene.

42 Ground. Close. Miscellaneous. Buddhism. Persons.
The lament continues over the failure to achieve enlightenment and live according to the Way of the Buddha.

	Tsuraki ni nomi ya	Why should they grow accustomed
	narawasaru beki	only to the anguish of neglect
37	michi aru mo	they still lead just lives
	katae wa nokoru	even in what stands of a dwelling
	yomogiu ni	lost in overgrowth

	Michi aru mo	They still lead just lives
	katae wa nokoru	even in what stands of a dwelling
	yomogiu ni	lost in overgrowth
38	shiru hito o shiru	where flowers blossom for all those
	hana no awaresa	who best know what flowers mean

	Shiru hito o shiru	The flowers blossom for all those
	hana no awaresa	who best know what flowers mean
39	ori ni au	and suiting with the time
	kasumi no sode mo	the haze drapes with its beauty
	iroiro ni	every kind of dress

	Ori ni au	Suiting with the time
	kasumi no sode mo	the haze drapes with its beauty
	iroiro ni	every kind of sleeve
40	kaeran sora mo	as the direction of return
	wakanu haru no no	is obscured across spring fields

	Kaeran sora mo	The direction of return
	wakanu haru no no	is obscured across spring fields
41	kane zo naru	the temple bell
	kyō mo munashiku	sounds on another day that passes
	sugi ya sen	empty of insight

	Kane zo naru	The temple bell
	kyō mo munashiku	sounds on another day that passes
	sugi ya sen	empty of insight
42	kikedomo nori ni	although instructed in the Law
	tōki waga mi yo	how far I wander from the Way

43 Ground. Close. Miscellaneous. Buddhism.
Kaneko classifies this as Grievance on the basis of "yowai" (old age), but *Ubuginu* gives Buddhism. Sōgi was in his seventy-ninth year when he wrote this and unquestionably speaks through of himself here. "Close" (chikaku) here plays against "far" (tōki) in 42.

44 Ground Design. Distant-Close. Autumn. Night. Radiance.
The first line has an extra syllable. This fifth moon stanza does not refer to "kokoro no tsuki," moon in the heart, which represents enlightenment. It is a natural moon, suggesting with 43 the need for enlightenment, a smooth transition to autumn, even if there is little verbal connection.

45 Ground-Design. Close-Distant. Autumn. Love. Rising Things. Peaks.
The mist shows why the moon could not be seen, but off to the east, where the moon rises above the hills, one may now hope to see the moon or gain a little respite from the pains of unfulfilled love-longing.

46 Design-Ground. Close-Distant. Autumn. Love. Trees.
The pines are on the hills of 46. This stanza tells why comfort should be had. It seems to be spoken by a friend of the woman who has been waiting in vain for her lover.

47 Ground-Design. Close-Distant. Miscellaneous. Love. Persons. Cultivation.
Several interpretations exist for "kokoro no sugi"; the one followed here is that the tree is a sign of love, as in *Kokinshū*, 18: 982, in which the woman invites a man to her place at Miwa Mountain: "Why not come and visit with me here? / (You can tell it by the cedar at the gate.)"

48 Ground. Close-Distant. Miscellaneous. Love. Residences.
The Close element depends on the allusion presumed in 47, and the interpretation of the vexed phrase. The gate (kado) also derives from the last line of the poem alluded to. The tone differs markedly. This completes a second run of five love stanzas.

Kikedomo nori ni
tōki waga mi yo
43   yowai nomi
hotoke ni chikaku
haya narite

Although instructed in the Law
how far I wander from the Way
    almost eighty years
bring me close to the Buddha's age
    without enlightenment

    Yowai nomi
hotoke ni chikaku
haya narite
44   mune naranu tsuki ya
miteru o mo min

    These eighty years
bring me close to the Buddha's age
    without enlightenment
the waxing moon that I behold
fails to illuminate my heart

Mune naranu tsuki ya
miteru o mo min
45   kiri haruru
yama ni nagusame
monoomoi

The waxing moon that has arisen
fails to illuminate the heart
    where the mist is clearing
in the eastern hills take comfort
    for unfilled desires

    Kiri haruru
yama ni nagusame
monoomoi
46   matsu oba aki no
kaze mo towazu ya

    Where the mist is clearing
in the eastern hills take comfort
    for unfilled desires
as autumn winds go to the pines
he will come if you can wait

Matsu oba aki no
kaze mo towazu ya
47   hito wa taga
kokoro no sugi o
tazunu ran

As autumn winds go to the pines
would he come if I but wait
    when some other heart
draws him to her like a cedar
    as a sign of love

    Hito wa taga
kokoro no sugi o
tazunu ran
48   kado furu michi no
taenu sae ushi

    Whose heart can it be
draws him to her like a cedar
    as a sign of love
although my gate is old the path
runs clear enough to show my pain

49 Design-Ground. Distant. Miscellaneous. Buddhism. Trees.
The only connection in imagery involves the assumption that the path goes through these fields to the temple, which is thought to be remote from any village. It is a faint image of a single person.

50 Design-Ground. Distant-Close. Winter. Clothes. Falling Things.
Moss-colored sleeves ("koke . . . koromode") designate the robes of a priest. Here it is also the real moss. The back of the second sheet ends with a proportion of stanzas on Buddhism and Love.

♦   ♦   ♦   ♦
♦   ♦   ♦   ♦

51 Ground-Design. Close-Distant. Winter. Person. Night.
Winter or autumn nights were proverbially long, so the suffering this one brings ("-waburu"—or "suffer"—governs winter as well as relating to what precedes) seems never to end. Although "oki-" means to be awake, in its sense of "fall" or "settle" it is an engo for "shimo" (dew) in 50.

52 Design-Ground. Close. Winter. Night. Radiance.
Again the syntax allows us to read "samuku naru" (grows colder) to apply to what follows as well as precedes. The long night of 51 is just ending with the first light, when winter was thought most appealing (this may well be a Design stanza). The sixth moon stanza.

53 Design-Ground. Distant. Miscellaneous. Birds. Plants.
This stanza also uses word play, with "shiruku" (distinct) yoking fore and after, and "-fushi" meaning a "matter" and a "joint" of a plant like bamboo. It is also an associated word with "ashi" (reeds); for once an English word, "stalks," suggests both meanings.

Kado furu michi no
taenu sae ushi
49 tsumagi koru
kage mo nodera wa
  kasuka nite

  Tsumagi koru
kage mo nodera wa
  kasuka nite
50 koke ni ikue no
shimo no koromode

   ♦ ♦ ♦ ♦
  ♦ ♦ ♦ ♦

Koke ni ikue no
shimo no koromode
51 okiitsutsu
mi o uchiwaburu
  fuyu no yo ni

  Okiitsutsu
mi o uchiwaburu
  fuyu no yo ni
52 tsuki samuku naru
ariake no sora

Tsuki samuku naru
ariake no sora
53 ashitazu mo
ukifushi shiruku
  ne ni tatete

Although his gate is old the path
runs clear enough to show his pain
  yet as he gathers wood
by the small temple in the fields
  he can just be seen

  As he gathers wood
by the small temple in the fields
  he can just be seen
the cold falls on the priestly sleeves
like frost on frost upon the moss

The cold falls on my priestly sleeves
like frost on frost upon the moss
  I cannot sleep
and fall to thinking of my troubles
  through the winter night

  I cannot sleep
and fall to thinking of my troubles
  through the winter night
the moon grows ever colder
fading in the sky at dawn

The moon grows ever colder
fading in the sky at dawn
  by the reeds the crane
also stalks about in anguish
  distinct in every cry

54 Ground-Design. Distant-Close. Miscellaneous. Waters.
The connection in images is that between the waves and the crane in the reeds by the shore. By itself the stanza would imply that the wind and waves are metaphors for human noise or tumult—in a household or in the world.

55 Ground. Distant-Close. Miscellaneous. Persons. Peaks. Waters.
Hills and streams imply different social groups, the whole differentiated society. Sōgi is thinking of the havoc of the Ōnin War and its long aftermath. It is not a very common subject in renga, but for examples see Yamada, *Renga Gaisetsu*, pp. 151-53. The social complaint seems somewhat Chinese.

56 Ground. Close. Miscellaneous. Persons.
Sōgi's low origins and his powers of humane observation showed him how the poor were suffering as the powerful struggled with each other for control. So rare is this subject in Japanese poetry that the Grievance classification appears not to include it.

57 Design-Ground. Distant-Close. Autumn. Plants. Falling Things.
"Tanomi" is to be taken both as "tanomi," what was hoped for, relied on, and as "ta no mi," the fruits of the fields, harvest. "Kakete" relates to the dew's settling on and ruining the grain and to autumn's coming on. With 56, that dew seems metaphorical for outside intrusions, incursions, or impositions.

58 Design-Ground. Close-Distant. Autumn. Residences. Plants.
Sōgi continues to plague the translator. "Kariho" means cut stalks of grain and also temporary hut, something "new thatched hut" misses by some distance. The dew of 57 is the agent for making the plants wither and fall.

59 Design. Distant-Close. Autumn. Birds. Clothes.
The beating of clothes (a way of cleaning them) is an image of great sadness, heightened here in complex ways involving autumn, twilight, time's passage, the feelings attributed to geese, and those of the speaker. The sounds of 58 and the first and third lines here are very like, especially the first line there and last here. This is the more mellifluous.

Ashitazu mo
ukifushi shiruku
ne ni tatete
54   kokorogokoro ni
sawagu namikaze

By the reeds the crane
also stalks about in anguish
distinct in every cry
feelings upon feelings rise
with the blustering wind and waves

Kokorogokoro ni
sawagu namikaze
55   yamakawa mo
kimi ni yoru yo o
itsu ka min

Feelings upon feelings rise
with the blustering wind and waves
shall we ever see
the time your reign brings lasting peace
to all hills and streams

Yamakawa mo
kimi ni yoru yo o
itsu ka min
56   ayafuki kuni ya
tami mo kurushiki

Shall we ever see
the time your reign brings lasting peace
to all hills and streams
and will the land not fall in ruin
with its commoners in distress

Ayafuki kuni ya
tami mo kurushiki
57   ueshi yori
tanomi o tsuyu ni
aki kakete

Will the land not fall to ruin
with its peasants in distress
since they tilled their fields
the harvest for which they hoped
is chilled with autumn dew

Ueshi yori
tanomi o tsuyu ni
aki kakete
58   kariho no kohagi
katsu chiru mo oshi

Since the fields were tilled
the harvest that raised great hopes
chills in autumn dew
bush clover by the new thatched hut
already is fallen here and there

Kariho no kohagi
katsu chiru mo oshi
59   koromo utsu
yūbe sugusu na
kari no koe

Bush clover by the new thatched hut
already is fallen here and there
while clothes are beaten
oh geese do not let the twilight pass
without your cries

60 Ground-Design. Close-Distant. Autumn. Night. Radiance.
Evening yields to night, and it seems the geese have still not cried. "Munashiki tsuki" is a strong conceit: empty moon. With this seventh moon stanza, we are two moons ahead of the stipulated number at this stage.

61 Ground-Design. Distant-Close. Miscellaneous. Love. Night. Falling Things.
Once more we hear the woman's complaint. The time must be later than 60, but the verbal connection is not very close.

62 Ground. Close-Distant. Miscellaneous. Love. Persons.
This exemplifies the image-free style often used in love stanzas. Unlike the case with Sōchō in *Three Poets*, however, Sōgi has matters under control, as the ease of progression from 60 to 65 shows.

63 Ground-Design. Close-Distant. Miscellaneous. Love.
The psychology seems very just. No reference is made to any person, and no nouns refer to persons here (in fact the stanza consists almost entirely of verbs and particles). Such being the case, it is not fully clear whether we should imagine the woman to be speaking to herself of "him" or "you," as if she had him beside her, which she does not; or whether this is to be imagined as sent with a letter. The first seems much more likely.

64 Ground-Design. Close. Miscellaneous. Love.
This is the last stage of his relations with her, when he even stops sending letters. The completeness with which she has been deserted is suggested by the fact that the only visitor or messenger she admits to having is the wind. So ends the front of the third sheet, with all its problems.

♦   ♦   ♦   ♦

	Koromo utsu	While clothes are beaten
	yūbe sugusu na	oh geese do not let the twilight pass
	kari no koe	without your cries
60	munashiki tsuki o	and as the moon moves on in vain
	uramite ya nen	must I lie down with bitter thoughts

	Munashiki tsuki o	As the moon moves on in vain
	uramite ya nen	must I lie down with bitter thoughts
61	towanu yo no	he did not come tonight
	kokoro yaritsuru	I thought no doubt it was the rain
	ame harete	but that has cleared

	Towanu yo no	He did not come tonight
	kokoro yaritsuru	I thought no doubt it was the rain
	ame harete	but that has cleared
62	mi o shiru ni sae	and what I know of what I lack
	hito zo nao uki	makes his unkindness all the worse

	Mi o shiru ni sae	What I know of my own faults
	hito zo nao uki	makes your unkindness all the worse
63	wasurene to	how could you have heard
	iishi o ika ni	I said I hoped you would forget me
	kikitsu ran	and why should you do so

	Wasurene to	How could he have heard
	iishi o ika ni	I said I hoped he would forget me
	kikitsu ran	and why should he do so
64	kaze no tayori mo	some rumors have come upon the winds
	kaku ya tayu beki	but why have his letters wholly ceased

♦ ♦ ♦ ♦

65 Design-Ground. Distant. Spring. Trees.

If the wind of 64 is taken as the central agent in the fall of the flowers, then this connection is Distant-Close. But this stanza suggests that the falling is largely in the past. As in 2, Sōgi seems not to assume the wind such an agent. The back of the third sheet begins as the whole sequence had, with a flower stanza, and the move from front to back of the third has not the usual continuation of topic or subtopic.

66 Design-Ground. Distant-Close. Spring. Residences.

The stanza sounds as if written about some former site of the capital. Only the location is left, with the long spring days warming in sadness for the past. The syntax is as relatively simple here as it has been agitated and compacted in 65 and many earlier stanzas.

67 Ground-Design. Distant. Spring. Persons. Radiance.

The phenomenon is that of "gossamer," or light shimmering in heat waves in the air. "Waga yo" may possibly mean "my world," but "ours" includes that, and in connection with 66 "waga yo" must be thought more general.

68 Design. Distant. Spring. Persons. Rising Things.

Sōgi has a special genius with stanzas using haze, and the connection—by juxtaposition—of this with 67 is beyond praise. The little boat is not far off the shore, but the sea is absolutely still. The haze cannot be distinguished from the sky, leaving the boat to hang by the haze from the sky and be held by it to the sea. So poor a thing as a fisherboat in so magical an atmosphere gives beauty to the transient phenomena of the Void.

69 Design-Ground. Close-Distant. Autumn. Night. Radiance. Waters.

It is a little later than 68, and the boat has now vanished into the darkness, leaving the speaker yearning for the moon. How overwhelming the experience is can be judged by the sudden shift from spring to autumn and the eighth moon stanza.

65

Kaze no tayori mo
kaku ya tayu beki
   hana wa haya
chiru sae mare no
   kure goto ni

Some have already yielded to the winds
but why have those ceased to blow
   the flowers have fallen
so that already few remain
   to go as each dusk comes

66

Hana wa haya
chiru sae mare no
   kure goto ni
hi nagaki nomi ya
furusato no haru

The flowers have fallen
so that already few remain
   to go as each dusk comes
spring comes at the ancient capital
where long days are its only pride

67

Hi nagaki nomi ya
furusato no haru
   itoyū no
arinashi o tada
   waga yo nite

Spring comes to the ancient capital
where long days are its only pride
   as a shimmer of light
seems both real and non-existent
   so does this world of ours

68

Itoyū no
arinashi o tada
   waga yo nite
kasumi ni kakaru
ama no tsuribune

As a shimmer of light
seems both real and non-existent
   so does this world of ours
with a line of haze for anchor
the fisherboat floats off at sea

69

Kasumi ni kakaru
ama no tsuribune
   nagamesen
tsuki na matare so
   nami no ue

With a line of haze for anchor
the fisherboat floats off at sea
   I long to see the view
oh moon do not delay your rising
   bright upon the waves

70 Ground-Design. Close-Distant. Autumn. Night. Waters.
If the moon would not rise, the night has been spent in vain. At this famous place something more might have been expected. For such use of Japanese place names, we have to look back to 12 and 13. "Akashi" also means "to dawn." The finest time of day in autumn is usually thought to be evening.

71 Ground-Design. Distant. Autumn. Love.
For some reason, Kaneko does not give the Love subtopic, which is traditional from waka. As often at this stage, Sōgi uses a Distant relation, although Kaneko does show that a poem in the *Senzaishū* (5, 313) connects the stag with the Akashi of 70.

72 Ground. Distant-Close. Miscellaneous. Love.
This stanza is an example of connection largely by juxtaposition. Such makes it seem natural following 71, but nothing in the words of either is shared. One or two examples of such connections give variety to a sequence, but too many would disjoint it.

73 Ground-Design. Distant-Close. Miscellaneous. Grievances.
The idea of a dusty world is essentially Buddhist, but it is a commonplace (like "vale of tears"). The six kinds of "dust" include colors, smells, tastes, etc. This might be thought to have a Buddhism subtopic, therefore, or even Love, as in certain waka. But I have followed Kaneko.

74 Design-Ground. Distant-Close. Miscellaneous. Grievances.
As with 66, this has the aura of an old capital, although here there remain some physical relics of the past. "Migiri" means "ishidatami," stones laid as flooring, something not used in ordinary houses.

75 Ground-Design. Close-Distant. Miscellaneous. Cultivation. Plants. Trees.
Within what had been the garden area, once no doubt walled or hedged, there are cultivated plants and trees now grown half wild. Beyond, such things have grown into a kind of wilderness. A well-realized conception.

	Nagamesen	I long to see the view
	tsuki na matare so	oh moon do not delay your rising
	nami no ue	bright upon the waves
70	tada ni ya aki no	the autumn night goes by in vain
	yo o Akashigata	as dawn lights the Akashi shore

	Tada ni ya aki no	It is in vain to pass the night
	yo o Akashigata	for dawn to light Akashi shore
71	tōzuma o	as the stag cries on
	urami ni taezu	with unbroken longing for his mate
	shika nakite	in some distant place

	Tōzuma o	The stag cries on
	urami ni taezu	with unbroken longing for his mate
	shika nakite	in some distant place
72	omoi no yama ni	and he would rid himself of life
	mi o ya tsuku san	on a mountain made of his desires

	Omoi no yama ni	Some would rid themselves of life
	mi o ya tsuku san	on mountains made of their desires
73	harau na yo	why brush away
	izuku ka chiri no	at the dust of this dreary world
	uchi naranu	since it lies everywhere

	Harau na yo	Do not brush away
	izuku ka chiri no	at the dust of this weary world
	uchi naranu	since it lies everywhere
74	migiri bakari o	some stones of palace flooring
	inishie no ato	are the sole traces of the past

	Migiri bakari o	Some stones of palace flooring
	inishie no ato	are the sole traces of the past
75	ueokishi	things had been planted
	hoka wa kusaki mo	but the shrubs and trees beyond
	nobe ni shite	tangle like a moor

76 Design-Ground. Distant-Close. Summer. Cultivation. Waters.
The connection with 75 involves its first line. Otherwise, everything is in marked contrast. This is a scene low in level, with the rice growing well.

77 Design-Ground. Distant. Summer. Love. Insects.
Fireflies, of course, lack voices, but the conceit is effective. "Ho" plays on "appearance" and "ear" of grain, so making a word association with "sanae" in 76.

78 Ground. Close-Distant. Miscellaneous. Love.
Like 77, this is on the waka topic of hidden love (shinobu koi): all the attempts to hide will not work. The usual conception is that the person loving reveals the fact in the face. "Iro" (color) also suggests the fireflies' light in connection with 77 and has associations with Love. As with the front of this third sheet, the back closes with Love, to be followed again by spring on the next side, although this time with continuance of the Love topic.

◆ ◆ ◆ ◆

◆ ◆ ◆ ◆

79 Design-Ground. Distant-Close. Spring. Love. Persons. Clothes. Rising Things.
The verb "hiku" (hikaru ran) relates to "kokoro" in 78 (kokoro ga hikareru) as to have one's heart taken or drawn by, and it is also an associated word with "kasumi" (haze). "Hikaru" also means to be radiant, colorful. The sense of color also remains in connection with 78 and with the sleeves. The conception of a sleeve of haze is very characteristic of this poet. The suggestion of beginning love (hatsu koi) implies that the man is embarked on a new affair.

80 Ground-Design. Distant. Spring. Travel. Peaks.
Only the rigors of traveling alone could make spring seem miserable. In earlier poetry, those who cross mountains or hills alone are usually lovers who do *not* find the spring miserable. Or if, as in "Ukifune" chapter in *The Tale of Genji* there is pain, the season is not spring. This stanza gives some surprise.

Ueokishi
hoka wa kusaki mo
nobe ni shite
76   kaze wa sanae o
wakuru sawamizu

Some things were planted
but the shrubs and trees beyond
    tangle like a moor
and in the water-flooded scene the wind
distinguishes the seedling rice

Kaze wa sanae o
wakuru sawamizu
77   koe o ho ni
ideji mo hakana
tobu hotaru

In the water-flooded scene the wind
distinguishes the seedling rice
    like fireflies in flight
hiding their anguished voice from others
    I suffer cruel restraint

Koe o ho ni
ideji mo hakana
tobu hotaru
78   iro ni kokoro wa
mienu mono ka wa

    Like fireflies in flight
hiding their anguished voice from others
    I suffer cruel restraint
the color of the heart glows forth
no matter how I hide my love

♦   ♦   ♦   ♦
♦   ♦   ♦   ♦

Iro ni kokoro wa
mienu mono ka wa
79   taga sode to
naseba kasumi ni
hikaru ran

The color of the heart shows forth
no matter how I hide my love
    what woman's sleeve
have I confused the bright haze with
    that it takes me so

Taga sode no
naseba kasumi ni
hikaru ran
80   haru sae kanashi
hitori kosu yama

    What woman's sleeve
have I confused the bright haze with
    that it takes my heart
for all its glories spring gives sorrow
as I cross these peaks alone

81 Design-Ground. Distant-Close. Spring. Grievances. Person. Birds.
A poem in the *Kokinshū* (9: 412) tells how the geese fly back to the north with one of their number missing, a famous poem by a woman regretting the loss of her husband. Here it is the one goose left, as the rest have flown to the world beyond. Each of the spring poems in this series (79-81) has a different subtopic.

82 Ground-Design. Close-Distant. Autumn. Grievances.
If in 81 Sōgi had termed the geese "kaeru kari" (returning), he could not make the transition he does here to autumn. Now the geese are not "returning" north but coming south. The stanza suggests that this is written before autumn, which the speaker doubts he will live to see.

83 Ground-Design. Close-Distant. Autumn.
Perhaps because it seems so simple to expect dawn after the proverbially long night of autumn (or winter), *Ubuginu* (p. 227) says it bad to add a stanza on dawn to one on "nagaki yo" (this long long night). One wonders what Sōgi will conceive of doing next.

84 Design-Ground. Close. Autumn. Night. Radiance.
The natural syntax would be "ware ni mieji to," which is changed here for stress on "mieji," which means something like, "Saying, 'I shall not appear to him.' " But since the speaker himself says the moon is crossing the sky, the moon means rather that she will grant him no pleasure. The syntax also places the initial verb (for not seeing) in a place natural after the last phrase in 83. The personification is very interesting. See 9 and 10. The ninth moon stanza.

85 Design-Ground. Close-Distant. Winter. Grievances. Clothes. Falling Things.
This and 86 present problems of classification. Kaneko thinks that "shigure" (drizzle) indicates winter, but it could also be autumn. I have followed him, however, since three stanzas on autumn suffice. But his statement that "shigure" and "sode" indicate love has no sanction in *Ubuginu*, which gives "sode no ka" (scent of the sleeves) as the only love "word." Also (still p. 198) it has: "With 'sode nururu' [sleeves are wetted] 'namida' [tears] may go two stanzas. But it is not a love stanza. . . ." On the other hand, it also tells us (301) that expressions such as "yoshi saraba" may be love or not.

81	Haru sae kanashi hitori kosu yama onoga yo wa kari no wakareji kazu tarade	For all its glories spring gives sorrow as I cross these peaks alone my life has been a loss like the one goose left to linger and all I loved have flown
82	Onoga yo wa kari no wakareji kazu tarade aki o kaken mo isa ya tama no o	My life has been a loss like the one goose left to suffer and all I loved have gone even vesting hopes in autumn what can I hope for from it all
83	Aki o kaken mo isa ya tama no o mi no usa wa toshi mo fu bakari nagaki yo ni	Even vesting hopes in autumn what can I hope for out of life my miseries are such that whole years pass by together on this long long night
84	Mi no usa wa toshi mo fu bakari nagaki yo wa mieji ware ni to tsuki ya iku ran	My miseries are such that whole years pass by together on this long long night the moon seems to slip away saying "Let him get no joy from me"
85	Mieji ware ni to tsuki ya iku ran yoshi saraba sora mo shigure yo sode no ue	The moon seems to slip away saying "Let him get no joy of me" if that is how it is the sky too may add its drizzle to that upon my sleeve

86 Ground. Distant-Close. Miscellaneous. Grievances.
The problem here is that "omoi" (yearnings) is the standard word for indicating Love, but that there are strong injunctions against just one Love stanza. Because neither Sōboku nor Shūkei as quoted by Kaneko mention Love here, I have presumed that this and 85 are Grievances stanzas. The other alternatives are that both concern Love or that 85 concerns Grievance and that Sōgi here breaks all precedent and has a single Love stanza.

87 Ground-Design. Close-Distant. Miscellaneous. Persons. Peaks.
There is the common association of mountains with strong winds.

88 Design-Ground. Close-Distant. Miscellaneous. Rising Things.
The path is faint and perilous, "hanging" (kake) among rocks; it seems to run out and be lost in clouds some distance ahead.

89 Design-Ground. Close-Distant. Miscellaneous. Waters.
The Yoshino was famous for its rapid current and dangerous course, which a *Kokinshū* poet (13, 673) compared to the risk of life and reputation in embarking on a love affair. The clouds of 88 are thought of as hiding the source asked about here. We have a named river "na no kawa."

90 Ground. Close-Distant. Miscellaneous. Grievances.
"Hayaku" (the distant past) also means rapidity, so following as if in the same stanza the "Yoshinogawa" of 89. Also, in that one excessive image in Japanese poetry, tears, we often read of "namida no se," a rapids of tears, so associating this with 89. There is again a degree of personification.

91 Ground-Design. Close. Miscellaneous. Grievances.
Everything is forgotten, and nothing is seen or heard—there are (in connection with 90) only tears for the losses sustained in old age.

Yoshi saraba
sora mo shigure yo
sode no ue
86 tagui dani aru
omoi naraba ya

If that is how it is
the sky too may add its drizzle
to that upon my sleeve
and let it join me as companion
to share the yearnings of my heart

Tagui dani aru
omoi naraba ya
87 tare kite ka
arashi ni taen
yama no kage

Let someone join me as companion
to share the yearnings of my heart
will no one come then
to help me endure the bitter storms
where the mountain looms

Tare kite ka
arashi ni taen
yama no kage
88 oku wa kumo iru
iwa no kakemichi

Will no one come
to help me endure the bitter storm
where the mountain looms
the perilous path among the crags
seems to close in gathering clouds

Oku wa kumo iru
iwa no kakemichi
89 ochisomeshi
takitsuse izuku
Yoshinogawa

The perilous path among the crags
seems to close in gathering clouds
what torrent starts
the waterfall that moves the rapids
of the Yoshino

Ochisomeshi
takitsuse izuku
Yoshinogawa
90 hayaku no koto o
namida ni zo tou

What torrent starts
the waterfall that moves the rapids
of the Yoshino
one should ask one's tears to tell
all about the distant past

Hayaku no koto o
namida ni zo tou
91 mono goto ni
oi wa kokoro no
ato mo nashi

I should ask my tears to tell
all about the distant past
everything that was
has vanished from my aged heart
leaving not a trace

92 Design. Distant-Close. Autumn. Residences. Plants. Night. Radiance.
The basic conception derives from a poem by Narihira (*Kokinshū*, 15: 747—not however alluded to) that the moon remains the same as people change. Here it shines with its wonted loveliness in the dew of the weeds overgrowing his old moon-viewing hut. This is the tenth and last moon stanza, two more than normal. So the front of the fourth sheet closes—as have all sides in this section—with bleakness or deprivation. The kyū or rapid close seems to begin here.

♦   ♦   ♦   ♦

93 Design-Ground. Close-Distant. Autumn. Clothes. Falling Things.
The moor with dew develops from the moon's shining on rampant weeds (with dew implied) in 92. Now a metaphorical dew is introduced with the named actual dew. Kaneko cites a poem by Priest Jien (1155-?1225; *Shinkokin-shū*, 15: 1338) which uses the phrases "nobe no tsuyu" and "sode yori suguru."

94 Ground-Design. Close-Distant. Autumn. Love. Peaks.
The movement from the moor to the mountains is accompanied by a causal sequence. Again and again in waka, renga, and haikai dew is said to be color-less but yet to affect the color of leaves. One is surprised to find love appearing so late in the sequence.

95 Ground. Distant-Close. Miscellaneous. Love. Persons.
The lament is that of a woman betrayed by her lover, although the tears of her complaint are more general.

96 Ground. Close-Distant. Miscellaneous. Love.
Buddhism does not ban suicide, although it does prohibit killing, even ani-mals. Taking one's life has long been thought the best way to end one's prob-lems and those one has made for others. In literature, a more common way for a distraught woman was to drown herself, as Ukifune attempts to do in *The Tale of Genji* (see the close of "Ukifune" and "Poetic Composition" ["Tenarai"]).

Mono goto ni
oi wa kokoro no
   ato mo nashi
92 medekoshi yado wa
   asajifu no tsuki

Everything that was
has vanished from my aged heart
   leaving not a trace
at the hut where I so loved the view
the moon still shines on rampant weeds

◆ ◆ ◆ ◆

Medekoshi yado wa
asajifu no tsuki
   nobe no tsuyu
93 sode yori oki ya
   narau ran

At the hut where I so loved the view
the moon still shines on rampant weeds
   perhaps this moor
learned to be beteared from dew
   settled on my sleeves

Nobe no tsuyu
sode yori oki ya
   narau ran
94 yama koso yukue
   iro kawaru uchi

Perhaps the moor
learned to be beteared from dew
   settled on my sleeves
leaves on the hills end in color
brought by a coldness like his heart's

Yama koso yukue
iro kawaru uchi
   tsure mo naki
95 hito ni kono yo o
   tanomame ya

Leaves on the hills end in color
brought by a coldness like his heart's
   how can I depend
on a world defined by someone
   lacking human feeling

Tsure mo naki
hito ni kono yo o
   tanomame ya
96 shinuru kusuri wa
   koi ni emahoshi

How can I depend
on a world defined by someone
   lacking human feeling
all I desire is a potion
to close a life of anguished love

97 Ground-Design. Close-Distant. Summer. Love. Plants.
One could argue that the classification should be Miscellaneous-Buddhism. In *Ubuginu* (p. 246) we read of "hachisu no chigiri": " . . . When the lotus throne is concerned, it is only Love." There is a Buddhist reference, but the *topic* is Love. Kaneko sees a change from desperation to a situation of happy love. This seems doubtful as the woman recalls a faithless lover's promise, especially in the last of a series of love stanzas.

98 Design-Ground. Distant-Close. Summer. Falling Things.
Yūdachi designates a summer shower that comes up quickly in the evening, pours very hard, and quickly passes on. "Tamayura" means briefly; "tama-" means beads, raindrops. We might have had a moon stanza in this last section by now, but we get none. As in *Three Poets*, the last side omits the moon stanza to emphasize "speed."

99 Design. Distant-Close. Miscellaneous. Rising Things. Night.
Kaneko assigns a Grievance subtopic, but *Ubuginu* does not for either "yume" (dream) or with "samuru" (wake from dreams). "Yume" generally means Love, and so particularly does "mihatenu yume" (unfinished dream), though that is merely part of the atmosphere here.

100 Design-Ground. Close-Distant. Miscellaneous. Radiance.
Kaneko classifies this as Grievance because of "waga kage" (my shadow), which *Ubuginu* does not allow. A splendid close to this wonderful sequence.

Shinuru kusuri wa
koi ni emahoshi
97   hachisuba no
ue o chigiri no
kagiri nite

All I desire is a potion
to close a life of anguished love
    such end is welcome
given the promise of our rebirth
    upon the lotus throne

Hachisuba no
ue o chigiri no
kagiri nite
98   chiru ya tamayura
yūdachi no ame

    The very end is welcome
given the promise of our rebirth
    upon the lotus throne
the beadlets from the sudden shower
rest a moment on the leaves and fall

Chiru ya tamayura
yūdachi no ame
99   kumokaze mo
mihatenu yume to
samuru yo ni

The beadlets from the sudden shower
rest a moment on the leaves and fall
    the wind-shattered clouds
are part of that unfinished dream
    from which I awake

Kumokaze mo
mihatenu yume to
samuru yo ni
100   waga kage nare ya
fukuru tomoshibi.

    The wind-shattered clouds
are part of that unfinished dream
    from which I awake
to see the shadow of my old age
cast by the light of a dying lamp.

PART THREE
FOUR HAIKAI SEQUENCES

EACH OF THE renku, or haikai sequences, that follow is in the kasen form of thirty-six stanzas that Bashō made the favored length. Three involve Bashō and his students, especially Bonchō and Kyorai, about whom something is said in the introduction to *Even the Kite's Feathers*. The two other participants are also introduced where appropriate. The fourth kasen is by Buson and Kitō and has a separate introduction.

In 1691, three years before Bashō's death, Kyorai and Bonchō jointly edited a collection, *The Monkey's Straw Raincoat (Sarumino)*. This consisted of four books of opening stanzas (hokku), about 400 by 118 poets, so that a purchaser of the volume could savor them separately or choose a stanza that seemed attractive and add stanzas alone or with some friends. The fifth book contained four kasen, of which the three given here are esteemed most highly. In major part, their quality and availability in a reliable edition has determined their selection. But another matter is also involved. *Even the Kite's Feathers* will give a reader new to haikai a fine idea of the usual sequencing and the usual conventions of a kasen. *Throughout the Town* presents a radical version, full of irregularities, variations, and in general a lower decorum. It has much more of the traditional haikai, non-standard tone, including comedy and surprise. *At the Tub of Ashes* offers not so much a mean between the other two, although it does do that, as the acme of the genius of Bashō and his friends in renku. For adequate counterpart in his other work, one would have to choose *The Narrow Road*. All three sequences come at the end of that period when Bashō set sabi as an ideal. Other qualities can be found in his earlier or later work, but, to most Japanese, these sequences represent his finest achievement in linked verse. The text is *Renga Haikaishū*, and the editors of the haikai section are Teruoka Yasutaka and Nakamura Shunjō.

Let me emphasize yet again that the assessments of stanza impressiveness and relatedness are my responsibility. They must be taken as suggestions or for guidance in the spirit that I hope the Preface to this study has suggested.

Even the Kite's Feathers

KYORAI, BASHŌ, BONCHŌ,
AND FUMIKUNI

(*Tobi no Ha mo no maki*)

IN THE third year of the Genroku period (1690) Bashō was living out of Edo. He had gone to stay at the Genjūan, or Unreal Hermitage, at Ishiyama near Lake Biwa. In the Seventh Month, he set off on a trip taking him here and there, including a visit to his native place, Ueno in Iga Province, the western part of present Mie Prefecture. The exact date of the composition of this kasen is not certain, but the opening stanza suggests that it was early winter, and probably the year was 1690, after Bashō had settled in Kyoto for a time.

As so often, Bashō appears second in a kasen. Perhaps he liked that turn, but it was also considered the guest's turn, the first being the host's. The hokku is composed by Mukai Kyorai, setting a chilly scene, with a not very attractive bird sleeked down by the cold rain. Kyorai (1651-1704) had been born into a samurai family, but he left the military life in his mid-twenties and went to Kyoto. He became a disciple of Bashō's and, along with Bonchō, furthered what is known as the shōfū—the Bashō style or school—in the area about Kyoto and Osaka. He edited *Sarumino* with Bonchō, and to such of his writings as *Kyorai Shō* (*Kyorai's Notes*) we owe much of our most valuable information about Bashō's critical principles, ways of composing, and even personality. Kyorai seems to have been a very modest person. After Bashō's death, he took almost no poetic followers, although it certainly would have been possible for him to present himself as one of the chief heirs and to profit immensely by doing so. The various kasen in which he participates show him to have been a remarkably gifted composer of linked verse, able to further a sequence with great freshness and naturalness, making each surprise seem inevitable. He is an especially fine team player, especially it would seem under Bashō's captainship.

Nozawa Bonchō (d. 1714) was born in Kanazawa in the Province of Kaga (present Ishikawa). He did some work in the medicinal line before becoming a disciple of Bashō sometime not too long before this kasen was composed. He parted company with Bashō during the master's late stage and change of style. He has great gifts in haikai, whether in renku as here, hokku, or other variations. He is perhaps a better poet than Kyorai and he is certainly often more striking, although not always as natural. Like Kyorai, he was counted among the ten finest of Bashō's followers, in spite of his defection.

Nakamura Fumikuni is not well known. His dates of birth and death are uncertain, although he came from Inuyama in Owari Province (Aichi Prefecture on the border of Gifu Prefecture). After some time with medicine, he went up to Kyoto, and then later left samurai service and went to Edo (Tokyo). His association with Bashō seems to be limited to the period of the composition of the kasen included in *Sarumino*. In this sequence he manages to hold his own with three of the greatest haikai poets of his day. "Fumikuni" is also pronounced Shihō.

The order of composing a kasen by four poets may vary somewhat (compare the following with that for *At the Tub of Ashes*). Let us designate our four poets by letters: A, B, C, D.

A Kyorai	C Bonchō
B Bashō	D Fumikuni

In the first sheet we get one repetition followed by two extra stanzas:

ABCD   BADC   ABCD   BADC   BA

And in the second sheet we get another repetition preceded by two extra stanzas:

CD   ABDC   BACD   ABDC   BACD

Since there are but six stanzas on the front of the first sheet and the back of the last, that orderly alternation is less apparent by sides.

First Sheet, Front	ABCDBA
First Sheet, Back	DCABCDBADCBA
Second Sheet, Front	CDABDCBACDAB
Second Sheet, Back	DCBACD

There are no vexing problems with this renku. In the first six or so preparatory stanzas, the jo, the seasons are winter and autumn, and we have some sense of travel and the remote. People do not seem to meet or make gestures to each other. It is a lonely beginning. The development section, the ha (7–30), goes through the seasons and seems to cover a considerable distance as well as a variety of people. The climax is brought by the Love stanzas toward the end of this part, with echoes of *The Tale of Genji* being altered into the more military terms of the Edo period, and at last into natural imagery. The fast conclusion (kyū, ca. 31–36) joins human activity and nature, bringing in travel again, and at last settling into spring imagery. Any reader coming to this kasen from renga will be struck by a number of things. The tone is often very much lower, and the variety of elements greater. The sense of a world of *things* has grown much stronger. Anyone can see that the sequence ends with a spring happier than the winter with which it begins.

The method used for translating and annotating renga has also been used here, with a few changes. Bashō spoke not of closely or distantly related verses but of heavily and lightly related verses, terms used in the commentary in ways that will be apparent. For purposes of distinguishing haikai from renga, in order that is to suggest something of the distinct world of haikai, I have introduced two categories into the commentary. One is of Products, things produced by human work. Such "thinginess" is part of the distinctly quotidian nature of haikai. The other category involves the class distinctions that meant so much in Edo Japan: Court, Military, Town, and Peasants. Waka had dealt with the first and renga sometimes also with the second. Haikai aspired to all four. As with other classifications, one of these is indicated as being used when the diction justifies it or when the sense seems to demand it. "When the sense seems to demand"—what a Japanese might term "kokoro no bushi" (the sense of Warriors) as opposed to "kotoba no bushi" (Warriors specified in words)—is susceptible of difference in interpretation. Because the ensuing translation and commentary are for those who want something more than a Japanese edition, I have enlarged on what will be found in such editions. Much more might be included: concern with motion in haikai as against the repose of renga, growing concern with day, with buildings and indoor scenes, with scenes nearer to hand, and with human experience less concerned with love.

Such matters will certainly be observable in the haikai sequences that follow. All four are kasen, and we begin with the most regular of them, "Even the Kite's Feathers." Its regularity (at least after the stanzas of its preface) conveys something of a norm. It also provides a useful transition from renga sequences and a useful auspice to less regular haikai sequences. This may seem faint praise. In fact it is one of the most esteemed of renku produced by Bashō and his followers.

1 Design. No relation. Winter. Birds.
Noun-ending rather than cutting-word such as "kana." "Hatsushigure" (early winter rain) designates Winter, unlike simple "shigure" (a Falling Thing in renga), which may be either Autumn or Winter. The cold scheme suggests an ink-wash drawing.

2 Design. Heavy-Light. Miscellaneous. Trees.
As the drizzle had affected the kite's feathers, the single gust of wind works on the dead leaves, both those on the ground and those still on the branches. Then all grows hushed once more, leaving the scene yet more desolate to sight and bleakly still. In connection with 1 the scene is wintry, but no word justifies the classification.

3 Ground-Design. Light-Heavy. Miscellaneous. Clothes.
Clothes imply a wearer, and humanity is introduced for the first time, like the leaves being affected by the elements. The person may be a traveler or some villager on a task.

4 Ground-Design. Light-Heavy. Miscellaneous. Animals. Products. Peasants.
Light bamboo is bent to spring forth and frighten away a badger who encounters it. Travel may be implied here, but no word justifies the topic. The person who has forded streams in 3 now comes on a house or a rural village scene.

5 Design. Light-Heavy. Autumn. Dwellings. Plants. Night. Radiance.
The first moon stanza appears as prescribed on the first front sheet and at the standard fifth stanza. We move into the isolated house of those who set the badger ward, probably in some mountain area. A lonely but lovely moonlight filters through ivy-covered lattice, casting dim shadows.

1   Tobi no ha mo
kaitsukuroinu
   hatsushigure
Kyorai

Even the kite's feathers
have been tidied by the passing shower
  of early winter rain

    Tobi no ha mo
kaitsukuroinu
   hatsushigure
2   hitofuki kaze no
ko no ha shizumaru
Bashō

Even the kite's feathers
have been tidied by the passing shower
  of early winter rain
stirred about by a gust of wind
the withered leaves grow still again

Hitofuki kaze no
ko no ha shizumaru
3   momohiki no
asa kara nururu
   kawa koete
Bonchō

Stirred about by a gust of wind
the withered leaves grew still again
  from morning onward
his trousers have been wetted
  in crossing streams

    Momohiki no
asa kara nururu
   kawa koete
4   tanuki o odosu
shinohari no yumi
Fumikuni

From morning onward
his trousers have been wetted
  in crossing streams
and he sees the bamboo bow
set to frighten badgers off

Tanuki o odosu
shinohari no yumi
5   mairado ni
tsuta haikakaru
   yoi no tsuki
Bashō

Not far from the bamboo bow
set to frighten badgers off
  and through lush ivy
crawling over the lattice door
  comes evening moonlight

6 Ground Stanza. Light-Heavy. Autumn. Persons. Trees.
The scene is still remote—perhaps a mountain village or temple—but the number of people grows. The "mo" of Kyorai's first line suggests that another person is referred to. So ends the first side of the first sheet, marked by consistent use of light-heavy relation and change in impressiveness of stanzas, ending with this first ground stanza.

◆   ◆   ◆   ◆

7 Design-Ground. Light-Heavy. Autumn.
The translation interprets the succession of stanzas to mean that the stingy person is also the artist, perhaps over-preoccupied with his work. Perhaps he is even unaware that the season is ending.

8 Ground. Light-Heavy. Miscellaneous. Clothes.
The translation follows one line of interpretation, identifying the persons in 8 and 7, even though such identification three stanzas in a row is frowned on. Knitted toed-socks (tabi) became fashionable in the 1680's as an import and were worn in cold weather. Tabi were usually made from woven cloth or leather.

9 Ground. Light. Miscellaneous.
The stanza provides a fine example of Light relation and of a Ground poem that is very plain in language without being simple. The mood of self-sufficiency is maintained, but the basis differs. Kyorai shows his full understanding of the art of sequence.

10 Design-Ground. Light-Heavy. Miscellaneous. Residences. Products. Peasants.
Although one interpretation holds that the shell is blown by a member of a religious group on a pilgrimage to summon others, the appearance of a village suggests that the person of 9, perhaps someone walking meditatively, comes on the sounds and time of the phenomenal world. The contrast is remarkable.

Mairado ni
tsuta haikakaru
  yoi no tsuki
6 hito ni mo kurezu
  meibutsu no nashi
Kyorai

Through the lush ivy
crawling over the lattice door
  comes evening moonlight
he will not give to anyone
the pears for which the place is known

◆　◆　◆　◆

Hito ni mo kurezu
meibutsu no nashi
  kakinaguru
7 sumie okashiku
  aki kurete
Fumikuni

He will not give to anyone
the pears for which the place is known
  while he takes pleasure
sketching pictures with brush and ink
  autumn nears its end

Kakinaguru
sumie okashiku
  akikurete
8 hakigokoro yoki
  meriyasu no tabi
Bonchō

While he takes pleasure
sketching pictures with brush and ink
  autumn nears its end
and what a joy he has in wearing
those fashionable knitted socks

Hakigokoro yoki
meriyasu no tabi
  nanigoto mo
9 mugon no uchi wa
  shizuka nari
Kyorai

What a joy there is in wearing
those fashionable knitted socks
  nothing that happens
while he refrains from talking
  breaks his inner quiet

Nanigoto mo
mugon no uchi wa
  shizuka nari
10 sato miesomete
  uma no kai fuku
Bashō

Nothing that happened
during the time without a word
  broke the great quiet
just as the village comes into view
a horn blows to tell of noontime

11 Ground-Design. Heavy-Light. Miscellaneous. Products.
No words authorize the summer classification this seems to deserve (see 12).
Now a peasant summoned by the horn in 10 rests for a bit after his noon meal.
The details acutely represent peasant life.

12 Design-Ground. Light. Summer. Cultivated Things.
The many positive associations of the lotus hover in this stanza, making its
connection with 11 one of contrast. The uncertainty as to connection of scene
keeps the connection light. Because the flower is given its name (is a na no
hana), this is not a flower stanza. (See 17.)

13 Ground-Design. Heavy-Light. Miscellaneous.
The association of a lotus pond with a temple is very natural; that and the general good feeling constitute the main connections. Since temples had lodgings
for visitors or travelers and served food, there is no Buddhist subtopic.

14 Ground-Design. Light-Heavy. Miscellaneous.
The connection with 13 exemplifies the narrative potential found in linked
poetry. The person here had been waiting for the soup at the end of the meal
and appreciates the host's kindness, but feels he must get on, as if business or
returning home motivated him.

15 Ground-Design. Light. Spring. Persons. Town.
Rodō, the T'ang poet Lu T'ung, was a minor poet and, like Fumikuni himself,
a master of tea. The stanza is connected only by contrast with 14. Since there
has been no flower stanza thus far (see 12 and note), Fumikuni here introduces
spring, making the stanza possible in 16 or 17.

11

Sato miesomete
uma no kai fuku
hotsuretaru
kozo no negoza no
shitataruku
Boncho

Just as the village came into view
the horn blew to tell of noontime
frazzled at the edge
the straw coverlet from last year
is smudged with his use

12

Hotsuretaru
kozo no negoza no
shitataruku
fuyō no hana no
harahara to chiru
Fumikuni

Frazzled at the edge
the straw coverlet from last year
is smudged with his use
the petals of the lotus flowers
fall one by one in splendor

13

Fuyō no hana no
harahara to chiru
suimono wa
mazu dekasareshi
Suizenji
Bashō

As petals of the lotus flowers
fall one by one in splendor
well-prepared soup
is first of all passed about
at Suizen Temple

14

Suimono wa
mazu dekasareshi
Suizenji
sanri amari no
michi kakaekeru
Kyorai

The well-prepared soup
is first of all passed about
at Suizen Temple
but pleading that eight miles remain
he sets off upon the road

15

Sanri amari no
michi kakaekeru
kono haru mo
Rodō ga otoko
inari nite
Fumikuni

Because eight miles still are left
they set off upon the road
and this spring as well
the servants loyal as Lu T'ung's
work another term

16 Design-Ground. Light-Heavy. Spring. Cultivation. Night. Radiance.
Bonchō solves a problem very well. The spring sequence begun in 15 must continue three stanzas, but a moon stanza is needed, and that is usually autumnal. So he advances spring a bit and gives a spring moon, with tree imagery that sets up Bashō for a flower stanza. In the four stanzas concluding this sheet (15-18) we see into the process of linking stanzas.

17 Design-Ground. Heavy-Light. Spring. Products. Cultivation. Plants.
The first flower stanza appears in the proper section and standard place. Having been set up and needing to join a flower to a moon stanza in the developmental stage (ha) of the sequence, Bashō must measure up without stopping things with too impressive a stanza. He gives a scene for viewing cherry flowers (always meant by "hana" in haikai) but without mentioning the people who would use the old basin.

18 Ground. Light-Heavy. Miscellaneous. Persons.
The high tone of the preceding stanza is altered in fine haikai style by the mention of anger, but it is not deflated—the anger is past. Also, connecting with 17, it seems that the speaker here has recovered his temper by working among the trees, perhaps as an attendant. The gamesome touch is very nice. Kyorai ends both the front and the back of the first sheet with Ground stanzas.

♦ ♦ ♦ ♦
♦ ♦ ♦ ♦

19 Ground. Light. Miscellaneous.
The lack of details in setting or other images prevents closeness of connection, but Bonchō intensifies the slight comic elements of 18. By writing the second Ground stanza in succession, he seems to put his successor on notice to write a Design-Ground or Design stanza.

20 Design. Light. Winter.
Fumikuni suddenly opens the scene to wide expanses and brings back winter for the first time. This impressive stanza is particularly renga-like, even to the yoking by "samuki" of the nouns preceding and following, a technique rarer in haikai. Snow is a falling thing in renga.

Kono haru mo
Rodō ga otoko
  inari nite
16   sashiki tsukitaru
tsuki no oboroyo
  Bonchō

    This spring as well
the servants loyal as Lu T'ung's
    work another term
the grafted trees reveal new growth
in moonlight on a hazy night

Sashiki tsukitaru
tsuki no oboroyo
  koke nagara
17   hana ni naraburu
  chōzubachi
  Bashō

The grafted trees reveal new growth
in moonlight on a hazy night
    covered with moss
the stone basin stands to one side
    of flowering cherry trees

  Koke nagara
hana ni naraburu
  chōzubachi
18   hitori naorishi
kesa no haradachi
  Kyorai

    Covered with moss
the stone basin stands to one side
    of flowering cherry trees
his mind has now been relieved
of the anger felt this morning

♦   ♦   ♦   ♦

♦   ♦   ♦   ♦

Hitori naorishi
kesa no haradachi
  ichidoki ni
19   futsuka no mono mo
  kūte oki
  Bonchō

His mind has now been relieved
of the anger felt this morning
    and in just one sitting
he has bolted down the rations
    for two full days

  Ichidoki ni
futsuka no mono mo
  kūte oki
20   yukike ni samuki
shima no kitakaze
  Fumikuni

    In just one sitting
they have eaten up the rations
    for two full days
the feel of snow brings on the cold
as northern winds blow on the isle

21 Design. Heavy-Light. Miscellaneous. Dwellings. Radiance. Peaks.
Kyorai particularizes, focuses, specifies in another excellent stanza: made possible in the larger economy by 18 and 19. This is haikai beauty in contrast to 20:
an ordinary lantern is lit, and the beauty of the scene is as much humble and
desolate as affecting. With 20, Emperor Gotoba's exile at Oki or Juntoku's at
Sado seems to be meant, deepening the sadness.

22 Ground-Design. Light-Heavy. Summer. Birds.
Bashō intensifies the haikai character of 21. In waka and renga the hon'i for
"hototogisu" is that there be a single one whose song one listens in vain to
hear. Yet he keeps the sense of problem: they will sing no more, suggesting
that the summer season designated by these birds is close to passing. Hence,
with 20, this is the sole stanza spent on a season, appropriately for summer or
winter.

23 Ground. Light. Miscellaneous.
The sudden shift tells us that another stage in the development (ha) section has
begun. In itself, this is wholly undistinguished, even prosaic. But for a sequence, Fumikuni's mastery is like that other kind shown by him in 15.

24 Ground-Design. Light. Miscellaneous. Love. Products. Residences.
The language is plain and does not justify a love classification, which is presumed by the allusion (honzetsu) to *The Tale of Genji*, where in "Yūgao" the
visit to a sick old woman leads to Genji's liaison with Yūgao. The recollection
raises the impressiveness of the stanza and perhaps suggests Court as a classification.

25 Ground-Design. Heavy. Miscellaneous. Love. Persons. Cultivation.
A clear-cut love stanza, this is haikai in language but timeless in conception: the
betrayed woman waiting, the lover who might come through the hedge, as
Narihira and countless literary lovers did after him. Some see an echo of
"Ukifune" in *The Tale of Genji*. The "k" alliteration is striking. Love appears
two-thirds through the sequence.

21

Yukike ni samuki
shima no kitakaze
　hi tomoshi ni
kururebe noboru
　mine no tera
　Kyorai

The feel of snow brings on the cold
as northern winds blow on the isle
　to light the lamp
at yet another dusk he climbs alone
　to the temple on the peak

22

Hi tomoshi ni
kururebe noboru
　mine no tera
hototogisu mina
nakishimaitari
　Bashō

To light the lamp
at yet another dusk he climbed alone
　to the temple on the peak
all the wood thrushes that he heard
have finished their summer songs

23

Hototogisu mina
nakishimaitari
　yasebone no
mada okinaoru
　chikara naki
　Fumikuni

All the wood thrushes that he heard
have finished their summer songs
　wasted to the bones
he still cannot summon strength
　to rise from his bed

24

Yasebone no
mada okinaoru
　chikara naki
tonari o karite
kuruma hikikomu
　Bonchō

Wasted to the bones
she cannot summon strength
　to rise from her bed
her visitor finds the place is cramped
and borrows carriage space next door

25

Tonari o karite
kuruma hikikomu
　uki hito o
kikokugaki yori
　kugurasen
　Bashō

He used to find my place so cramped
he borrowed carriage space next door
　his neglect is heartless
if only he would come again to see me
　through my mock-orange hedge

26 Design-Ground. Heavy-Light. Miscellaneous. Military. Products.
Lovers part in the morning. Kyorai alters the aura of court nobility in the preceding to a more contemporary scene, as the woman hands the sword to her lover, who had slipped in through the hedge of 25. It is not clear whether the "Ima ya" of farewell is imagined to be said/thought by the woman alone.

27 Ground-Design. Heavy-Light. Miscellaneous. Products.
Left by her lover, who will probably be long in returning, the woman feels great agitation. The stanza could hardly stand apart but is a splendid contribution to the sequence, both for its connection with 26 and the possibilities it leaves open.

28 Ground. Light. Miscellaneous. Military.
Fumikuni achieves a major change: in sex of the speaker and of the situation justifying agitation. Another interpretation holds that the person here is an Asura, one of the opposing demons in Indian and other Buddhism.

29 Design. Light. Autumn. Night. Radiance.
In a major departure—even greater in some ways than 23—Kyorai introduces autumn after six miscellaneous poems and gives the third moon stanza in its approved position. His successor is put on his mettle. The moon fades into a lovely morning sky.

30 Design. Heavy-Light. Autumn. Peaks. Waters.
Bashō specifies the location of the scene in 29—some few miles from Kyoto, enough for imagination to play—one of the eight famous views of Lake Biwa. The joining of noun-elements by *no* particles recalls waka poetry in one of the styles of the *Shinkokinshū*, the eighth imperial collection (beginning of 13th century). The development (ha) section has led up to two design poems. Frost is a falling thing in renga.

♦ ♦ ♦ ♦

Uki hito o His neglect was heartless
kikokugaki yori but he went again to visit her
kugurasen through the mock-orange hedge
26 ima ya wakare no now is the time of lovers' parting
katana sashidasu and she helps him put on his sword
Kyorai

Ima ya wakare no At the time of lovers' parting
katana sashidasu she helped him put on his sword
27 sewashige ni left all restless
kushi de kashira o with her comb she worried her hair
kakichirashi messing its lines
Bonchō

Sewashige ni In a restless state
kushi de kashira o with his comb he worries his hair
kakichirashi messing its lines
28 omoikittaru summoning determination
shinigurui mi yo to hazard his life in battle
Fumikuni

Omoikittaru He summoned determination
shinigurui mi yo to hazard his life in battle
29 seiten ni in the chill blue sky
ariakezuki no the yet remaining moon dissolves
asaborake in the light of dawn
Kyorai

Seiten ni In the chill blue sky
ariakezuki no the yet remaining moon dissolves
asaborake in the light of dawn
30 kosui no aki no as autumn comes to Biwa Lake
Hira no hatsushimo and to Mount Hira with first frost
Bashō

♦　♦　♦　♦

31 Ground-Design. Light-Heavy. Autumn. Residences. Trees. Cultivation.
The first line continues the waka diction. A preoccupied poet, buckwheat, and a thief make a characteristic haikai combination. So the back of the second sheet and the conclusion (kyū) begin. From this still point with stealthily quick movement outside, the last section of the poem speeds up.

32 Ground-Design. Light-Heavy. Winter. Clothes.
Bonchō accepts the scene and its preoccupied figure, but he moves the season ahead to winter. Since the 35th stanza is the standard place for the last flower (and therefore spring) stanza, we anticipate a progress that gives us speed in the kyū or fast conclusion.

33 Ground-Design. Light-Heavy. Miscellaneous. Travel.
Bashō not only introduces a traveler but has him well on his trip, so giving a sense of speed. The poetic diction of the third line contrasts with that for the scene in the first and second, a technique characteristic of Bashō and very hard to emulate successfully.

34 Ground-Design. Heavy-Light. Miscellaneous. Products.
What the travelers see at very early morning in a deserted area suggests a leap ahead several days beyond the time of 33. The changed location makes further development feasible. Clouds are rising things, as is smoke, in renga categories.

35 Design-Ground. Heavy-Light. Spring. Residence. Products.
The second flower stanza comes at its appointed place. The legacy from 34 is a deserted, humble place, but the beauty is there in a nice connection with the reddish clouds of 34. Bonchō's stanza fits in very well. Comparison with Bashō's first moon stanza (5) will help distinguish the abilities of the two poets.

Kosui no aki no
Hira no hatsushimo
31   shiba no to ya
soba nusumarete
uta o yomu
Fumikuni

Autumn comes to Biwa Lake
and to Mount Hira with first frost
    his buckwheat stolen
the hermit in the wattled hut
    goes on writing poems

Shiba no to ya
soba nusumarete
uta o yomu
32   nunoko kinarau
kaze no yūgure
Bonchō

His buckwheat stolen
the hermit in the wattled hut
    goes on writing poems
and will adjust to padded clothes
now that cold winds come with the dark

Nunoko kinarau
kaze no yūgure
33   oshiōte
nete wa mata tatsu
karimakura
Bashō

I shall adjust to padded clothes
now that cold winds come with the dark
    jostled by others
I sleep poorly and set out again
    on the rigors of travel

Oshiōte
nete wa mata tatsu
karimakura
34   tatara no kumo no
mada akaki sora
Kyorai

Jostled by others
they slept poorly and set out again
    on the rigors of travel
the foundry foot-bellows makes clouds
reddening the sky before dawn breaks

Tatara no kumo no
mada akaki sora
35   hitokamae
shirigai tsukuru
mado no hana
Bonchō

The foundry foot-bellows makes clouds
reddening the sky before dawn breaks
    they are making cruppers
at the isolated house whose window
    looks on cherry flowers

36 Design-Ground. Light-Heavy. Spring. Trees.
Fumikuni closes with a double contrast in color—between the old and the new leaves of the loquat (an evergreen), and between them and the flowers of the cherry trees. But the connection with 35 is otherwise very Light. The sense of fresh green growth gives the sequence the usual positive ending.

	Hitokamae	They are making cruppers
	shirigai tsukuru	at the isolated house whose window
	mado no hana	looks on cherry flowers
36	biwa no furuha ni	against the old loquat leaves
	konome moetatsu.	the new sprout luxuriantly.
	Fumikuni	

2

Throughout the Town

BONCHŌ, BASHŌ, AND   (*Ichinaka wa no maki*)
KYORAI

THE DATE OF this sequence is not wholly clear, but it seems to be the summer of 1690, when Bashō was staying for a time with Bonchō, and probably late in the Sixth Month, when the summer heat has just built up and still seems novel. Because it is unusual to have the hokku a moon stanza, the sequence is also known as *The Summer Moon* (*Natsu no tsuki no maki*).

The three poets participating are those of *Even the Kite's Feathers*, except that Fumikuni is dropped and Bashō is left with two close disciples: Bonchō and Kyorai. (See pp. 277-78 above.) The result is considerable freedom of handling, almost as if the three knew each other's minds so well that they explored the nature and boundaries of haikai sequence. The variety and pacing are remarkable, as comparison with the much more conventional sequence, *Even the Kite's Feathers*, would show. On the other hand, this sequence is harder to interpret in many places, and at times the variance in glossing is considerable. For various reasons, then, it is desirable to read *Even the Kite's Feathers* before this sequence. Doing so gives, above all, the expectations that are fulfilled, frustrated, and transcended here.

The order of composition for three poets necessarily differs from that for four. In fact, the simplest possible order is followed in the alternation throughout of Bonchō, Bashō, and Kyorai.

In the total sequence, there is a somewhat higher proportion than usual of Miscellaneous stanzas. About half is the usual proportion to the seasonal stanzas. The general proportion tells us less, however, than the proportion of parts. In the initial prefatory section (jo) three Summer stanzas are followed by three Miscellaneous. In the developmental section (ha, 7-30) there are but ten Seasonal stanzas among twenty-four. The proportion of Seasonal stanzas drops yet farther in the fast finale (kyū, 31-36), being but two of six. After the initial Summer stanzas, the season is never referred to again. And the other of the lesser two seasons, Winter, has but one stanza (10) which follows three Spring stanzas (7-9). Sequences not seldom move from one season to its predecessor, but such succession is especially appropriate to the unconventional nature of *Throughout the Town*. The long second section of the sequence (7-30) turns with the fifteenth stanza to oscillation between Autumn and Miscellaneous stanzas. When Spring is brought in at the very end, its beauties are very much in the haikai vein, and very unlike renga or waka. From beginning to end it is full of surprises. Its imagery is often low, but it is in some ways particularly human because of that. And with a couple of exceptions, the sequential connectedness of this kasen is brilliant.

1 Design-Ground. No relation. Summer. Night. Radiance. Town.
Bonchō's hokku lacks the cutting-word (kireji) more or less usual to an opening stanza. Because of the season of composition, which is well realized here, and the fact that an otherwise unspecified moon belongs to autumn, he uses the phrase "natsu no tsuki." A *Summer* moon stanza as hokku is deliberately unconventional.

2 Ground. Heavy. Summer. Residences.
In connection with 1, this stanza imagines people everywhere coming out of their houses at night, complaining of the heat, and trying to find a breeze as well as to appreciate the moon. This is quite definitely and unusually a Ground stanza, which is unusual for a waki or second stanza. The hokku and waki are usually Design or Design-Ground stanzas.

3 Design-Ground. Heavy. Summer. Grasses. Cultivation. Peasants.
The stanza ends as the third is supposed to, in "—te," but since the third usually lowers in impressiveness after the first two, the rise in this stanza above 2 is quite novel. The diction has a fine literary quality. The heat of 2 is considered as the nurture for an early crop.

4 Ground-Design. Light. Miscellaneous.
Connecting with 3, this seems to presume people, probably peasants, readying a meal after inspecting or caring for the rice fields. There is not much fish, and the existing charcoal is made to do duty. But the connections are not very firm. Bashō was reported to say that the fourth stanza should not have Heavy relation.

5 Ground. Light. Miscellaneous. Products.
The provincial scene has not yet come to know the silver coinage that had been circulating in Edo, and so still uses barter. Some read "gin mo mishirazu" for the second line. The sense of travel is very strong, but by itself the stanza might imply impatience on returning home from a less backward area.

1
    Ichinaka wa
   mono no nioi ya
    natsu no tsuki
   Bonchō

        Throughout the town
     above the welter of smelly things
        the summer moon

    Ichinaka wa
   mono no nioi wa
    natsu no tsuki
2 atsushi atsushi to
   kado kado no koe
   Bashō

        Throughout the town
    above the welter of smelly things
        the summer moon
  how hot it is, how hot it is
  says a voice at every house-gate

    Atsushi atsushi to
   kado kado no koe
3   nibangusa
   tori mo hatasazu
    ho ni idete
   Kyorai

    How hot it is, how hot it is
  says a voice at every farm-gate
     although the weeds
  have not been worked a second time
    the rice comes into ear

    Nibangusa
   tori mo hatasazu
    ho ni idete
4 hai uchitataku
   urume ichimai
   Bonchō

     Although the weeds
  have not been worked a second time
    the rice has come to ear
  the charcoal ash is shaken off
  the dried sardine broiled at noon

   Hai uchitakaku
   urume ichimai
5   kono suji wa
   kane mo mishirazu
    fujiyusa yo
   Bashō

    The charcoal ash is shaken off
  the dried sardine broiled at noon
     but in this back country
  the use of coins is not yet heard of
    what a bother to travelers

6 Ground-Design. Light. Miscellaneous. Products.
The preceding stanza left little chance of connection. Kyorai appears to change the speaker of the preceding into the person carrying the sword here, and observe him from another's viewpoint. So ends the front of the first sheet, with stanzas deliberately held toward the "Ground" impressiveness and fluctuating widely in relation.

♦   ♦   ♦   ♦

7 Design-Ground. Light-Heavy. Spring. Insects. Plants.
A delightful, witty addition to 6, this is yet on the Light side in connection because of change in topic to Spring and because (as 8 shows) there is no necessary close connection with 6. "Kawazu" (frog) is Spring in classification and, because of the Chinese character, is "insect," not "animal." "Yūmagure" is the period between dusk and full dark. More of Bonchō's humor lies ahead.

8 Design-Ground. Heavy-Light. Spring. Plants. Night. Radiance.
It is not clear how many people are involved or what their sex may be, but in poetry it is often a woman who picks shoots. The tone rises greatly, even in connection with 7. Cause and effect assist in making a Heavy connection.

9 Design-Ground. Light-Heavy. Spring. Buddhism. Trees.
A new kind of seriousness enters with a little accident in this world. The stanza continues the spring season, but seems to place it in the past. This first flower stanza comes properly in the backside of the first sheet, but it is very early— toward its beginning rather than its end.

10 Ground-Design. Light-Heavy. Winter.
The move from Spring to Summer or Autumn is more usual. The sense seems to relate well to 9, but, as 11 shows, it has no close connection to a religious subject. The "sumi-" of the second line rules out travel as a subtopic. Nanao is in present Ishikawa prefecture.

Kono suji wa
kane mo mishirazu
fujiyusa yo
6   tada tohyōshi ni
nagaki wakizashi
    Kyorai

In this back country
the use of coins is not yet heard of
    what a bother to travelers
but he is an odd one to be talking
and swagger with an enormous sword

♦　　♦　　♦　　♦

Tada tohyōshi ni
nagaki wakizashi
7   kusamura ni
kawazu kowagaru
    yūmagure
    Bonchō

He is an odd one to carry on
swaggering with an enormous sword
    he quakes in fright
from a frog croaking in the weeds
    as twilight thickens

Kusamura ni
kawazu kowagaru
    yūmagure
8   fuki no me tori ni
ando yurikesu
    Bashō

She jumps with fright
at the frog's croaking in the weeds
    as twilight thickens
so in search of butterburr shoots
her shaking hand puts out the lamp

Fuki no me tori ni
ando yurikesu
9   dōshin no
okori wa hana no
    tsubomu toki
    Kyorai

While hunting butterburr shoots
I shook the lamp and put it out
    my waking to the Way
came long ago at that season
    of budding flowers

Dōshin no
okori wa hana no
    tsubomu toki
10   Noto no Nanao no
fuyu wa sumiuki
    Bonchō

His waking to the Way
came long ago at that seasons
    of budding flowers
now at Nanao Bay in Noto
the winter cold is hard to bear

11 Design-Ground. Heavy-Light. Miscellaneous. Grievances.
It may be that this stanza is a category lower (Ground-Design), but this well represents the spirit of haikai, blending wry comedy with full seriousness. The blend is perfect. In his youth the speaker chewed fish unthinkingly. Grown old and toothless, it is another matter. The Noto peninsula of 10 is well known for fish.

12 Design-Ground. Light. Miscellaneous. Love. Persons. Residences.
Kyorai effects a wonderful light movement from Grievances to Love. His diction is effective, and his conception fresh. It seems unnecessary to assume with some that there is an allusion to "Suetsumuhana" in *The Tale of Genji*, since the main details differ, and this does not require allusion to create its atmosphere. As with moon and flower stanzas, here Love makes an unusually early appearance.

13 Ground-Design. Heavy-Light. Miscellaneous. Love. Persons. Products.
This and the next stanza are very difficult to assess. The interpretation followed holds that this is a Love stanza, since it is true that Love should be continued more than one stanza, but the evidence is not easily given. Some think that the scene is a noble house, and that the peeping maids do not actually knock down the screens. The humor is typical of Bonchō.

14 Ground-Design. Light. Miscellaneous. Residences. Trees.
This is even harder to deal with, and commentators vary widely. It is not clear who is speaking of whom, or why Bashō connects a bath with 13 or finds its furnishings so depressing. In my opinion, he has simply failed to realize his conception, and this is a poor stanza.

15 Design-Ground. Light-Heavy. Autumn. Plants.
After the uncertainties of 13 and especially 14, this renga-like stanza is welcome for its clarity. Joined with 15, it seems to pick up "wabishiki" (forlorn) as an attributive adjective for "uikyō" (fennel). The suggestion of fragrance is also welcome and is the first since the beginning of the sequence.

11

Noto no Nanao no
fuyu wa sumiuki
  uo no hone
shiwaburu made no
  oi o mite
    Bashō

At Nanao Bay in Noto
the winter cold is hard to bear
  all that I can do
is suck upon the bones of fish
  and think of old age

12

Uo no hone
shiwaburu made no
  oi o mite
machibito ireshi
komikado no kagi
    Kyorai

All that he can do
is suck upon the bones of fish
  thinking of his age
as he lets the mistress' lover
through the side gate with his key

13

Machibito ireshi
komikado no kagi
  tachikakari
byōbu o taosu
  onagodomo
    Bonchō

The mistress' lover was let in
through the side gate with a key
  stretching for a peek
the young maidservants overturn
  the folding screen

14

Tachikakari
byōbu o taosu
  onagodomo
yudono wa take no
sunoko wabishiki
    Bashō

As they stretch forward
the young maidservants overturn
  the folding screen
the split bamboo drainboard gives
a forlorn appearance to the bath

15

Yudono wa take no
sunoko wabishiki
  uikyō no
mi o fukiotosu
  yūarashi
    Kyorai

The split bamboo drainboard gave
a forlorn appearance to the bath
  and to the seeds of fennel
that are all blown off their plants
  by the evening storm

16 Ground. Heavy-Light. Autumn. Persons. Residences.
The diction is quite unpoetic ("tera ni kaeru ka"), but the conception follows 15 and its storm very well. The question stresses the presence of an observer of the lonely scene, while also entering into the experience of the solitary priest.

17 Design-Ground. Light-Heavy. Autumn. Persons. Animals. Night.
   Radiance.
This is not very clear as a connected stanza. One interpretation holds that the priest of 16 goes one way, the monkey-master another. The usual interpretation is that all people must pass through the phenomenal world. This famous stanza, it comes in the standard place for a flower stanza. "Aki no tsuki" is strange—a moon belongs to autumn unless otherwise specified.

18 Ground. Light. Miscellaneous. Persons. Peasants.
Kyorai appears thrown off balance by 17. He contrasts a peasant of honest character with the vagabond life of the monkey-master. The tone is growing sober (cf. 6-9), and one pleasure of reading on is seeing how a shift will be effected. This stanza ends the second side of the first sheet.

◆ ◆ ◆ ◆
◆ ◆ ◆ ◆

19 Ground. Light. Miscellaneous. Trees. Waters.
This connects ever so slightly with 18 in the use of numbers and general poverty of the area. We are now to the bleakest stage of this sub-sequence, with no human creature in sight. The cutters of the logs go unmentioned, although the cold scene does not promise well for their existence.

20 Ground-Design. Heavy. Miscellaneous. Clothes.
Some commentators appropriately enough classify this stanza as winter, but "tabi" (leather socks) apparently did not designate winter until later. (See *Renga Haikaishū*, p. 450, st. 8.) A fastidious person from the capital seems to have got his walking tabi soiled in the country.

Uikyō no
mi o fukiotosu
   yūarashi
16   sō yaya samuku
tera ni kaeru ka
   Bonchō

The seeds of fennel
are all blown off their plants
   by the evening storm
will the priest return to the temple
as he feels the cold increasing

Sō yaya samuku
tera ni kaeru ka
   saruhiki no
17   saru to yo o furu
aki no tsuki
   Bashō

Will the priest return to the temple
as he feels the cold increasing
   the monkey-master
ages with his monkey and the world
   beneath the autumn moon

Saruhiki no
saru to yo o furu
   aki no tsuki
18   nen ni itto no
jishi hakaru nari
   Kyorai

The monkey-master
ages with his monkey and the world
   beneath the autumn moon
each year it is but a peck of rice
but the land-tax is paid in full

♦ ♦ ♦ ♦
♦ ♦ ♦ ♦

Nen ni itto no
jishi hakaru nari
   go-roppon
19   namaki tsuketaru
mizutamari
   Bonchō

Each year it is but a peck of rice
but the land-tax is paid in full
   where five or six logs
still green from cutting lie asoak
   on the boggy ground

Go-roppon
namaki tsuketaru
   mizutamari
20   tabi fumiyogosu
kuroboko no michi
   Bashō

Where five or six logs
still green from cutting lie asoak
   on the boggy ground
his fine leather socks grow dirty
as he walks along the muddied path

21 Ground-Design. Heavy-Light. Miscellaneous. Persons. Animals.
The movement of 20 suddenly bursts forth in a superb connection, showing why the footgear in 21 are soiled. There is some problem as to point of view, but the scene is a splendid one along the roadside.

22 Ground-Design. Heavy-Light. Miscellaneous. Persons. Town.
Interpretations differ somewhat on just what happens in the encounter, much as in most accidents. But shock if not collision seems to affect the astounded apprentice as he walks around the corner of the house into the street.

23 Ground-Design. Light. Miscellaneous. Residences. Town.
The action is stilled. The situation is bleak. Perhaps the location is nearby 22, but, after quite heavy connections, Bashō gives a model of Light connection that does not violate sequence as, for example, 17 does.

24 Design-Ground. Light-Heavy. Autumn. Cultivation.
In connection with 23, the scene remains bleak, as if the peppers had been hung up at the eaves (pretty much what "tenjōmamori" means) of a deserted house to dry. But color, time, and autumn enter to enrich the stanza.

25 Ground-Design. Light. Autumn. Clothes. Night. Radiance.
The humble occupation of one who seeks any means to eke a living is made possible and brightened by the autumn moonlight. The contrast typifies Bon-chō's art. The third moon stanza usually comes four stanzas later.

21

Tabi fumiyogosu
kuroboko no michi
  oitatete
hayaki ouma no
  katanamochi
Kyorai

His leather stockings grow dirty
as he hurries along the muddied path
  the sword attendant
is pulled off at breakneck speed
  by his master's fast horse

22

Oitatete
hayaki ouma no
  katanamochi
detchi ga ninau
mizu koboshitari
Bonchō

The sword attendant
is pulled off at breakneck speed
  by his master's fast horse
making the nearby apprentice spill
the water bucket that he holds

23

Detchi ga ninau
mizu koboshitari
  to shōji mo
mushirogakoi no
  uriyashiki
Bashō

Near where an apprentice spills
the water bucket that he holds
  a house is up for sale
its broken doors and windows covered
  with straw matting

24

To shōji mo
mushirogakoi no
  uriyashiki
tenjōmamori
itsu ka irozuku
Kyorai

A house is up for sale
its broken doors and windows covered
  with straw matting
when was it that its chili peppers
took on their ripened color

25

Tenjōmamori
itsu ka irozuku
  kosokoso to
waraji o tsukuru
  tsukiyo sashi
Bonchō

When was it that the chili peppers
took on their ripened color
  stealthily stealthily
he plaits straw into sandals
  in bright moonlight

26 Ground-Design. Light-Heavy. Autumn. Insects.
The main connection involves the idea that autumn nights are long, and so we move from waking to sleeping. The sex of the waker is variously given. The translation follows one line. Fleas ("nomi") usually designate summer, which is why Bashō must specify autumn to connect with 25.

27 Ground-Design. Light-Heavy. Miscellaneous. Products.
A box set up to catch a mouse or rat falls without success. With 26, the sound wakes the sleeper to the sensation of fleas. The play on different senses in this part of the development section (ha) is very fine.

28 Ground-Design. Heavy-Light. Miscellaneous. Products.
Another aspect of a misfitting household is shown, and in a lovely connection. This is the fourth Ground-Design. But the other characteristics have been changing steadily.

29 Design-Ground. Light-Heavy. Miscellaneous. Residences.
Bashō himself was given either to locking himself up in his hermitage or returning to it only briefly before setting out again. Like the cover on the box in 28, this place does not fit the returned hermit.

30 Design-Ground. Heavy-Light. Miscellaneous. Court.
The old hermit of 29 is overjoyed to have lived long enough to be invited to submit his waka for the compiling of an imperial collection. The assessment of class and relation here depends on the interpretation that a poetic recluse like Priest Nōin (998-?1050), Kamo no Chōmei (1155-1216), or, most likely, Priest Saigyō (1118-1190) is meant.

♦   ♦   ♦   ♦

THROUGHOUT THE TOWN — 311

Kosokoso to
waraji o tsukuru
tsukiyo sashi
26   nomi o furui ni
okishi hatsuaki
Bashō

    Stealthily stealthily
he plaits straw into sandals
  in bright moonlight
and shaking fleas from the bedcovers
she wakes to early autumn

Nomi o furui ni
okishi hatsuaki
  sono mama ni
27   korobiochitaru
  masuotoshi
Kyorai

Shaking fleas from the bedcovers
she wakes to early autumn
  as the half-gallon box
set up as a trap falls in the night
  with a hollow thud

  Sono mama ni
korobiochitaru
  masuotoshi
28   yugamite futa no
awanu hambitsu
Bonchō

    The half-gallon box
set up as a trap falls in the night
  with a hollow thud
with its lid warped out of line
the storage box cannot be closed

Yugamite futa no
awanu hambitsu
  sōan ni
29   shibaraku ite wa
  uchiyaburi
Bashō

With its lid warped out of line
the storage box cannot be closed
  for a little while
he remains at his hermitage
  and then is off again

  Sōan ni
shibaraku ite wa
  uchiyaburi
30   inochi ureshiki
senju no sata
Kyorai

    For a little while
I remain at my hermitage
  and then am off again
happy in old age that my poems
have won place in a collection

♦   ♦   ♦   ♦

31 Ground-Design. Close. Miscellaneous. Love.
Bonchō appears to imagine a poet as speaker—perhaps Ariwara Narihira (825–880), who was also thought a famous lover—so connecting with 30. The backside of the second sheet begins with the second love sequence in this ka-sen. This is very late and has the effect of intensifying this fast finale (kyū) sec-. tion of six stanzas, in which Spring and Flowers must yet appear.

32 Design. Heavy. Miscellaneous. Love. Persons. Court.
Ono no Komachi (fl. c. 850) was famous for her beauty and as a poet and lover. Her wretched old age was the subject of nō plays and other literary treatment. This famous stanza also seems detachable, but unlike 17 it contributes excel-lently to the sequence. In renga the classification would probably be Griev-ances here and in 29, because of the language.

33 Ground-Design. Heavy-Light. Miscellaneous. Grievances.
One reason is old age, and another the situation in 32. Effort will be required if anything like the usual positive ending of a sequence is achieved.

34 Ground-Design. Light. Miscellaneous. Residences.
In connection with 33, the image of the empty house is very dispiriting. The actual language suggests a rather splendid place, however, and if Bonchō has not done the usual thing and introduced spring here, he has set up Bashō.

35 Design-Ground. Light. Spring. Persons. Insects. Cultivation.
The flower stanza comes as usual here. Like so much else in this kasen, how-ever, the stanza is very much modified from usual simple beauty by the per-son's good-humored contemplation of lice on a fine warm day beautiful with flowers. Lice were thought to emerge from clothes when warm weather came. With 34, the person here must be some kind of caretaker during absence, a very light connection, something Bashō frequently uses in this kasen.

31

Inochi ureshiki
senju no sata
   samazama ni
shina kawaritaru
   koi o shite
Bonchō

Happy in my old age that my poems
have won place in a collection
   now this and now that
governed the circumstances
   of my love affairs

32

   Samazama ni
shina kawaritaru
   koi o shite
ukiyo no hate wa
mina Komachi nari
Bashō

   Now this and now that
governs the circumstances
   when we are in love
and the amorous world's end
is Komachi grown a hag

33

Ukiyo no hate wa
mina Komachi nari
   nani yue zo
kayu susuru ni mo
   namida kumi
Kyorai

The end of the amorous world
is Komachi grown a hag
   but for what reason
do one's eyes grow dim with tears
   even sipping gruel

34

   Nani yue zo
kayu susuru ni mo
   namida kumi
orusu to nareba
hiroki itajiki
Bonchō

   What is the reason
that his eyes grow dim with tears
   even sipping gruel
while his lord is not in residence
and the wide hall stands vacant

35

Orusu to nareba
hiroki itajiki
   te no hira ni
shirami hawasuru
   hana no kage
Bashō

While his lord is not in residence
and the wide hall stands vacant
   under cherry flowers
he watches as new spring lice
   crawl upon his palm

36 Design-Ground. Heavy-Light. Spring.

Haze is an image for Spring early or late. Here it hangs in the still, warm air and promotes drowsiness. It is a rising thing in renga. The "speed" of this last section is technical, with the crowding of Love and Spring and also with other variations. Only two Spring stanzas is rather unusual. Otherwise, the kasen ends in a quiet that has alternated with great agitation.

Te no hira ni
shirami hawasuru
     hana no kage
36 kasumi ugokanu
hiru no nemutasa.
Kyorai

Under cherry flowers
he watches as new spring lice
     crawl upon his palm
the spring haze hangs motionless
at the drowsy midday hours.

3

At the Tub of Ashes

BONCHŌ, BASHŌ, YASUI, AND   (*Akuoke no no maki*)
KYORAI

THIS KASEN was composed sometime toward the end of the 8th or the beginning of the 9th month of 1690 at the Unreal Hermitage (*Genjūan*). Bonchō began with the first stanza, and the other three followed: Bashō, Yasui, and Kyorai. Okada Yasui, a specialist in tea ceremony in Nagoya, lived to the age of 85, dying in 1743. It was sometimes said that his style of stanzaic composition was characterized by a narrative emphasis. The other three poets are familiar from the preceding haikai sequences.

This kasen probably represents the peak of Bashō-style renku. The four poets were all well known to each other and all at the height of their powers. In *Haikai Dialogues* (*Haikai Mondō*), Bashō is reported to have proposed for this sequence, "Let's squeeze the juice from our bone marrow," and the charge to do their utmost was fulfilled. The collection, *The Monkey's Straw Raincoat* (*Sarumino*), has long been termed the *Kokinshū* of haikai, the equivalent of the first imperial collection of waka. Within it, this is surely the finest sequence, always varied and immensely satisfying.

The editors of the text used here have characterized various stanzas, and their designations give us one kind of useful interpretation. They find artistic elegance in 7 and 8; pungent expression of the world of common people in 9 and 10; conviction of evanescence in 16 and 17, 32 and 33; concrete expressiveness in 3; lightness of connection in 6; the changing yet harmonious style of the collection *A Sack of Charcoal* (*Sumidawara*) in 20; and exemplary expression of sabi in 21 and 27.

Other descriptions are possible. There are no mistakes made. More positively, the pacing is at once fresh and natural, as are also the variations from stanza to stanza and within the prescribed kasen form. The flower stanzas appear where expected (17, 35), but the moon stanzas do not (3 instead of 5, 15 instead of 13, 25 instead of 29), and yet the moon stanzas are of the usual number and fall in the right sections. Besides, there is an appropriate reason for the variation each time.

Another striking general feature involves the proportion of Seasonal to Miscellaneous. Usually the Miscellaneous stanzas more or less equal or slightly exceed the seasonal. In *Even the Kite's Feathers*, nineteen of the thirty-six stanzas are Miscellaneous, and, as we saw, that is a very regular sequence. The otherwise unusual *Throughout the Town* has twenty-one Miscellaneous stanzas. *At the Tub of Ashes* differs in having only fourteen Miscellaneous stanzas to twenty-two Seasonal. All the seasons are represented, something which does not always happen: Spring with 8, Summer with 4, Autumn (the time of composition) with 9, and Winter with 1. Moreover, the Miscellaneous stanzas are sometimes compromised as it were in having important subtopics that prevent their being "plain miscellaneous" (tada no zō). Stanzas 11 and 12 have Miscellaneous-Love; 22 also has Travel; 30 has Shintoism; and 32 Evanescence. In any haikai sequence, the proportion of Seasonal stanzas is normally highest in the first section, the front of the first sheet (1-6). As other elements are introduced in the developmental section (7-18 and 19-30) the proportion of Seasonal stanzas tends to decline as Miscellaneous topics are introduced for variation. The last section, the second side of the second sheet (31-36), is hardest to characterize, since its "speed" is achieved in widely different ways. Here is the pattern of Miscellaneous stanzas in the four sides of the quite regular or conventional kasen, *Even the Kite's Feathers*:

1-6	3, 4
7-18	8, 9, 10, 11, 13, 14, 18
19-30	19, 21, 23, 24, 25, 26, 27, 28
31-36	33, 34.

By contrast, here are those in *Throughout the Town*:

1-6	4, 5, 6
7-18	11, 12, 13, 14, 18
19-30	19, 20, 21, 22, 23, 27, 28, 29, 30
31-36	31, 32, 33, 34.

Since the first three stanzas of the opening should be of the same season, *Throughout the Town* has as many Miscellaneous in that section as can be included. The proportion drops greatly to fewer than usual in 7-18. In 19-30, however, nine of the twelve are Miscellaneous. And in 31-36 all that can be are, since 35 is a flower and therefore Spring stanza, which must be continued at least another stanza to 36.

At the Tub of Ashes follows the general kasen pattern of increasing proportion of Miscellaneous stanzas through the four parts of its thirty-six. Their rarity will be evident, however, and those stanzas with important subtopics (e.g., 11 and 12, Love) are set in parentheses:

1-6	4
7-18	8, (11), (12), 13
19-30	20, (22), 26, 27, (30)
31-36	31, (32), 33, 34.

There is but one Miscellaneous poem in the first section, and there are only four in the next, two of which are qualified. Thereafter the proportion grows markedly, and especially toward the end. It can be inferred from this what one might have guessed otherwise, that Seasonal stanzas *tend* to convey more repose, and that Miscellaneous stanzas *tend* to add new elements or give a sense of "speed." Half the Miscellaneous stanzas in this sequence fall in its last third, and almost a third of such stanzas come in the last sixth.

The order of composition used by the four poets writing this kasen follows that employed in *Even the Kite's Feathers* (see above, p. 278). There is one variation. Instead of having the last two stanzas written in the natural order of Yasui and then Kyorai, that order is reversed. Perhaps the reversal was to give Kyorai the flower stanza, since he was an abler poet than Yasui. But my private guess is that his wholly irregular flower stanza was an idea that occurred to him on the spot and that he begged to compose out of turn. That would account even better for Bashō's calling him self-indulgent.

Such description is skeletal and gives little sense of the vitality and harmonious beauty of *At the Tub of Ashes*. These splendid qualities owe something to what has been spoken of thus far, and especially perhaps to the high proportion of Seasonal stanzas. Something more is owed to quality and tone of individual stanzas, as a comparison of the last two here with the last two in *Throughout the Town* will show in a moment. But no more serious mistake can be made about linked verse than to see it apart from linking, and when individual stanzas come to claim priority, haikai suffers as a sequential art. In the stanzas that follow, the art of haikai sequence is at its finest, and for that one could not wish a thing different.

1 Design. No Relation. Autumn. Insects. Products. Waters.
Ashes are kept in a tub outside the house for such uses as scouring or otherwise cleaning kitchen objects. During a dry period the tub ceases to drip. That silence is intensified by the sounds of the crickets. An excellent hokku, open to various development, it has a noun-ending rather than cutting word (kireji). The insects are named.

2 Design-Ground. Heavy-Light. Autumn. Night. Radiance. Products.
The scene moves indoors to one who might be listening. As the oil grows low (like the water ceasing to drip), he falls asleep for want of light to make activity possible. Autumn nights are proverbially long, so early sleep means lengthy sleep.

3 Design. Heavy-Light. Autumn. Residences. Products. Night. Radiance.
The first moon stanza comes two before its standard place, and the white light streams on the slightly green new mats, a beautiful image. The first three stanzas begin with a sounds.

4 Ground-Design. Light-Heavy. Miscellaneous. Products.
It seems that friends are gathering in the room of 3. Ten cups make up two sets. The host is pleased to be able to afford as much, as he apparently was not before. The positive mood is retained, but the language and imagery are less impressive as well as somewhat distantly connected.

5 Ground-Design. Heavy-Light. Spring. Court.
The festive air of 4 is maintained, now at a celebration of the court. A poem by Priest Saigyō is recalled (*Sankashū, Zoku Kokka Taikan*, 8166), but the diction here is not especially elevated.

1 Akuoke no   At the tub of ashes
  shizuku yamikeri   dripping sounds yield to stillness
   kirigirisu   as crickets chirp
  Bonchō

  Akuoke no   At the tub of ashes
  shizuku yamikeri   dripping sounds yield to stillness
   kirigirisu   as crickets chirp
2 abura kasurite   in his lamp the oil grows low
  yoine suru aki   and autumn brings him early sleep
  Bashō

  Abura kasurite   In the lamp the oil grows low
  yoine suru aki   and autumn brings him early sleep
3 aradatami   the floor matting
  shikinarashitaru   freshly laid out in the chamber
   tsukikage ni   shines in the moonlight
  Yasui

  Aradatami   the floor matting
  shikinaroshitaru   freshly laid out in the chamber
   tsukikage ni   shines in the moonlight
4 narabete ureshi   the host beams over ten sake cups
  tō no sakazuki   set out neatly for his party
  Kyōrai

  Narabete ureshi   What a joy to see ten sake cups
  tō no sakazuki   set out neatly for a party
5 chiyo fu beki   for New Year's feasting
  mono o samazama   every good thing is called for
   nenobi shite   to propose long life
  Bashō

6 Design. Light-Heavy. Spring. Birds.
Warblers are associated with snow on the boughs of plum trees in flower. Here the scene is wide, and the (named) bird cannot be seen. The front side of the first sheet has had stanzas of unusually consistent impressiveness. We can expect the development (ha) section (7-30) to show greater variety. Snow is a falling thing in renga.

◆ ◆ ◆ ◆

7 Ground-Design. Light-Heavy. Spring. Persons. Animals. Military.
The second part begins with a sudden burst of action and an element of humor lacking before. The contrast between the warbler and softly falling snow with this genre scene is very haikai-like.

8 Design-Ground. Light-Heavy. Miscellaneous. Peaks.
Yasui slows the action, not just with the clouds hanging but by naming the mountain where they are (near present Kobe). The scene once more opens up, but with a typical modification by clouds obstructing the view. Clouds are a rising thing in renga.

9 Ground-Design. Light. Summer. Fish.
It is a humble scene, apparently close to the sea, and, according to one explanation, "kamasugo" (the fry of marine pike) is a dialect word in the Osaka area (as 8 is situated near Kobe). The stillness of 9 is slightly altered with the summer breeze.

10 Ground-Design. Light-Heavy. Summer. Persons. Insects. Peasants.
"Kuchido" perhaps should read "kuido" or "kudoko" and seems to be low speech, but is otherwise mellifluous. The "k" alliteration in 9-10 involves the much softer Japanese pronunciation of consonants. The new scene moves inland from the seashore.

Chiyo fu beki
mono o samazama
nenobi shite
6 uguisu no ne ni
tabira yuki furu
Bonchō

For New Year's feasting
every good thing is called for
to propose long life
and with the warbler's song the snow
comes down lightly over all

♦ ♦ ♦ ♦

Uguisu no ne ni
tabira yuki furu
7 noridashite
kaina ni amaru
haru no koma
Kyorai

With the warbler's song the snow
comes down lightly over all
galloping for a ride
he finds the young spring stallion
will not yield to reins

Noridashite
kaina ni amaru
haru no koma
8 Maya ga takane ni
kumo no kakareru
Yasui

Galloping for a ride
he finds the young spring stallion
will not yield to reins
as there upon Mount Maya
clouds hang on the lofty peak

Maya ga takane ni
kumo no kakareru
9 yūmeshi ni
kamasugo kueba
kaze kaoru
Bonchō

While there upon Mount Maya
clouds hang on the lofty peak
at summer supper
as he is eating saury minnows
the breeze brings fragrance

Yūmeshi ni
kamasugo kueba
kaze kaoru
10 hiru no kuchido o
kakite kimi yoki
Bashō

At summer supper
as I am eating saury minnows
the breeze brings fragrance
and there is something that feels good
in scratching where the leech had bit

11 Ground-Design. Light. Miscellaneous. Love.
This is an extreme example of light relation. The connection lies in the strenu-
ousness of the service from which the woman now has a day or so of respite.
The work and the longing had combined to exhaust her. This and the preceding stanza are easily assessed as to connection but in impressiveness may well
be thought Design-Ground.

12 Ground-Design. Heavy-Light. Miscellaneous. Love. Persons. Military.
If we follow the interpretation that this recalls the first book of *The Tale of
Genji*, the class is Noble rather than Military. But this seems much more like
various post-court stories and suggests the concubine of a military lord rather
than the usual court situation in which the woman waits.

13 Ground-Design. Light. Miscellaneous. Persons. Products.
This stanza well illustrates a kind of connection that looks Close (by juxtaposition) but in fact is Light. It is desirable to have one or two such as these, but too
many would disjoint the sequence, as too Heavy relation would make all seem
the same. The Japanese is obscure as to point of view and person described.

14 Design-Ground. Light-Heavy. Autumn. Night. Radiance.
This second moon stanza comes in the standard place. Since all Japanese like
baths, someone who is specially said to bask in them must be an old person, a
person with little work, or a dandy. But the moon each night is appreciated. A
fine haikai combination.

15 Design-Ground. Heavy-Light. Autumn. Residences. Town.
In this somber stanza autumn seems to move right through the town past
empty buildings that also hasten on—in time (fukeyuku). The passage of time
is beautifully and sadly evoked.

11

Hiru no kuchido o
kakite kimi yoki
   monoomoi
kyō wa wasurete
   yasumu hi ni
Yasui

There is something that feels good
in scratching where the leech had bit
   the pains of longing
are such that she wishes to forget
   on a day free from service

12

Monoomoi
kyō wa wasurete
   yasumu hi ni
mukaese hashiki
tono yori no fumi
Kyorai

The pains of longing
are such that she wishes to forget
   on a day free from service
but a love letter from her lord
urgently requires her return

13

Mukaese hashiki
tono yori no fumi
   kintsuba to
hito ni yobaruru
   mi no yasusa
Bashō

A love letter from her lord
urgently requires her return
   what complacency
there is in hearing people say
   she is fortune's child

14

Kintsuba to
hito ni yobaruru
   mi no yasusa
atsufurozuki no
yoiyoi no tsuki
Bonchō

What complacency
there is in hearing people say
   that one is fortune's child
and basking in a fine hot bath
each night with the moon in view

15

Atsufurozuki no
yoiyoi no tsuki
   chōnai no
aki mo fukeyuku
   akiyashiki
Kyorai

Basking in a fine hot bath
each night with the moon in view
   throughout the town
autumn also hastens on
   by vacant buildings

16 Ground. Light-Heavy. Autumn. Evanescence.
In itself, this stanza has only Autumn in common with 15, but Evanescence grows so well out of that stanza as to give some "heaviness" of connection. This is the first Ground stanza, and has a certain flat moralizing to it, in preparation for a contrasting flower stanza. Dew is a Falling Thing in renga.

17 Design-Ground. Light-Heavy. Spring. Evanescence. Persons. Clothes. Trees.
Using the religious emblematic status of dew rather than its seasonal emblem of autumn, Bashō moves to spring from autumn, a somewhat violent movement, especially since the flower imagery works so strongly from the beginning of this stanza. This is the proper location for the first flower stanza. After the positive nature of much earlier, this is very sober for this stanza.

18 Design-Ground. Light-Heavy. Spring. Plants.
In 17 it seemed the speaker would become a recluse. Here he is on the road at a named place. Both stanzas regret the passing of an aspect of Spring. Japanese pickle many different vegetables, but this particular one seems to be a local specialty produced in Spring.

♦ ♦ ♦ ♦
♦ ♦ ♦ ♦

19 Design-Ground. Heavy-Light. Spring. Birds. Peaks.
It seems to be assumed here that the traveler of 18 is going southwest and the birds are returning northeast—to what was thought their proper home. There are now five stanzas in a row alternating real and figurative motion.

20 Ground-Design. Light. Miscellaneous. Residence. Trees. Farming.
Kyorai brings the action to rest at a mountain scene (the thatch is of twigs, not straw). Here is a human home in contrast to that for the titmice in 19. But since no human creature is mentioned as present, the scene appears very still.

Chōnai no
aki mo fukeyuku
  akiyashiki
16 nani o miru ni mo
  tsuyu bakari nari
    Yasui

Throughout the town
autumn also hastens on
  by vacant buildings
all the world offers to our sight
is covered with the moment's dew

Nani o miru ni mo
tsuyu bakari nari
  hana to chiru
17 mi wa sainen ga
  koromo kite
    Bashō

All the world offers to our sight
is covered with the moment's dew
  as cherry blossoms fall
so I have reached the time for robes
  that tell of priestly life

Hana to chiru
mi wa sainen ga
  koromo kite
18 Kiso no suguki ni
  haru mo kuretsutsu
    Bonchō

As cherry blossoms fall
so have I reached the time for robes
  that tell of priestly life
in Kiso the pickled greens
taste as if the spring is ending

♦ ♦ ♦ ♦
♦ ♦ ♦ ♦

Kiso no suguki ni
haru mo kuretsutsu
  kaeru yara
19 yamakage tsutau
  shijūkara
    Yasui

In Kiso the pickled greens
taste as if the spring is ending
  it seems the titmice
fly home northward as they follow
  the loom of the mountains

Kaeru yara
yamakage tsutau
  shijūkara
20 shiba sasu ie no
  mune o karageru
    Kyorai

It seems the titmice
fly homeward as they follow
  the loom of the mountains
the last twig thatching has been bound
to the ridge pole on the cottage roof

21 Design-Ground. Light. Winter.
The mountain atmosphere of 20 associates with the wind blowing from the north here, but the connection is light. The stillness of the house in 21 has contrast in the violent sky seen over a considerable distance.

22 Ground-Design. Light-Heavy. Miscellaneous. Travel. Products. Night. Radiance.
After enduring the bitter weather of 21, the traveler arrives at lodging to find a considerate host. The lamp is probably a simple box with apertures for light and air, but the image of its light is very comforting.

23 Ground. Heavy-Light. Autumn. Love. Persons.
The situation of the woman waiting in vain for a faithless lover is standard, but Kyorai skillfully uses 22 to his ends. The introduction of both Love and Autumn in a Ground stanza is rather unusual, since they are both subjects of high price. The "mo" in the second line means women's as well as men's wisdom.

24 Ground-Design. Light-Heavy. Autumn. Love. Animals.
The stag's cries are traditional, but the wolf is so novel as to make impressiveness difficult to judge. Apparently the wolf's male wisdom helps no more here than the woman's in 23, but there seems some comic misogyny in the change to wolves. "Omoigusa" (wanton-flowers) are ominaeshi, patrinia, and the Japanese names suggest passion.

25 Design. Heavy-Light. Autumn. Grasses. Night. Radiance. Peaks. Court.
At a desolate site, but brightened with moonlight, the faithful guard waits out Autumn and his life, hearing the wolf cry in the wilds. Bashō introduces the third moon stanza with great effect as the last of three Autumn stanzas but four before its usual place. The waka-like diction of the first two lines plays against the sinified word in the last.

21
Shiba sasu ie no
mune o karageru
fuyuzora no
are ni naritaru
kitaoroshi
Bonchō

The last twig thatching has been bound
to the ridge pole on the cottage roof
   the winter sky
has been shaken into disarray
   by the northern storm

22
Fuyuzora no
are ni naritaru
kitaoroshi
tabi no chisō ni
ariakashi oku
Bashō

The winter sky
has been shaken into disarray
   by the northern storm
as a welcome to the traveler
the host brings a floor lamp for the night

23
Tabi no chisō ni
ariakashi oku
susamajiki
onna no chie mo
hakanakute
Kyorai

To welcome her distant lover
she brought a floor lamp for the night
   utterly useless
her vaunted female wisdom
   also ends in nothing

24
Susamajiki
onna no chie mo
hakanakute
nani omoigusa
ōkami no naku
Yasui

Utterly useless
her vaunted female wisdom
   also ends in nothing
what feelings stir the wanton-flowers
as the wolf cries out for his mate

25
Nani omoigusa
ōkami no naku
yūzukuyo
oka no kayane no
gobyō moru
Bashō

What feelings stir the wanton-flowers
as the wolf cries out for his mate
   reeds upon the hillside
shine in the moonlight where the guard
   stands by the royal tomb

26 Ground-Design. Heavy-Light. Miscellaneous. Waters.
The desertion of the scene is intensified. The "mo" after "hito" may imply in connection with 25 that the guard does not use the water, and by itself that animals do not use it, or that no one at all uses it, stressing the absence of anyone at the scene.

27 Ground-Design. Light. Miscellaneous. Persons.
This very light linking uses little more than contrast to connect: between the objective, factual character and dreariness of 26 and the unbelievable tales told with such relish here.

28 Ground. Light-Heavy. Summer. Town.
The humor is very similar to that in 27, condescending but goodnatured. To compensate, a different person is implied, the impressiveness is changed, and a season is freshly introduced. The old-style *sushi*—fish pressed on rice—designates Summer.

29 Design. Light. Summer. Cultivation. Peasants.
The stanza rises in impressiveness over recent ones, freeing itself with a Light relation to 28, but connecting by season and rice plants. This is a very Japanese scene. Bonchō reveals a talent different from his humor in *Throughout the Town* and here begins the most memorable run of stanzas in this kasen.

30 Design-Ground. Light-Heavy. Miscellaneous. Shinto. Residences.
The prosaic quality of the stanza is a decorum for this kind of simple but, to a Japanese, impressive scene in a named place. Others might wish to give it a lower impressiveness. Its connection of the lovely rice in 29 with native divinities is very effective. The "yoki" means something like "rich with gods," not "fresh" as in 29, they being two distinct characters.

♦　♦　♦　♦

Yūzukuyo
oka no kayane no
   gobyō moru
26   hito mo wasureshi
akasobu no mizu
Bonchō

Reeds upon the hillside
shine in the moonlight where the guard
   stands by the royal tomb
everybody has neglected
the well holding brackish water

Hito mo wasureshi
akasobu no mizu
   usotsuki ni
27   jiman iwasete
   asobu ran
Yasui

Everybody has neglected
the well holding brackish water
   one can enjoy
letting the tale-teller swagger on
   with his tall stories

Usotsuki ni
jiman iwasete
   asobu ran
28   mata mo daiji no
sushi o toridasu
Kyorai

One can enjoy
letting the tale-teller swagger on
   with his tall stories
again he brings out with a flourish
the *sushi* that he thinks so grand

Mata mo daiji no
sushi o toridasu
   tsutsumi yori
29   ta no aoyagite
   isagi yoki
Bonchō

Again brought out with a flourish
the *sushi* that is thought so grand
   far beyond the dike
the lush green rice plants in the fields
   give freshness to the sight

Tsutsumi yori
ta no aoyagite
   isagi yoki
30   Kamo no yashiro wa
yoki yashiro nari
Bashō

Far beyond the dike
the lush green rice plants in the fields
   give freshness to the sight
the precincts of the Kamo shrine
suggest the many gods within

     ◆   ◆   ◆   ◆

31 Ground-Design. Light. Miscellaneous. Persons. Town.
The high tone and peacefulness of 30 are altered. In connection with 30, this suggests a busy market at the entrance to the Kyoto shrine. By itself, it gives the tonal contrast.

32 Design-Ground. Light. Miscellaneous. Evanescence.
The thematic connection with 31 is clear. But the imagery sets it quite apart. The internal contrast is between Japanese and sinified diction in the two lines. Both recall Sōgi's famous "shigure no yadori," the hermitage in drizzling rain. Rain is a falling thing in renga.

33 Design. Light-Heavy. Miscellaneous. Birds.
Again a thematic connection diminished by differing imagery. This symbol of peace and understanding of the Law gives surprising stillness in the fast (kyū) finale of the kasen. The stipulation of time and place in the sequence no doubt decreases the near sanctity of the image of a bird in water, on one leg, its head under its wing, free from phenomenal flow.

34 Ground-Design. Heavy-Light. Miscellaneous. Grasses. Waters.
The atmosphere of 33 continues, but now there is motion and less dignified language ("shoroshoro"). The imagery well associates with that in 33, but this whole stanza has new elements. The final "ran" has none of the old presumptive meanings in waka and functions as a copula plus cutting-word.

35 Ground-Design. Light. Spring. Trees.
Only light relation enables Kyorai to make this stanza the flower-stanza it should be. He violates decorum by giving a named flower, which does not count in renga or haikai for a flower stanza. Bashō is said to have approved, because of the colloquial expression "hara ippai," a bellyful, which has different associations in English.

31	Kamo no yashiro wa yoki yashiro nari 　monouri no shirigoe takaku 　nanori sute *Kyorai*	The precincts of the Kamo Shrine suggest the many gods within 　the strolling peddler loudly calls his wares in shortened names 　as he passes by
32	Monouri no shirigoe takaku 　nanori sute ame no yadori no mujō jinsoku *Yasui*	The strolling peddler loudly calls his wares in shortened names 　as he passes by no more than cover from a shower is human life in ceaseless flux
33	Ame no yadori no mujō jinsoku 　hiru neburu aosagi no mi no 　tōtosa yo *Bashō*	No more than cover from a shower is this world in ceaseless flux 　sleeping at noon the body of the blue heron 　poised in nobility
34	Hiru neburu aosagi no mi no 　tōtosa yo shoroshoro mizu ni i no soyogu ran *Bonchō*	Sleeping at noon the body of the blue heron 　poised in nobility where the waters trickle trickle the rushes sway in utter peace
35	Shoroshoro mizu ni i no soyogu ran 　itozakura hara ippai ni 　sakinikeri *Kyorai*	Where the waters trickle trickle the rushes sway in utter peace 　the drooping cherries have flowered in such loveliness 　as fills me to the top

36 Design-Ground. Heavy-Light. Spring. Night.

We end with spring at its height, the cherry blossoms of 35 dimly visible at dawn (a night word). The "sangatsu" instead of "yayoi" purposely lowers the tone, stressing the traditional beauty of spring dawn in a fresh way.

Itozakura
hara ippai ni
sakinikeri
36   haru wa sangatsu
akebono no sora.
Yasui

The drooping cherries
have flowered in such loveliness
as fills me to the top
spring glories in the third of months
with dawn's first glowing in the sky.

4

Peony Petals Fell

FROM *PEACHES AND PLUMS* (*Botan chitte no maki*)
BUSON AND KITŌ

THIS IS THE only ryōgin or two-person sequence included here. Its two poets are Taniguchi (later Yosa) Buson (1716-1783), the greatest haiku poet after Bashō, and his partner, Takai Kitō (1741-1789), who appears to have become a follower of Buson's haikai style at about the age of thirty. Although he tried to continue Buson's style after his master died, Kito's own death a few years later ended a major bastion of it. According to the story, when Kitō called on Buson one evening in 1780, the master said that he had been sporting with haikai for half a century and had not many more years to go. His friend seemed to him to be a haikai poet also, so why should they not have a try at a two-poet sequence? Beginning in the Third Month, or late spring, they composed until the eleventh, ending with two sequences. Among the features that will seem unusual in *Peony Petals Fell* is this lengthy composition. That is rather reminiscent of Sōgi's solo renga given in the previous part. If Sōgi's intention had been to write a model renga, Buson and Kitō appeared to have set out to do as they pleased and certainly to enjoy themselves.

Something of Buson's particular humor in the haikai style emerges in his Preface. As will be seen, he claims that they wrote four kasen, but that the Spring and Autumn sequences were somehow lost. (Of course they never existed.) Someone later asked for something to publish, and rummaging in old papers, Buson found the Summer and Winter sequences. (Actually, they were published soon after composition.) And so on. Even the choice of seasons is unusual, since Spring and Autumn are of far greater price in Japan, and for good reason. The title, *Momo*

Sumomo sounds rather odd, and is so no less because neither peaches nor damson plums are appropriate to Summer or Winter. The companion sequence, *The Wintry Woods* (*Fuyu Kodachi no Maki*), begins in a yet more comic way. The humor of this Summer sequence is not quite so obvious, and it comes more consistently at the end than at the beginning.

The two poets evidently knew very well what to expect of each other and often make gestures of one kind or another, as when Kitō makes the first stanza a moon stanza in *The Wintry Woods*. Taking their time, they produced some really outstanding stanzas. In judging impressiveness, one does not assess quality purely and simply. It is a question of elevation and decorum as well. Many Ground stanzas are extremely interesting, whereas a Design stanza can be rather conventional. There is hardly an uninteresting stanza in this sequence, and the range is very considerable. As in other haikai sequences many liberties are taken here with various conventions. Yet in all but one particular this sequence is no more radical than many by Bashō, and in some ways it is less. The aestheticism and humor come to be expected in things like plays between what is very Japanese and what is Chinese, or in the frustrations of life. The oil vendor keeps on gossiping next door when one wants a delivery now. The poor palanquin bearer has no one to hold up the other end (an especially fine stanza). A little rural shrine has more gods than it needs. The sequence really sparkles with wit and imagination.

The one exceptional particular referred to happens to be very serious. Very, very few of the stanzas have anything approaching usual haikai re-latedness. Nothing in *Peony Petals Fell* at all approaches the very close, albeit humorous, connection between the first and second stanzas of *The Wintry Wood*. So Distant or Light are the relations—and especially in Kitō's additions—that any attempt to judge relatedness is so difficult as to verge on impossibility. Any two critics will always come up with some variation, in assessing renga as well as haikai. But the extremes usually emerge rather clearly. When, however, so much is extreme, it becomes difficult to guess what normality might be. Even the poets' contemporaries voiced some complaint.

If the assessments given are correct, of the possible thirty-five relations (the hokku can have none), twenty-eight are either Light or Light-Heavy, six Heavy-Light, and one Heavy. Many of the Light have basically no relation at all, at least apart from contrast or juxtaposition. This works very well about once a sequence. It does not work so well when it comes to prevail. To have fifteen—nearly half of the thirty-five—relations Light makes near nonsense of the idea of a sequence. Of the fifteen, Kitō wrote nine—although he also wrote the only stanza of Heavy relation and twice as many (four to two) of Heavy-Light.

One can read this sequence in two major ways. It can be appreciated for its brilliant stanzas. There are too many good ones for a proper sequence, but that fault can be borne with. Or one can read it as a symptom of the obsolescence of linked verse. It is difficult to say that an art is dying when we see it practiced by such brilliant people. But this is a sequence that often seems to be closer to a series of haiku than to haikai. If the best minds had to take such extreme measures to make haikai seem important in their time, there cannot have been much hope for the continuing greatness of the sequential aspects of the art.

With this problem so evident, one does not worry so much about other matters, such as the relation of this sequence to what seems enduringly important in human affairs. Actually, our poets come off well in that respect since they do know very well what matters—even if they seem remote from it, reluctant to be involved. Although the individual stanzas should afford very great interest, the longer one has worked with renga and haikai, the less satisfactory a sequence this seems to be. It can only be the special conditions of sequential art that could lead one to complain of what is in many ways so brilliant in its individual parts.

The unusual abundance of lightly related stanzas makes judgment of the progression difficult in this renku. It seems, however, that the prefatory section (1-6, the front of the first sheet) is elevated, rather grave, and with some element of mystery or exoticism (as in stanzas 4 and 6). The long Development section (7-30, the back of the first sheet and the front of the second) plays on the motifs of the first section, adding humor and a wider variety of experience, including Love along with social groups higher and lower. The conclusion (kyū), which is supposed to have speed of some kind (31-36, the back of the second sheet), begins to accelerate earlier, as so often in sequences. From stanzas 29-30 (the last two of the development section), we have a sense of agitation in human affairs to stanza 31. Then the agitation is successively that of animals, divinities, and a person (32-34), and the sequence closes with two spring poems (35-36), the last one coming to a quiet close.

A kasen by two poets could have its thirty-six stanzas composed in simple alternation. That seems to have been thought too monotonous, however. We discover in this kasen that there is simple alternation in the two long parts of the Development section (7-18, 19-30). In the former Kitō begins and Buson follows; in the latter, the reverse is true. In the shorter first and last sections the order is non-symmetrical. In the first, Buson begins, Kitō does two stanzas, Buson two, and Kitō the last. In the conclusion, Kitō begins and there follow stanzas by Buson and then Kitō. The section ends with two by Buson and a last by Kitō. This can be diagrammed by considering Buson poet A and Kitō poet B.

1-6	ABBAAB
7-18	BABABABABABA
19-30	ABABABABABAB
31-36	BABAAB

It is difficult not to feel that, if the art of linked sequences must come to an end, this one gives the proper sense of an ending. Apart from the high quality of its stanzas, it has many contrasts, comedy, innovation, glances back to renga and waka, and above all a sense that the wryly variegated pageant of life is available to human art.

(*Momosumomo*)

AT ONE TIME we had sequences on each of the four seasons. Those on spring and autumn have been lost, while these on summer and winter yet remain. Someone suggested that publication might be desirable, and here to hand were those two kasen that had been laid aside for so long a time. This made me laugh and say that such was the happiness of haikai that it was really something both belonging to fashion and not belonging to fashion, very much like running around a circle, chasing after someone. It seems that poetic fashions that precede pursue those that fall behind. How, in the realm of fashion, can we distinguish before or after? So it is that from day to day I express my own taste, composing today's kind of haikai today and tomorrow's tomorrow. For a title I have chosen *Peaches and Plums*, and anyone reading it will find nothing of the old-fashioned or of the up-to-date. Such is the grand intent of this sequence.

—*by Buson*

1 Design. No Relation. Summer. Cultivation.
Buson has resuscitated an old hokku to begin this sequence. "Botan" and "shakuyaku" are both translated "peony," but the latter is botanically closer to the usual species in the United States. "Botan" has somewhat more Chinese association. It had names such as "king of flowers" and was a favorite with Buson. He uses a noun ending instead of a cutting-word such as "kana."

2 Design. Light. Summer. Night. Radiance.
The moon is in the twentieth day of its cycle as it fades into the sky at dawn. (Since "tsuki" is not used, this is not a moon stanza.) Buson praised this waki stanza. In other haikai, Kitō connects flowers with moonlight: here the silent fall of peony petals perhaps relates to the moon's faint light as it fades.

3 Ground-Design. Light. Miscellaneous. Persons. Residences.
Usually the season of the hokku is continued through this stanza. Kitō does not, perhaps because summer (and winter) are less esteemed. The only tangible connection with 3 seems to be "hiraku" here with "-ake" there, both of which may mean "to open." The "ran" termination is appropriate for this stanza.

4 Ground. Light-Heavy. Persons. Miscellaneous.
Apparently, the old man becomes this apparition, clearing his throat to draw attention. If so, some degree of heaviness exists in the relation to 3. The ghost appearance has a fairy-tale quality about it.

5 Ground-Design. Light. Miscellaneous. Products. Trees.
Apparently the connection with 4 is with its fairy-tale atmosphere and a long-long-ago sense of time's passage here. Nettle-trees are thought of as suitable to an area of houses.

BUSON AND KITŌ

1   Botan chitte
uchikasanarinu
    ni-sanpen
   Buson

        Peony petals fell
piling one upon another
    in twos and threes

       Botan chitte
uchikasanarinu
    ni-sanpen
2   uzuki hatsuka no
ariake no kage
   Kitō

        Peony petals fell
piling one upon another
    in twos and threes
the waning moon of early summer
shines but faintly as dawn breaks

       Uzuki hatsuka no
ariake no kage
3   suwabukite
okina ya kado o
    hiraku ran
   Kitō

        The waning moon of early summer
shone but faintly as dawn broke
    clearing his throat
the old gentleman opens the gate
    with a lofty air

       Suwabukite
okina ya kado o
    hiraku ran
4   muko no erabi ni
kitsuru hengue
   Buson

        Clearing his throat
the old gentleman opens the gate
    with a lofty air
while choosing a son-in-law
there has come this apparition

       Muko no erabi ni
kitsuru hengue
5   toshi furishi
chimata no enoki
    ono irete
   Buson

        While choosing a son-in-law
there came that apparition
    as many years go by
the town's overgrown nettle-tree
    submits to the axe

6 Design-Ground. Light. Miscellaneous. Travel.
The diction of this impressive stanza is highly sinified, and the extensive scene is more Chinese than Japanese. Kitō apparently associates the action in 5 with the story of Emperor Yang of the Sui (7th century), who had a great canal made. The story was current in Japan as *Zui no Yōdai Gaishi* (*The Extra History of Emperor Yang of the Sui*).

♦ ♦ ♦ ♦

7 Ground. Heavy-Light. Summer.
The traveler of 6 has become a poet happy to visit places celebrated in verse (utamakura). Fever (okori) is the seasonal word. This stanza is as Japanese as 6 is Chinese. We return to Summer for one stanza after four Miscellaneous stanzas.

8 Design. Light. Autumn. Cultivation. Peasants.
Since cold comes to the mountains earlier than to low areas, autumn is not yet late in general. It is a lovely scene of terraced paddy-fields up the slope, brown with the heavy rice stalks. The only relation to 7 must be that the person's place is located, but this is not specified as to any famous, named place.

9 Design. Heavy-Light. Autumn. Night. Radiance. Birds.
This lovely scene fits well with 8, since autumn is most esteemed poetically for its evenings. In renga or waka the birds would probably be geese, but the scene is otherwise traditional. This is the first moon stanza, which usually is thought best to come eight positions later, although many exceptions exist.

10 Ground-Design. Light-Heavy. Autumn. Persons. Residences.
The diction suggests proper sensibility but feelings stronger than are usually felt. "Hitori" means the person is alone. To lean against a door is fresh but hardly very poetic in connection with the moon of 9.

Toshi furishi
chimata no enoki
  ono irete
6 hyakuri no kugachi
tomari sadamezu
  Kitō

As many years go by
the place's overgrown nettle-tree
  submits to the axe
the land mass stretches a hundred leagues
without a place to spend the night

♦ ♦ ♦ ♦

Hyakuri no kugachi
tomari sadamezu
7   utamakura
okori ochitaru
  kinō kyō
  Kitō

The land mass stretches a hundred leagues
without a place to spend the night
  to see famous places
has lowered my malarial fever
  yesterday and today

  Utamakura
okori ochitaru
  kinō kyō
8 yamada no oda no
wase o karu koro
Buson

  To see famous places
has lowered his malarial fever
  yesterday and today
the little paddies in the mountains
have rice already ripe for harvest

Yamada no oda no
wase o karu koro
9   yūgetsu ni
okurete wataru
  shijūkara
  Kitō

The little paddies in the mountains
have rice already ripe for harvest
  the flock of titmice
cross belatedly at evening
  before a waxing moon

  Yūgetsu ni
okurete wataru
  shijūkara
10 aki o ureite
hitori to ni yoru
Buson

  The flock of titmice
cross belatedly at evening
  before a waxing moon
sensing the autumn sadness
he leans rapt against the door

11 Ground. Light. Miscellaneous.
The humorous side of haikai appears here. The relation to 10 is very tenuous. Those strong feelings for autumn are now changed to the sufferings of illness. Since traditional Japanese medicines were usually powdered, their flavors would be clearly tasted.

12 Ground-Design. Light. Miscellaneous. Products.
Taima Temple was founded many centuries before by a court lady and was famous for its peonies. The connection with 11 seems to be that that sick person has sent a letter to his native place, Taima. A "furoshiki" is a cloth square used for wrapping and carrying.

13 Ground. Light. Miscellaneous. Persons. Residences. Town.
Oil-vendors carried buckets of fuel for lamps and other domestic purposes. Something like rape-seed oil is probably implied, as also the gossipy nature of the vendors. The speaker wishes to be served, and this impatience with waiting seems to be attributed to a person in Taima waiting for the letter of 13 as a connection between the stanzas. A nice haikai town scene.

14 Design-Ground. Light-Heavy. Winter.
The second line is very waka-like, and the scene is lovely. The lightness of the relation derives from its being based chiefly on establishing the scene of 13; the heaviness derives from dusk's being a time when a person would be especially desirous of the oil and from a sense of isolation intensified.

15 Ground. Heavy. Winter. Residences, Animals.
For once Kitō gives a stanza of heavy relation. The great snowfall of 14 is taken as bringing the wolf to a village in some remote mountain area.

11
Aki o ureite
hitori to ni yoru
　me futaide
nigaki kusuri o
　susurikeru
　Kitō

Sensing the autumn anguish
he leaned rapt against the door
　eyes shut tightly
he swallowed down the medicine
　so bitter in taste

12
Me futaide
nigaki kusuri o
　susurikeru
Taima e modosu
furoshiki ni fumi
Buson

Eyes shut tightly
he swallowed down the medicine
　so bitter in taste
to Taima comes as reply
a letter in a *furoshiki*

13
Taima e modosu
furoshiki ni fumi
　tonari nite
mada koe no suru
　abura-uri
　Kitō

To Taima comes as reply
a letter in a *furoshiki*
　one still hears the voice
of that oil-vendor who remains
　at the house next door

14
Tonari nite
mada koe no suru
　abura-uri
sanjaku tsumoru
yuki no tasogare
Buson

One still hears the voice
of that oil-vendor who remains
　at the house next door
accumulating three full feet
the snow lies in the twilight

15
Sanjaku tsumoru
yuki no tasogare
　e ni uyuru
ōkami uchi ni
　shinobu ran
　Kitō

Accumulating three full feet
the snow lies in the twilight
　starved of its food
the wolf stalks quietly along
　to the side of the house

16 Ground. Light-Heavy. Miscellaneous. Persons.
Once one guesses that a hunter's wife is meant, there is some heaviness of relation. Because he takes the lives of animals, his wife is cursed with the affliction
that causes her shame and grief.

17 Design-Ground. Light. Spring. Buddhism. Persons. Trees.
A beautiful young woman gives up her long hair to assist in raising funds for a
new temple bell. The scene is one of beauty and sacrifice, and the metamorphosis of the woman in 16 seems to be the sole relation.

18 Design. Heavy-Light. Spring. Buddhism.
The Western Paradise is meant. This places the scene of 17 at dusk, but it also
connects in its Buddhist elements and suggests that the woman's virtuous act
will be rewarded at the end. The diction is particularly waka- and renga-like.
An auspicious ending to the first sheet.

◆　◆　◆　◆
◆　◆　◆　◆

19 Design. Light-Heavy. Spring. Products. Military.
Buson refers to a general of the Taira (Heike), who went down to defeat at the
battle of Dannoura to the west in Japan. The setting sun of 18 now seems
ominous. Over a great gulf of time and distance, Buson recalls the sounds of
the bowstrings, sounds misted over by the beauty of a spring haze. A splendid
stanza.

20 Ground. Light. Miscellaneous. Persons. Court.
"Hakase," or "doctor," implies no vulgar astronomer. Presumably Kitō associated with the end of Noritsune in 19 the possibility of prediction. But the
relation is so light that even his contemporaries criticized its tenuousness.

	E ni uyuru	Starved of its food
	ōkami uchi ni	the wolf stalks quietly along
	shinobu ran	to the side of the house
16	ikuchi no tsuma no	the hare-lipped wife of the hunter
	tada naki ni naku	does nothing else but weep and weep
	Buson	

	Ikuchi no tsuma no	The hare-lipped wife of the hunter
	tada naki ni naku	does nothing else but weep and weep
17	kanei aru	for a bell-casting
	hana nomi tera ni	at a temple full of cherry flowers
	kami kirite	she cuts her lovely hair
	Kitō	

	Kanei aru	For a bell-casting
	hana nomi tera ni	at a temple full of cherry flowers
	kami kirite	she cuts her lovely hair
18	haru no yukue no	the destined end of springtime
	nishi ni katabuku	is sunset in the Buddha's west
	Buson	

♦　♦　♦　♦
♦　♦　♦　♦

	Haru no yukue no	The destined end of springtime
	nishi ni katabuku	is sunset in the Buddha's west
19	Noto-dono no	Noritsune's fate
	tsuru oto kasumu	is lost in the hazed-over sound
	tōkata ni	of bowstrings far away
	Buson	

	Noto-dono no	Noritsune's fate
	tsuru oto kasumu	is lost in the hazed-over sound
	tōkata ni	of bowstrings far away
20	hakase hisomite	the intent astrologer foretells
	toki o uranau	the right hour for the prince's birth
	Kitō	

21 Ground. Light-Heavy. Miscellaneous. Animals. Birds.
According to a story in the *Analects*, a follower of Confucius understood bird-talk and predicted assassination. He was imprisoned until further revelations by sparrows showed him to be right. The Japanese atmosphere of 20 is altered to Chinese (although Japanese also think some bird cries ominous). The connection lies in prediction.

22 Design. Light-Heavy. Summer. Trees. Cultivation. Peasants.
The words of 21 are taken as setting a rural scene. Otherwise the connection is tenuous. The distance here is about half a mile, which is enormous for the usually terraced small Japanese fields. The trees grow to about twenty feet and are used medicinally.

23 Design. Light. Miscellaneous. Peaks.
Mt. Asama is a volcano in Nagano and Gumma Prefectures. The relation to 23 is one of contrast between a view near at hand and a distant one. In renga, smoke is a Rising Thing. Buson imagines that the shower has ceased and across the clear portion of the sky extends the rainbow above the peak.

24 Design-Ground. Light. Miscellaneous. People. Residences. Court.
It is not clear whether this should be a third-person or first-person presentation. Imperial messengers would put up in the houses of important provincial people as they went across the countryside. Apart from the honor, the hosts would receive latest news from the court. This figuratively bright atmosphere and the literally bright atmosphere of 23 offer the sole relation.

25 Design-Ground. Light-Heavy. Miscellaneous. Waters.
The fish are imagined to be the food offered to the messengers of 24. The first character (the "e-" of *Edo*) is deliberately read "kō" by Buson out of his love of things Chinese. It renders an air of the exotic to verses that might connect by very Japanese details, such as imperial messengers and fish.

21
Hakase hisomite
toki o uranau
    awa oishi
uma taorenu to
    tori nakite
Buson

The intent astrologer foretold
the right hour for the prince's birth
    carrying millet
the horse collapsed with the load
and birds cried of death

22
    Awa oishi
uma taorenu to
    tori nakite
ōchi sakichiru
nawate hatchō
Kitō

    Carrying millet
the horse collapsed with the load
    and birds cried of death
sandalwood flowers bloom and fall
where the field ridge stretches far away

23
Ōchi sakichiru
nawate hatchō
    tachiaenu
niji ni Asama no
    uchikeburi
Buson

Sandalwood flowers bloom and fall
where the field ridge stretches far away
    from Mount Asama
the puffs of smoke strive upwards
    even to the rainbow

24
    Tachiaenu
niji ni Asama no
    uchikeburi
chokushi no oyado
mōsu ureshisa
Kitō

    From Mount Asama
the puffs of smoke strove upwards
    even to the rainbow
what a joy to offer lodging
to the emperor's messengers

25
Chokushi no oyado
mōsu ureshisa
    kō ni etaru
ajika no uo no
    hara akaki
Buson

What a joy to offer lodging
to the emperor's messengers
    the fish carried off
in baskets from the great river
    are red-belly trout

26 Design-Ground. Light. Winter.
The winter sky of an island country is capricious, here producing seemingly contrary phenomena that are very attractive together. Once again, Kitō gives us a very tenuous relation. Hail is a Falling Thing in renga.

27 Ground. Light. Miscellaneous. Love. Persons.
The relation amounts only to contrast: season in 26, human affairs here. The Love is that of an older man for a younger, something common enough in temples and camps. As other sequences have shown, haikai delights in surprises like this (standard renga followed the waka tradition of heterosexual love).

28 Ground. Light-Heavy. Miscellaneous. Love. Persons.
I follow the usual interpretation here: replacing the older man in 27, the girl is anxious to meet the lad. Having prettied herself up to meet him, she does not want any of her elaborate work undone before they meet. The absence of clear longing also makes this an unusual love stanza.

29 Design-Ground. Light-Heavy. Autumn. Night. Radiance.
This second moon stanza comes in the conventional place, but this stanza is also unusual in not specifically mentioning the moon (tsuki). "Izayoi" is the first night after the full moon. The relation is a little heavier: many people here, the one or two in 28; pleasure there, business here. Again contrast rather than linkage is employed.

30 Ground-Design. Heavy-Light. Autumn. Products.
The front of the second sheet ends with this (for Kitō) heavy relation between continuing sound of the fulling blocks and the busy people of 29. Human exertions continue to make autumn less "poetic" than in renga and waka.

♦　♦　♦　♦

Kō ni etaru
ajika no uo no
　　hara akaki
26　hi wa sashinagara
mata arare furu
　Kitō

The fish carried off
in baskets from the great river
　　are red-belly trout
even while the sun is shining
more hail falls from the winter sky

Hi wa sashinagara
mata arare furu
　　mishi koi no
27　chigo neriide yo
　　dōkuyō
　Buson

Even while the sun is shining
more hail falls from the winter sky
　　to see him was to love
if only he would come out again
　　for the temple rites

　　Mishi koi no
chigo neriide yo
　　dōkuyō
28　tsuburi ni sawaru
hito nikuki nari
　Kitō

　　When she saw she loved him
if only he would come out again
　　for the temple rites
pretty with her hair got up
the girl wants no one to jar her

Tsuburi ni sawaru
hito nikuki nari
　　izayoi no
29　kuraki hima sae
　　yo no isogi
　Buson

Pretty with her hair got up
the girl wants no one to jar her
　　even in the dusk
before the waning moon appears
　　all keep at business

Izayoi no
kuraki hima sae
　　yo no isogi
30　shikoro utsu naru
Bamba Matsumoto
　Kitō

　　Even in the dusk
before the waning moon appears
　　all keep at business
at Bamba beside Lake Biwa
fulling blocks beat without a pause

◆　◆　◆　◆

31 Ground. Light-Heavy. Autumn. Persons. Products.
The wretched life of the man is represented in the double frustration of being unable to work and having a cold autumn rain fall (rain is, of course, a Falling Thing in renga). The constrained life of 30 is intensified here, making a sad comedy of life, and gives some heaviness of relation. A splendid stanza.

32 Ground. Heavy-Light. Miscellaneous. Birds.
The world's miseries now have birds as representatives, and not very elevated ones at that. The sense of doubleness also relates to 31. Buson has evidently observed that 27-31 have dealt with human affairs and sees a change is necessary.

33 Ground. Light-Heavy. Miscellaneous. Shinto.
This is a rather comic notion that a little rural shrine can be so rich in the animistic divinities. It gives a scene for 32 and shares some idea of competition (though as implication rather than words).

34 Ground. Light. Miscellaneous. Persons.
Gemba appears to be the name of someone like a steward for the property of a religious establishment or some landowner. He is either quick to act or litigious (or both?). Once again the comic spirit holds as we skirt the senryū border of haikai. Since the next stanza should be the second flower stanza, we can only wonder what its tone will be like.

35 Ground-Design. Light-Heavy. Spring. Persons. Residences. Cultivation.
This illustrates the Japanese proverb, "Choose food over flowers." The connection would be heavy if the words of the stanzas justified it, but this illustrates the tendency of many stanzas to fit by juxtaposition and yet to have little relation except by ingenuity. The second flower stanza comes in its usual place.

31
Shikoro utsu naru
Bamba Matsumoto
  kagokaki no
bōgumi taranu
  aki no ame
Kitō

At Bamba beside Lake Biwa
fulling blocks beat without a pause
  the palanquin bearer
needs someone to bear the other end
  as autumn rain comes down

32
Kagokaki no
bōgumi taranu
  aki no ame
tobi mo karasu mo
achira mukiiru
Buson

The palanquin bearer
needs someone to bear the other end
  as autumn rain comes down
a kite and a crow face off
disputing space over there

33
Tobi mo karasu mo
achira mukiiru
  tatari nasu
tanaka no shōsha
  kansabite
Kitō

A kite and a crow face off
disputing space over there
  standing in the field
the little shrine is haunted
  with competing gods

34
Tatari nasu
tanaka no shōsha
  kansabite
sude ni Gemba ga
kuji no makeiro
Buson

Standing in the field
the little shrine is haunted
  with competing gods
already Gemba is at law
on a suit without much chance

35
Sude ni Gemba ga
kuji no makeiro
  hana ni utoki
mi ni hatagoya no
  meshi to shiru
Buson

Already Gemba is at law
on a suit without much chance
  with his rice and soup
the provincial taking lodging
  has no taste for flowers

36 Design. Heavy-Light. Spring. Night. Radiance.

The loveliness of this stanza contrasts markedly with most of the preceding six stanzas of the sequence. The relation is nicely associational—after the evening meal a lamp will be needed. Of course the feelings differ greatly, and the relation may be somewhat lighter than specified.

Hana ni utoki
mi ni hatagoya no
  meshi to shiru
36 mada kureyaranu
haru no tomoshibi.
  Kitō

With his rice and soup
the provincial taking lodging
  has no taste for flowers
a lamp lights the evening hours
as the spring season lingers on.

GLOSSARY

Glossary

EACH entry is italicized, and words italicized within an entry are entered elsewhere in the Glossary. Renga and Haikai are both meant unless otherwise indicated.

See also the Figures.

A. JAPANESE TERMS

Ageku. The last stanza in a sequence.

Aki. Autumn, with the other seasons and Zō, one of the principal topics.

Bunraku. Popular theatre using puppets of large size operated by three men to narrative recitation and musical accompaniment. Now a subsidized art. The modern term for jōruri.

Chōka. The "long poem," alternating 5- and 7-syllable lines till the final 7-syllable couplet; flourished in the 8th century; one of the principal forms of *Waka*—with *Tanka*, which were also used as envoys to chōka.

Chōrenga. "Long renga" as opposed to *Tanrenga*, "short renga." This is the properly linked renga or *Kusarirenga* that emerges in the 12th century and becomes the standard kind.

Daisan. The third stanza in a sequence.

Dokugin. A sequence composed by one person.

Engo. Verbal association within a stanza or between stanzas.

Furimono. Falling thing, a motif category in *Renga* for snow, rain, dew, hail, etc. Opposed to *Sobikimono*.

Fushimono. Originally a stipulated directive for a *Renga* sequence, such as "person" (hito), Cathay (kara), etc. Later added perfunctorily after composition to give part of the title.

Fuyu. Winter, a topic for a sequence; as *Aki*.

Gojūin. A 50-stanza sequence.

Ha. See *Jo-ha-kyū*.

Haibun. Prose written by a *Haikai* master, interspersed with *Hokku*; sometimes a travel record.

Haikai. Properly, "haikai no renga," the non-standard or *Mushin* kind opposed to *Ushin* or standard *Renga*. Of lower language and subject, it became serious and reached its zenith in the 17th and 18th centuries. A haikai sequence is now called Renku; formerly "haikai" meant both the kind of poetry and such a sequence; opposed to *Renga* and *Waka*.

Haiku. From a phrase, "haikai no ku." A poem of three lines in 5, 7, 5 syllables like a *Hokku* but without sequential development. It emerged in the 19th century.

Hana no ku. A flower stanza, appearing at certain places in a sequence.

Hankasen. An 18-stanza sequence, half a *Kasen*, used chiefly in *Haikai*.

Haru. Spring; like *Aki* a major topic in a sequence.

Hiraku. Any stanza other than: *Hokku* (the first), *Waki* (the second), *Daisan* (the third), and *Ageku* (the last); or sometimes meaning any but the first.

Hokku. The first or base stanza in a sequence, three lines in 5, 7, 5 syllables. In that, like *Kami no ku* and *Haiku*.

Hokku-waki. Identical in parts with *Tanrenga*, two stanzas, *Hokku* plus *Waki*.

Hon'i. The principle of essential character for poetic imagery and diction; such as spring rain (harusame) is always gentle, haze (kasumi) designates solely spring—even when in fact such things need not be so. Again, that the wood thrush (hototogisu) is longed for but very seldom heard, though in fact it sings a good deal.

Honkadori. Allusion with levy on a "foundation poem" (honka) for words, with rules as to the degree of change and other conditions necessary.

Honzetsu. Like *Honkadori*, but allusion to a prose work, with levying on the prose wording unnecessary.

Hyakuin. A 100-stanza sequence, the standard *Renga* number and used also in *Haikai*.

Iisute. A short sequence of an irregular number of stanzas.

Ji. Ground stanza, one plain in words and conception, as opposed to *Mon* or Design stanzas. Following Konishi Jin'ichi, this book distinguishes four grades of impressiveness: ji or Ground; jimon or Ground-Design; monji, or Design-Ground; and *Mon*, Design.

Jiamari. Supernumerary syllables to a line. Japanese poets not seldom write supernumerary lines but never lines with fewer than the stipulated number of syllables (jitarazu).

Jingi. Shinto, a subtopic of sequences; such subtopics include numerous others such as *Koi* (love), *Tabi* (travel), *Shakkyō* (Buddhism), etc.

Jo-ha-kyū. Sequence rhythms taken from court music and passed on to *Nō.* See Figure 2. A Jo or "preface" is a dignified, calm preparatory first part, emphasizing seasonal stanzas. A Ha or development is the longest section, introducing variety and more stanzas on *Zō* (Miscellaneous) topics and on agitating subtopics such as *Jukkai* (Grievance) and *Koi* (love). A *Kyū* or fast finale achieves a sense of speed in its brief conclusion (the length of a jo) by various means and concludes decorously, usually affirmatively.

Jukkai. Grievance, a subtopic of sequences; like *Jingi.*

Kami no ku. In *Tanka* the first three lines in 5, 7, 5 syllables, followed by the shimo no ku in 7, 7 syllables. Sequences alternate these two "ku," beginning with a kami no ku and ending with a shimo no ku. Identical in form with *Hokku* and *Haiku.*

Kabuki. A popular drama using male actors, often giving versions of *Nō* or *Bunraku* plays, but having many stories of its own. Still performed.

Kasen. A sequence of 36 stanzas, named after the "Thirty Six Poetic Saints" (Sanjūrokkasen) of *Waka.* Made the standard *Haikai* or *Renku* sequence length by Matsuo Bashō.

Koi. Love, a major subtopic; like *Jingi.*

Kokoro. With *Kotoba* one of the two principal terms in classical Japanese poetics. By itself it means conception, heart, mind, spirit—the affected and conceiving element in the poet or poetry. To have kokoro (kokoro aru, *Ushin*) is to have taste or to be right, proper, fitting.

Kokorozuke. Stanza connection by conception rather than by diction, as opposed to *Kotobazuke.*

Kotoba. Like *Kokoro* one of the two principal terms in classical Japanese poetics. It designates words, diction, materials, elements—the expressive and expressed elements in a poet or poem.

Kotobazuke. Stanza connection by words rather than by conception, as opposed to *Kokorozuke.*

Ku. A stanza of a linked sequence. See *Hokku*, *Waki*, *Daisan*, *Hiraku*, *Ageku* for specific stanzas. It also means a specific stanza, such as *Hana no ku*, a flower stanza. Also a prosodic unit, such as *Kami no ku* or *Shimo no ku*. Also a "line of verse" for Chinese or modern Japanese poetry.

Kusarirenga. See *Chōrenga*.

Kuzari. Omission or suspension of a work or topic for a specific number of stanzas: as yume (dream) must come at intervals of eight stanzas; unnamed insects (mushi, tada no mushi) but once in a hundred stanzas; etc.

Kyōgen. Farces that were formerly performed as interludes for *Nō*, often featuring master and servant, husband and wife, thieves, etc. Still performed.

Kyū. See *Jo-ha-kyū*.

Maekuzuke. "Attaching to the preceding stanza." A movement for popularizing *Haikai*.

Monogatari. "Relating things." Prose fiction with or without some number of poems. In utamonogatari, the prose exists as an excuse to introduce poems. In tsukurimonogatari there may be poems, but the prose fiction is the reason for being.

Mon. An impressive or Design stanza; see *Ji*.

Mujō. Transience, a subtopic such as *Jingi*.

Mushin. "Lacking in kokoro, heart." Opposed to *Ushin*; see also *Kokoro*. "Mushin renga" was a prototype of *Haikai*. The term designates a wide range of the non-standard from some small violation of decorum to the comic and even scatological.

Natsu. Summer, a major topic; like *Aki*.

Nadokoro. A named place, place name, one of the bases for stanza connection.

Nagori no ori. The last sheet on which a sequence was set down.

Na no . . . A named something, as na no mushi (named insect); cf. *Nadokoro*.

Ni no ori. The second sheet of four for setting down 100 stanzas.

Nō. A kind of drama featuring two principal characters and their attendants, a small orchestra, and a chorus that takes no part in the action.

These plays were once quite lively; they are now slow, stately, and indebted to *Renga* for the *Jo-ha-kyū* rhythm (see Figure 2) and for other aesthetic principles taken ultimately from *Waka*.

Nisemono. Dissembled, assumed, or metaphorical version of something, for which the stipulations of the thing itself meant literally do not apply. "Kokoro no matsu" (pine in the heart) is not classified as tree.

Omote. The front of a sheet on which stanzas are set down. Cf. *Ura*.

Ori. A sheet, usually named, as Sho-ori, Nagori no ori, etc.

Oriku. Acrostic haikai.

Renga. The serious linked poetry in a standard form of 100 stanzas, that reached its zenith in the 15th and 16th centuries.

Rengaawase. A match or competition in which sets of renga sequences were opposed. Cf. *Utaawase*.

Rengashi. The renga masters or teachers, often priests.

Renku. The modern name for a sequence of *Haikai* by analogy with *Renga*, but not a term used by Bashō, etc.

Ryōgin. A sequence composed by two people.

Sangin. A sequence composed by three people.

San no ori. The third sheet on which a 100-stanza sequence is set down.

Senku. A sequence of 1,000 stanzas and in practice 10 *Hyakuin*, or 100-stanza sequences.

Shakkyō. Buddhism, a subtopic; like *Jingi*.

Shimo no ku. See *Kami no ku*.

Shin. Close or heavy connection, relation of stanzas. as opposed to *So*, Distant or Light. Following Konishi Jin'ichi, this book distinguishes four degrees of closeness: shin (Close); shinso (Close-Distant); soshin (Distant-Close); and shin (Distant). For haikai this study uses Bashō's terms: jū or Heavy instead of shin; and kei or Light instead of so.

Sho-ori. The first sheet on which a sequence is set down.

So. See *Shin*.

Sobikimono. Rising thing, a category of motif in *Renga* including smoke, clouds, haze, etc., and opposed to *Furimono*.

Tabi. Travel, a subtopic like *Jingi*.

Tanka. "Short poem," with *Chōka*, the major form of court poetry, and after the 8th or 9th century the dominant one. Five lines in 5, 7, 5, 7, 7 syllables. Tanka provide linked poetry with the resources for *Honkadori*.

Tanrenga. Short Renga. See *Chōrenga*.

Tsukeku. An attached or connected stanza, and therefore any after the *Hokku*. Also often used to designate connection and its art.

Tsuki no ku. A moon stanza, appearing at certain places in a sequence.

Ura. The back of a sheet on which a sequence is set down.

Ushin. Possessed of heart: see *Kokoro* and *Mushin*. The implications are of the standard, the serious, what meets proper criteria.

Utaawase. A poetic match or competition, in which two *Tanka* are brought forward at a time for judgment.

Waka. In its largest significance, Japanese poetry as opposed to Chinese. Used in this book to represent poetry that flourished before linked poetry: that is, court poetry, and in particular *Chōka* and *Tanka*.

Wakan renku. Sequences linking stanzas of Japanese poetry and verses of Chinese.

Waki. The second stanza of a sequence.

Yōen (Yōembi). An aesthetic idea, usually designating a concept of beauty with some brightness or charm.

Yongin. A sequence composed by four poets.

Yoyoshi. A sequence of 44 stanzas.

Yūgen. An aesthetic idea, originally in *Waka* of a profound, mysterious, and often obscure kind. In *Renga* and *Haikai*, as thereafter in *Nō*, it usually designates the highest standard of beauty, not necessarily mysterious, etc.

ZŌ. "Miscellaneous," with the four seasons (*Haru*, *Natsu*, *Aki*, *Fuyu*) the alternative topic in linked poetry. In *Waka* zō designates a category in which no one season or other topic such as love (koi), travel (tabi), predominates. In linked poetry, the only topics are the seasons and zō, with the rest relegated to subtopical status. A sequence usually consists of half, or slightly more, zō stanzas.

Zuiga. The excess 50 stanzas composed on the 5th day of writing a *Senku*.

B. English Cross-Listing

This listing by categories will assist the reader's use of the Japanese terms.

Impressiveness. See *Ji*, *Mon*.
Motifs. See *Furimono*, *Sobikimono*.
Relatedness. See *Shin*, *So*.
Rhythm. See *Jo-ha-kyū*.
Sequences. See
    (a) Kinds: *Haikai, Renga, Renku, Wakan Renku;*
    (b) Divisions: *Nagori no ori, Ni no ori, San no ori, Sho-ori;*
    (c) Lengths: *Iisute, Hankasen, Hyakuin, Kasen, Senku, Yoyoshi.*
Stanzas. See *Ageku, Daisan, Hiraku, Hokku, Tsukeku, Waki;* also *Kami no ku, Shimo no ku.*
Subtopics. See *Jingi, Jukkai, Koi, Mujō, Shakkyō, Tabi.*
Topics. See *Aki, Fuyu, Haru, Natsu, Zō.*

Index

This list includes names, titles, and subjects in Part One as well as names and titles from the introductions and commentary in Parts Two and Three.

Titles, terms, etc., are entered under the Japanese versions; English translations are also given as cross references.

For those authors cited who have written more than one study used in this book, short titles are given in the entries under their names.

Dates are given for historical Japanese persons.

This book has been composed and printed by
Princeton University Press
Designed by Jan Lilly
Edited by R. Miriam Brokaw
Typography: VIP Bembo
Paper: Warren's Olde Style

Library of Congress Cataloging in Publication Data

Miner, Earl Roy.
  Japanese linked poetry.

  Bibliography: p.
  Includes index.
  1. Renga—History and criticism.   2. Haikai—History
and criticism.   3. Japanese poetry—To 1868-
—History and criticism.   4. Renga—Translations into
English.   5. Haikai—Translations into English.
6. English poetry—Translations from Japanese.   I. Title.
PL732.R4M5   895.6'.009   78-51182
ISBN 0-691-06372-9